Gendered Spaces in Argentine Women's Literature

Gendered Spaces in Argentine Women's Literature

Marta Sierra

GENDERED SPACES IN ARGENTINE WOMEN'S LITERATURE
Copyright © Marta Sierra, 2012.

All rights reserved.

First published in 2012 by
PALGRAVE MACMILLAN®
in the United States—a division of St. Martin's Press LLC,
175 Fifth Avenue, New York, NY 10010.

Where this book is distributed in the UK, Europe and the rest of the world, this is by Palgrave Macmillan, a division of Macmillan Publishers Limited, registered in England, company number 785998, of Houndmills, Basingstoke, Hampshire RG21 6XS.

Palgrave Macmillan is the global academic imprint of the above companies and has companies and representatives throughout the world.

Palgrave® and Macmillan® are registered trademarks in the United States, the United Kingdom, Europe and other countries.

ISBN: 978–0–230–12085–3

Library of Congress Cataloging-in-Publication Data

Sierra, Marta, 1968–
    Gendered spaces in Argentine women's literature / Marta Sierra.
    p. cm.
    ISBN 978–0–230–12085–3 (hardback)
    1. Argentine literature—History and criticism. 2. Women—Argentina.
 3. Gender identity in literature. 4. Space and time in literature I. Title.

PQ7623.W6S54 2012
860.9'3520420982—dc23   2011044513

A catalogue record of the book is available from the British Library.

Design by Newgen Imaging Systems (P) Ltd., Chennai, India.

First edition: May 2012

To Alan and Alejandro, with much love.

To my grandmother, Evarista, who instilled in me the love for literature.

And to Jan, whose unconditional love took me to wondrous places.

Contents

List of Figures — ix
Poetry Permissions — xi
Acknowledgments — xiii

Introduction: Gendered Spaces in Argentine Women's Literature — 1

Chapter 1   Displacing Domesticity: Cosmopolitanisms, Travel Writing, and Narratives of the Home — 21

Chapter 2   "Of Other Spaces": Staging Repression in the Works of Griselda Gambaro and Diana Raznovich — 63

Chapter 3   Global Patagonia: Rewriting the National Space — 113

Chapter 4   Poetic Crossovers: The Paradoxical Spaces of Women's Poetry — 157

Notes — 199
Bibliography — 217
Index — 235

Figures

1.1 Alejandro Leveratto, Victoria Ocampo's House in Rufino de Elizalde y Castilla, Palermo Chico, Buenos Aires (built by Alejandro Bustillo, 1928). Used with permission of Alejandro Leveratto. Fotografía©alejandroleveratto.   44

1.2 Victoria Ocampo's House in Rufino de Elizalde y Castilla (sketch). Used with permission of Architect Martha Levisman, President Asociación Civil ARCA, Archivos de Arquitectura Contemporánea Argentina.   44

1.3 Literary Meeting at Victoria Ocampo's house in Rufino de Elizalde y Castilla in 1931. Used with permission of Fundación Sur.   45

1.4 Victoria Ocampo's House in Rufino de Elizalde y Castilla (stairs detail). Used with permission of Architect Martha Levisman, President Asociación Civil ARCA, Archivos de Arquitectura Contemporánea Argentina.   45

3.1 Usuhaia Prison (hallways), site of the installation *Diario de la luna caníbal*. Used with permission of Belén Gache.   146

3.2 *Diario de la luna caníbal* (video still). Photograph taken from inside a prison cell. Used with permission of Belén Gache.   148

3.3 *Diario de la luna caníbal* (video still). Usuhaia Prison (exterior). Behind, the Cinco Hermanos Mountains. Used with permission of Belén Gache.   149

3.4 *Diario de la luna caníbal*. Promotional image for the installation. Used with permission of Belén Gache.   150

Permissions

El jardín and *Sur,* included in *Tener lo que se tiene* by Diana Bellessi, Buenos Aires, pages 469, 515, 612, 608, and 609. © 2009, Adriana Hidalgo editora. Reprinted with permission of Adriana Hidalgo editora.

"Vitraux del Exilio" and "Más sol en la Jornada," *Partir, digo* by Luisa Futoransky. © 2010, Libros del Aire. Reprinted with permission of Libros del Aire, Madrid.

"Jonás, Jonás," "Nuevo barco ebrio," "Llanos del sur," "Coraçao da Guanabara," *Babel, Babel* by Luisa Futoransky. © 1968, Ediciones La Loca Poesía. Reprinted with permission of Ediciones La Loca Poesía.

"La coleccionista" "Cartulina de Ljubjana," "Llanos del sur," "Tiananmen, 4 de Junio, 1989," "El patio y los abuelos," "Consignas al navegante," and "Poética Jueza de la mi sombra," *Prender de gajo* by Luisa Futoransky. © 2006, Calambur Editorial. Reprinted with permission of the author and Calambur Editorial (www.calambureditorial.com).

Islandia. A Poem by María Negroni. Translated by Anne Twitty. Pages 13, 10, 19, 69, 94, 97, 103, and 153. © 2001, Station Hill, Barrytown LTD. Reprinted with permission of Station Hill Press, Inc.

Night Journey by María Negroni. © 2002, María Negroni. Translation of poems and introduction © 2002, Princeton University Press. Reprinted with permission of Princeton University Press.

A section of chapter 4, "Global Patagonia: Rewriting the National Space," appeared as "Global Patagonia: Belén Gache's Nomadic Writings," in *Transnational Borderlands in Women's Global Networks: The Making of Cultural Resistance.* eds. Clara Román-Odio and Marta Sierra. Reprinted with permission of Palgrave-Macmillan.

Acknowledgments

A book is never written alone. The idea for this study began about seven years ago in a series of conversations my friend and colleague, Clara Román-Odio, and I began with the topic of gender and space, which resulted in the coedition of a special issue for the journal *Letras Femeninas, Global and Local Geographies: the (Dis)locations of Contemporary Feminisms* (33.1, Summer 2007) and the publication of a second volume on methodological reflections on the topic and its relationship to transnational feminisms, *Transnational Borderlands: The Making of Cultural Resistance in Women's Global Networks* (New York: Palgrave-MacMillan, 2011). The nurturing intellectual collaboration, along with friendship and encouragement by Clara, is a central force behind this book.

To my colleagues at Kenyon College, I owe the support of an open and caring intellectual community who has encouraged my intellectual growth for the past seven years. I am particularly indebted to Linda Metzler, Travis Landry, and Daniel Harnett, who volunteered their time to read drafts and generously commented on my work. Outside Kenyon, Marcy Schwartz has offered her unconditional support throughout the years by reading sections of the manuscript and giving crucial advice during this intellectual journey. My colleague at the University of Buenos Aires, Perla Zusman, shared her wealth of knowledge of cultural geography. I am forever grateful for her generosity and kindness and the rigor of her comments on several ideas about the book. Perla and I cotaught a graduate seminar at the University of Buenos Aires, which provided much insight to the complex disciplinary connections between geography and literature. I am very grateful to the students in this seminar who helped me rethink the topic of gendered spaces from a different geopolitical perspective. Amy Kaminsky, who I later learned served as the anonymous reviewer for Palgrave, provided me with comments and insights that have enriched the contents, language, and structure of the manuscript. This book is, without a doubt, a much better product thanks to her. I am also thankful to Francine Masiello for her professional support throughout the years. The course on "The South" that she taught at the University of Tucumán in 2005 provided much insight in the preliminary stages of my investigation.

Several research trips were made possible by the financial support of different grants by Kenyon College. I am grateful to those who shared this journey throughout the years with me. The writers whose work I address in the following pages have been friends, mentors, and dear companions whom I met on different occasions. Diana Bellessi and I met for the first time at her house in Buenos Aires six years ago. Our conversations about what it means to read, write, and think in the North or in the South have been invaluable in my understanding of how location impacts the production and circulation of knowledge. Luisa Futoransky contributed her caustic sense of humor and unconditional friendship. Her ironic views about nationalism and memory helped me to rethink my own affiliations to ideas of nation and identity. I still remember with much affection her visit to Kenyon College in 2007, the visit to that old cemetery, and the blond at the local bank who would later become a protagonist of one of Luisa's poignant poems. María Negroni and I shared an ongoing conversation across many places: Buenos Aires, Brooklyn, and Buenos Aires, again. As one of the characters in her poetry and fiction, I often feel entrapped in a virtual geography connecting different times and spaces. Belén Gache's generous friendship and support, first from Buenos Aires and later from Madrid, has allowed me to understand the notion of place from a fantastic, sometimes even surreal perspective. I also owe Sylvia Iparraguirre a debt of gratitude for my interest in travel literature and shipwrecks. My understanding of the history of Patagonia and Tierra del Fuego would be incomplete without her insights and her breadth of knowledge on the topic.

Writing in a foreign language is a wondrous and, at times, mysterious experience. I owe special thanks to Loretta Godfrey, who helped me edit the entire manuscript and who carefully checked for proper format in references and bibliography. Her professionalism and generosity with her time made this adventure easier and more enjoyable. When a translation of the works in Spanish was not available, my colleague and friend, Cindy Schuster, was in charge of all the literary translations. The elegance, beauty, and precision of her translations made a unique contribution to this work.

And finally, to Alan, who shares with me the joys and burdens of life. Without his loving help and support, I would not have been able to accomplish this task. And to Alejandro, born a year later than the initial ideas for this book. His joyous face, his happiness, and his innocence accompanied me as I saw him and this project grow.

Introduction: Gendered Spaces in Argentine Women's Literature

A mysterious tree planted in the middle of the desert; the roaring fire in the nearby *pajonal;* the dense silence disrupted only by wild sounds of strange birds and animals; the unchanged appearance of the desert. Such are the powerful spatial images that populate the pages of *La cautiva,* the poem that Esteban Echeverría published in 1837. This foundational imaginary geography evokes a vivid landscape for the eyes of the reader, namely that of the desert as a barbaric space that the writer feels compelled and yet challenged to represent. Argentine literature sought, in the decades that followed, to rewrite this symbolic space as both a literary and a political project. *La cautiva* not only sets in place an imaginary function for this landscape at the literary level, it also fundamentally associates it to gender and racial relationships of hegemony and domination; for instance, through the equation of the wild landscape to the indigenous populations described through a Dante-esque portrayal of *el malon* and its raiding tactics to sweep the precarious colonial settlements in the Pampas. The spatial iconography of the desert also addresses gender tensions through the introduction of the female captive, María, and her role in civilizing the barbaric space. At times, an almost supernatural character displaying an extreme endurance in dealing with the hardships posed by the desert, María also exhibits stereotypical feminine traits when she demonstrates an unusual capacity to feel and be passionate about her role as the savior of Brián from the dark forces of nature. She acts as his ideal partner, and when his debilitated body cannot carry out patriotic duties, she intervenes with her dagger as a valiant combatant to complete his tasks. *La cautiva* ends, however, as a tale of the martyrdom of both Brián and María, signaling that such a project of conquering and domesticating space is doomed to failure until the institutional mechanisms of the nation are set in place.

A cautionary tale about the challenges that lie ahead for the intellectual and political leaders of the nation, *La cautiva* lays the groundwork for a spatial imaginary that will later be exploited for the purposes of an aggressive colonization and population of what the romantic generation of Echeverría, and later Sarmiento, perceived as the inhabited territory of the desert. Contrary to European Romanticism, an urban intellectual movement desiring to abandon civilization to go back to nature, Romanticism in Argentina and in Latin America in general goes against this utopian vision of nature by exploring the hostile forces of a natural world as obstacles for the civilizing projects of the nation-states in formation; Romanticism and its images of nature were identified above all with individual freedom and an incipient nationalism (Franco, *An Introduction* 46). As Jens Andermann states in his study of "power maps" in nineteenth-century Argentine literature, this first moment in the perception of the national space is one of "apperception," wherein the subject, in this case the Romantic writer, claims the territory from which he feels displaced, as the national project is yet to be determined within the political structure of the nation (*Mapas del poder* 21). Later authors, such as the Gauchesca writers of the 1880s literary generation, would appropriate this space and code it as national by transforming it into a "place of memory" through a debate on the national patrimony (ibid.). The formation of the national territory took place between 1879 and 1884 and accompanied this literary project of defining the national space. As Perla Zusman and Sandra Minvielle state, the formation of the nation-state in Argentina was a planned process that implied the "invention of a territory," which involved the occupation—by the use of military force in the majority of cases—of the perceived "empty" internal territories that, in fact, were populated by indigenous peoples. This process also necessitated the definition of international limits leading to conflicts with neighboring Brazil and Chile at the end of the nineteenth century, economic investment in the areas recently added to the country, and, in the ideological field, the formation of representations of a modern nationality (Zusman and Minvielle). Literature and the incipient geographical discourse of the late nineteenth century played a leading role in linking the symbolic functions of the nation-state and its material powers over the territories it controlled and in transforming the "territorial consciousness," the perception of the country as an empty or deserted space, into a "social construction of space," the imagined or invented space with political, economic, and social functions, as defined by Zusman and Minvielle (Navarro Floria).

La cautiva shows the complexity of spatial categories within this literary and political project of inventing a national space. In this poem, space refers, not to what Edward Soja calls the experienced or "materialized spatiality," but rather to images of the spatial conceived as a social representation (Soja, "Thirdspace" 266). More important, this text by Echeverría points to the central role women play in this process of imagining space. In *Gendered Spaces in Argentine Women's Literature*, I inquire into the construction of imaginary geographies in literature and how they establish a dialogue with prevalent spatial constructions in Argentine society of the twentieth century. More specifically, I examine the role of space in establishing gendered relations and the ways in which literature addresses the production of gendered spaces. I suggest that, through seizing literary representations of space, women writers in Argentina create alternative or virtual spaces as sites of possibility and resistance against the social positions women have historically occupied in Argentina. The women's literature included in this study shows the construction of alternative spatialities and the writers' search for a place within the literary and social histories of the country. What is the precise nature of spatial representations in women's literature? And how do they impact the role women occupied within Argentina's literary and social life? I intend to answer these questions from an analytical perspective that examines representations of gendered spaces in women's literature in Argentina from 1920 to 2000. Further, I posit the centrality of literary representations in a dialogue that women writers establish between literary and social formations of gendered spaces.

The complexity of literary spaces and their connection to social processes brings to the fore a series of methodological issues. In reviewing how literary studies have considered spatial representations, I found the textual analysis of space to be insufficient for the type of answers my study seeks to provide. My interest in symbolic dimensions of space transcends the goal of describing space through a series of literary tropes. In the words of Henri Lefebvre, the descriptive level evidenced by certain literary studies reduces "space itself to the status of a message, and the inhabiting of it to the status of a reading" (7). Prevalent questions in theories on space by human geographers similarly address the issue of representation as a central element in connecting different dimensions of space as a perceived, conceived, and lived reality. As explained by Lefebvre, space is first perceived as a "spatial practice" that embraces "production and reproduction and the particular locations and spatial sets characteristic of each social formation"; spatial practice gives cohesion to society through a level of competence and performance (33). It is also a social conception tied to the production of a spatial order by scientists, planners, and urban planners, and as such, it organizes social relationships. Last, space is also a "lived reality"; it overlays physical space, making symbolic uses that seek to change and appropriate the two spatial realities previously described (39). The term "geographical imagination," originally coined by David Harvey in his 1973 foundational text, *Social Justice and the City,* is very useful for understanding the representational dimensions of space as a social reality. In this book, Harvey seeks to breach the gap between sociological and geographical imaginations of space and primarily analyzes how space is a social entity from the perspective of how we perceive it and how it affects our lives (13). The genealogy of this concept traces to Lefebvre's seminal book, *The Production of Space,* and his notions about spaces as socially produced and conceptualized by relationships of power, ideology, and knowledge. Later geographers such as Edward Soja further developed this idea. In *Postmodern Geographies: The Reassertion of Space in Critical Social Theory,* Soja states that space is produced through a sociospatial dynamic whereby social and spatial structures interact; a society is thus not only a temporal but also a spatial construct (127). Time, space, and matter are inextricably connected; social life must be seen as a producer and a product of spatiality, and social and spatial structures are dialectically intertwined in social life. The term *spatialization* refers to the ways in which space is produced according to different power variables where the social intervenes in the perception and construction of space. According to Soja, spatiality is thus an arena for struggles over social production and reproduction, whereby different social practices either maintain or challenge existing spatialities (130).

The context of these redefinitions is the "spatial turn," or a reassertion of space into the social sciences, turning away from a historicism that primarily focused on time as the key force in creating a modern consciousness since the nineteenth century (Warf and Arias 3). Prevalent in theories that seek to explain such spatial dimensions of the social is an emphasis on the power-laden nature of spatiality. For instance, studies by Lefebvre, Harvey, and Soja focus on how space is central to the structure and functioning of capitalism as a coherent whole, and postcolonial readings of space and mapping, as Alison Blunt and Gillian Rose state, unearth the hegemonic colonial power that sustains the politics of representation embedded in such spatial imagery (8). As expressed by Derek Gregory, the notion of a "geographical imagination" addresses the ways in which power, knowledge, and spatiality interact, what he describes as "the politics of spatiality" (xi). Blunt and Rose also propose that spaces are imbued with an imaginary quality, as there is a discursive construction that constitutes space through struggles of power and knowledge (5). Thus, the above geographical theories provide important methodological frames for understanding the role of cultural productions such as literature in assessing symbolic functions of space and spatiality in social relations. Literary representations of space can be described by using Michel Foucault's term of "heterotopias" as the "counter-sites of enacted utopias" in which "the real sites, all the other real sites that can be found within the culture, are simultaneously represented, contested and inverted" (24). As such, literary productions offer an alternative way of questioning the formation and validation of spatializations of power and the construction of spatial images through literary history. For instance, this theorization is implicit in the description of regional literary traditions by Antonio Cornejo Polar and Antonio Benítez-Rojo. When referring to the Andes and the Caribbean, they both point to the failures of certain spatial constructs to describe the cultural and literary heterogeneity of the area they analyze. Cornejo Polar stresses, for instance, the existence of "heterogeneous literatures" in the Andes region that intersects two or more sociocultural spatialities characterized by bilingual and multiple cultural identities (16–17). In reflecting upon the spatial and cultural complexities of this area, Cornejo Polar describes it as a series of "internal archipelagos" (179–80). The spatial formation of literary histories also occupies Benítez-Rojo in *La isla que se repite. El Caribe y la perspectiva postmoderna* [*The Repeating Island: The Caribbean and the Postmodern Perspective*] as he describes the Caribbean as fragmentary and heterogeneous where certain spatial models, such as center-periphery, are inappropriate for theorizing the literary and cultural histories of the region. By using the notion of chaos, he proposes instead that the Caribbean resembles the spatial construct of a "repeating island" through "processes, dynamics, and rhythms that emerge within the marginal, the residual, the incoherent, and the heterogeneous" (iv). In both instances, Cornejo Polar and Benítez-Rojo question a prevalent set of literary cartographies that do not account for the complexities of social spatialities.

Cornejo Polar and Benítez-Rojo examine how nationalist and imperialist ideologies impose a false spatial order that is insufficient to describe the "lived" spatial realities in the Andes and the Caribbean. In a similar way, additional literary studies have focused on political uses of space that, during the nineteenth century, sought to define the spatiality of the Latin American nations in the making. The literature representing national frontiers in Argentina and Chile, as Álvaro Fernández Bravo explains, depicts the marginal space of national borders as both an unfinished physical reality claiming to be ordered by statesmen and intellectuals and as an enunciatory location from which to establish a discourse about the needs and imperatives for nation-building (41). As a semantic condensation of the national identity, the frontier embodies an empty space that gives ideological support to the territorial expansion and internal colonization throughout the nineteenth century; literary discourses "textualize" its spatial dimensions and transform them into writing (11). As such, literature impacts the symbolization of space as it spatializes historic time and shows the conflicting struggles in the history of colonization and territorialization during the nineteenth century. The ordering of space for political aims is also considered in postcolonial critical studies such as Sara Upstone's *Spatial Politics in the Postcolonial Novel*. Upstone claims that literature can contest colonial spatial orderings by "re-visioning" the colonial space and its implied identity formations. Contrary to the colonial space, she proposes that postcolonial narratives construct a "post-space" that contests "the fantasy of space as a medium that is capable of being ordered, the myth of a 'natural' territory based on geographical landmarks." As such, these narratives "overwrite the colonial space" by erasing the original text—the colonial space as a textuality—and layering over it new traces that expose "how unachievable is the order and homogeneity that the colonial division of space projects" (6). Therefore, literary productions play an important role, not only in establishing and sustaining political projects of ordering of the social space, but also as tools for rewriting oppressive spatializations and proposing virtual geographies of emancipation.

Human geographers similarly study spatial constructions as dynamic entities that allow for a reinterpretation of hegemonic relations of social domination. Echoing definitions by Lefebvre of a "lived" dimension in spatial realities that disrupts any ideological ordering of space, Soja proposes the notion of a "third space," stating that in this capacity, social space is neither inherently real nor imagined, but rather a chaotic, ever-changing experience of existing in it, from which we can "interpret, and act to change the spatiality of human life." As such, a "third space" is an encompassing approach to defining the spatial as a social construction that fosters "collective political action against all forms of human oppression" ("Thirdspace" 269). In the same way, Homi Bhabha, reflecting on how hegemony constructs enunciatory positions that are based on material and symbolic locations, proposes a "third space" of enunciation, one that "makes the structure of meaning and difference an ambivalent process, destroys the mirror of representation," and ensures that "the meaning and symbols of culture have no primordial unity or fixity" where cultural and material locations can be appropriated, translated, rehistoricized, and read anew (37). Such space is an "alien territory" where it is possible to articulate a "culture's hybridity," an in-between space that is "based not on the exoticism of multiculturalism or the diversity of cultures, but on the inscription and articulation of culture's hibridity" (38). In these theorizations, the relation between space and representation is rather complex; space is the product of a representational social logic that constantly redefines the spatial as a result of the interactions between the perceived, conceived, and lived dimensions of social spaces. As such, we need to think of space as a dynamic simultaneity that literary productions reflect on a given moment of this dialectical relation. Thus, literature holds a key role in producing enunciatory positions described as "third spaces" by means of crafting a relation of appropriation and translation of social spaces and by bringing to the fore the complex set of cultural and political negotiations embedded in social spatialities.

In the complex spatialities of power built both in society and in literature, a number of variables such as sex, gender, class, and nationality intervene. As evidenced by the previous literature review, although space has gained importance as a tool for social transformation, the important aspect of gender relations is often left out or only marginally conceptualized in geographical and literary studies of the topic. Feminist methodologies and theories offer, in this regard, an additional perspective for understanding and conceptualizing space as a social product. Feminisms have traditionally seen space as central both to masculinist power and to feminist resistance. The opposition between the public and the private is central in feminist critiques of gendered spatial segregation, as demonstrated by Daphne Spain's study *Gendered Spaces*. As explained by Spain, gender is not only at the basis of spatial segregation, it also reinforces gender stratification; social spatial divisions reduce women's access to knowledge and thereby reinforce their lower status relative to men's (7). Most feminist studies center on how this spatial segregation confines women to the realm of the domestic in patriarchal societies, whereas the public realms of culture, politics, and the economy remain spheres dominated by men. Feminists of color in the United States have also sought to redefine gendered social spaces in terms of race and social class and have proposed new spaces based on their experiences of exploitation and resistance, such as Chicana theories on the borderlands, or African American redefinitions of the home and the domestic. Transnational feminisms, on the other hand, focus on location and the decentering of cartographies of knowledge and power by questioning, for instance, the construction of third-world women as peripheral subjects in Euro-American feminist theories and methodologies. Centered on what we could call the local-global predicament of women's studies, transnational feminists highlight the need to redefine Immanuel Wallerstein's "world-system" in favor of "scattered hegemonies"; that is, the existence of complex and multiple subjectivities and power dynamics across complex and scattered locations, which replace the dominance of a Western homogeneous subject at the base of the dependence theories and spatial models coined by Wallerstein (Grewal and Caplan 12). Jacqui Alexander and Chandra Mohanty analyze the cartographies of knowledge and power that are at the foundation of feminist genealogies (*Feminist Genealogies* 16). Moreover, they question the creation of hierarchies of place within women's studies and the U.S. academy in general in a moment when thinking about place and location has an impact on the social and ethical responsibilities academics bear as producers of knowledge ("Cartographies" 27). Thus, such critical reflections on how location produces and reproduces power relations within and beyond the academy is key to understanding that reflections on space and representation are not only at the core of women's issues, but also at the center of a critique of imperialism and neocolonialism. The critical revision of location put forward by transnational feminist methodologies and theories offers an additional perspective on how space and place shape political and social struggles experienced by, not only women, but also by other marginalized populations. Furthermore, the idea of a transnational or cross-border feminist solidarity opens up new ways for understanding different "practices, spaces, and temporalities... into ideological and geographic proximity with one another in ways that produce connectivity and intersubjectivity (albeit a tense or uneven one) rather than absolute alterity" ("Cartographies" 40).

As these feminist studies demonstrate, notions of space and place structure complex models for defining identity and building power dynamics that have a deep impact on women and other underrepresented social groups. In *Space, Place and Gender,* Doreen Massey points to the need to reformulate conceptualizations of space and place; gender relations shape spatialities from the perspective of an "ever-shifting geometry of social / power relations" (3). Traditionally, "place" has been defined as something fixed and associated with gender connotations that represent it as the "local," or the feminine, whereas "space" has been conceived as fluid, universal, theoretical, abstract, or conceptual, frequently identified with the masculine (10). Massey further argues against such definitions, in particular the exclusivist claims to places—nationalist, regionalist, and localist—conceived of as sites of nostalgia bounded in a singular, fixed, and unproblematic understanding of identity. On the contrary, the space and place binary should be understood, according to Massey, from a constantly shifting dynamic in which "localities can in a sense be present in one another, both inside and outside at the same time... a view which stresses the construction of specificity through interrelations rather and through the imposition of boundaries and the counterposition of one identity against another" (7). By dismantling the space and place binary, Massey analyzes the political uses of both categories in constructing gendered spatialities. The concept of "articulation" is particularly useful in her theorizations on the topic. A place is a point of articulation, a particular moment in the intersecting porous spatial networks embedded in it that, over time, "have been constructed, laid down, interacted with one another, decayed and renewed" (120).

Massey's methodological claims provide an important framework for analyzing how women writers have addressed prevalent conceptualizations of space and place in Argentina. First, the discussion of places as sites of an identity politics sheds light on the critical role that the authors considered in this study play against gendered spatial identities that have marginalized women since the nineteenth century as social agents within the country's literary and social life. Contrary to a reification of place, the works studied here describe places as paradoxical and complex entities that produce symbolic renegotiations of gender relations. Second, by understanding places as articulations in larger porous networks of gendered spatial relations, we can conceive of literary spatializations as depictions of these articulations in key moments in the spatial imaginary of the country. Although this study centers mainly in the spatial, the temporal dimension is relevant, as Massey states; gendered spaces are not to be read in terms of static constructions but rather as sites of symbolic encounters constantly shifting place where both space and identity come unbounded. The search for a place refers to those sites where women find a temporary commonality of experience, where literature can be the place for constructing alternative identities and locations.

Accordingly, I have identified four representative stages in which significant shifts in the Argentine cultural landscape allow for a fruitful study of the production of gendered spaces in women's literature during the twentieth and beginning of the twenty-first century: immigration and the impact of international feminism (1910–1920); cosmopolitanism, domesticity, and the literary scene (1920–1950); authoritarianism and the return to democracy (1970–1990); and the local-global connections of the 1990s and the 2000s. Although the first period will not be addressed in this study because of space limitations, I believe it represents an important stage in setting the foundations of the production of gendered spaces in women's literature as a complex, and at times, paradoxical attempt to both challenge spatial imagery and build a new one. The notion of a "place" acquires, in the productions by women writers considered in this study, different connotations. For instance, in a global world where placelessness seems to be the rule, the poetry of Diana Bellessi, Luisa Futoransky, and María Negroni invites reflection on how places still possess a symbolic role in defining identities and languages. However, those poetic places are paradoxical constructions, fragile and vulnerable sites on the brink of collapse where the woman poet challenges the many uses dominant ideologies have made of the idea of place in the literary and political history of the country. We can read Bellessi's notion of a poetic South, as depicted in her collection *Sur* (1998), against the notions of a literary South that Jorge Luis Borges and Victoria Ocampo understood as a site where national and cosmopolitan imaginations of place come together. Bellessi's South, however, refers to other geographical imaginations; it is not a site for a cosmopolitan reinvention of nationalism, as in Borges and Ocampo, but rather the place where the woman poet, along with the indigenous populations of America, silenced and disappeared by official discourses and pervasive colonization campaigns since the nineteenth century, can finally find a voice within the violent histories of the continent. Contrary to a nationalist rhetoric that made the South into a literary trope for the foundation of cultural dynasties in the country, Bellessi readdresses the formation of this literary place as a site of a decolonization and decentering of the literary culture. Further, her poetry engages in a geopolitical definition of the South by displacing this literary location from a Euro-American to a Pan-American paradigm that also challenges how Argentina has imagined itself as a site of cosmopolitism since the foundation of its literary culture in the nineteenth century.

What is the location of women's literature within the complex spatial networks of social image reservoirs? The issue of women and location is central in recent feminist studies, such as Susan Stanford Friedman and her ideas on a "locational approach" for feminism, which by using a "geopolitical literacy," acknowledges the production of "changing societal stratifications and movements for social justice" in different locations (5). The local is a place of enunciation, states Elspeth Probyn; feminism needs to work "more deeply in and against the local" in order to examine, for instance, how certain local experiences may be "denied and ordered into the periphery" (186). As such, the local has been reified as the "location of radical openness and possibility," where social spaces can be "interrupted, appropriated, and transformed through artistic and literary practice" (hooks 153). The women writers studied here deconstruct oppressive spatialities through the powers of literary language; after all, as bell hooks states, "language is a place of struggle" (145). They propose alternative locations that position women as critical agents in the politics of knowledge production embedded in cultural institutions of the country. The imaginary locations described here are paradoxical; they bring together spatialities that are otherwise mutually exclusive, such as the center or the margin, the inside and the outside (Rose 140). Such paradoxical spaces resist the exclusions of hegemonic spatialities structured around what Rose calls the "territoriality of masculinism" wherein social subjects can imagine themselves within and outside the boundaries of hegemonic masculinism. Such space, rather than being at the foundations of disciplinary expertise and power, is precarious and fluctuating (160). From this liminal perspective, the woman writer is able to envision imaginary geographies. As Bellessi states, she is the armored Amazon or the naked Arthemise standing "in between the city—the culture's canon—and the deep wilderness... [from where] she opens the window to otherness, and observes the world, the human condition" (*Lo propio* 36). As rich and intricate virtual geographies, the women's literature included in this analysis interrogates both how location creates marginality and how it could be transformed into a site for women's empowerment and resistance.

My book addresses the formation of a "critical location" in women's literature through a discussion of a series of discourses based on intricate spatial dynamics, such as domesticity, exile, and globalization. I inquire into how categories of home and away, placement and displacement, dwelling and travel, and location and dislocation shape imaginations of place and the role they came to play in women's literature, as well as in the formation of literary and cultural genealogies. Previous critical studies have considered these spatial images in Argentina from different perspectives. A substantial body of critical works addresses travel literature in relation to the formation of national identity in Argentina and Latin America. Studies by Mónica Szurmuk on women's travel writing and the formation of images of self and national identity during the period from 1850 to 1930, and by Beatriz Colombi and the "intellectual journeys" of writers between 1880 and 1915 are just two examples worth mentioning. Other critics address the formation of the Argentine territory from a combined perspective of literary and geographical studies. Ernesto Livon-Grosman describes the establishment of "imaginary geographies" as "assemblages" in nineteenth-century travel narratives about Patagonia. Jens Andermann analyzes literary representations of space establishing cartographies of power that create nationalist identity discourses. And Álvaro Fernández Bravo links literary representations of the frontier to the development of a national identity in the nineteenth-century literatures of Argentina and Chile. The studies by Livon-Grosman, Andermann, and Fernández Bravo demonstrate how spatial formations show the anxieties of a nation in the making and the role of literature in the political projects of the country's cultural elites. To use Fernández Bravo's term, spatial constructs such as the frontier are "synecdoches" of the nation, places to build modernization projects that create a national narrative of identity formation.

My study establishes a dialogue with previous literary criticism that focuses on spatial constructions as represented in discourses on nation-building; it unveils the ramifications of the nineteenth-century literary and political project of defining the national space into twentieth- and twenty-first-century women's literature. Previous studies on literary representations of space are based primarily—if not exclusively—on a methodology that comes from literary and cultural studies; in contrast, my book finds in human geography's recent developments a rich model for addressing spatial constructions in literature from a cross-disciplinary perspective. Further, I examine literary works from the perspective of feminist conceptualizations of space and place, as evidenced in feminist geographers' understanding of spatialization processes as gender-based, theorizations by women of color in the United States, and transnational feminisms about space as a central category in creating oppressive locations for women and as a site for women's intervention and agency. *Gendered Spaces in Argentine Women's Literature* gives a comprehensive view of different spatialities in Argentina, such as the ideas of a national territory, the home, and the city. It addresses the considerable silence in existing scholarship about the role of gender in the study of spatial constructs in the literary histories of the country. The decision to focus exclusively on the women's perspective on gendered spatial relations responds to the belief that it has been systematically left out or underrepresented in studies on space and the formation of national identities in Argentina. Women's literature brings to the fore, as evidenced in this study, the centrality of space and place in determining gendered relations. Within this context, it demonstrates what Jean Franco describes as "the struggle for interpretative power" that has led women to "plot" against the imaginary nature of master narratives (*Plotting Women* xii). The time period included here is quite broad; thus, women's literature demonstrates different levels of agency and feminist commitment, but in all cases, it shows how women with more or less social power resorted to "subterfuge, digression, disguise, or deathly interruption" (xxiii) to challenge spatializations of power in twentieth- and twenty-first-century Argentina.

In the process of building imaginary geographies, the women authors considered in this study engage in a form of activism that Francine Masiello describes, when referring to the period of transition to Argentine democracy, as coming forth "not just in daily life but also in the realm of art and letters" ("Este pobre" 247–48). In a society that systematically has erased women and minorities and has reduced them to projections of a masculine culture of utopian or dystopian spaces, women have engaged in a subdued and yet powerful redesigning of Argentina's cartographies of power. For instance, in the 1910s and 1920s, international feminisms redefined women's place in the public culture by addressing issues of family law, health care, and working conditions for women and children. Pioneers of this struggle, Gabriela Coni, Fenia Chercov Repetto, Raquel Caamaña, and Carolina Muzzili, published in the socialist newspaper *La Vanguardia* and in *La Prensa*, report discourses and travel accounts that challenged women's role in the culture of the period. Alfonsina Storni also made public her critical perspectives in articles that appeared in *La Nación* and *La Nota* between 1919 and 1920. These early twentieth-century feminists confronted nationalist ideas on motherhood and the seclusion of women to the private scene of the home; they also contested the descriptions of Buenos Aires as a modern metropolis of European design by describing the marginal locations and experiences of women living, in many cases, in deplorable conditions or working in factories side by side with children. These writings challenged the production of the city as a space for *flânerie* and for the cultivation of literary games celebrating unrestricted mobility, like avant-garde poetry by Oliverio Girondo—for instance, his *20 poemas para ser leídos en el tranvía* (*Twenty Poems to be read in a Trolley Car*)—by depicting what Lefebvre calls the "lived reality" of women, appropriating the production of the city as a masculine literary geography. As Masiello states, by the twentieth century, the Argentine woman in the public sphere was the outsider who "set the boundaries between intelligibility and irrationality; she defined the limits between the high and low cultures, between elite and popular responses; and finally, she allowed men to mark the difference between civilization and savagery" (*Between* 9). In these early feminisms, the struggles for civil and family rights were a clear attempt to challenge the experiences of spatial segregation that women endured as a consequence of gender constructs like those described by Masiello. For instance, in 1911, Julieta Lanteri, one of the founders of the Association for University Women, cast her vote challenging state regulations that forbade women to vote, and in 1919, she ran for a position in the congress and, after being forbidden to do so, organized a fictitious electoral day in the streets of Buenos Aires in which many women had the chance to "vote" for the first time (Barrancos 97–99).

During the last decades of the twentieth century and at the turn of the twenty-first century, women's literature acquired an unquestionably central role. Nelly Richard states that the rise of Latin American feminism (and the questioning of hegemonic gender identity formations generally) may be, in the long run, the most radical and radicalizing expression of Latin American postmodernism (quoted in Beverly and Oviedo 8). Although the term "postmodernism" acquires different connotations in Latin America and at times causes many controversies among intellectuals, Beverly and Oviedo explain that the postmodernist turn coincides with the rapid and extensive spread of feminism and women's organizations in the region, and it provoked "the emergence of a postmodernist, but still explicitly socialist, form of political agency in Latin America" (12). Within the context of the "complexity of Latin America's own 'uneven modernity' and the new developments of its hybrid (pre- and post-) modern cultures…" (4), Latin American postmodernism has witnessed the empowerment of peripheral subjects and new forms of questioning the effects of modernity and coloniality in the continent. In Argentina, the cultures of postmodernism are also tied to the questioning of authoritarianism when gender, as Masiello states, "becomes a detonator of what has long been suppressed and offers crucial connections to a critical awareness in formation" (*Art* 40). We cannot affirm that women's literature is solely an effect of a postmodern culture because, as Franco demonstrates in *Plotting Women,* it has maintained the power to challenge hegemony since the colonial period. However, many authors considered here, such as Griselda Gambaro, Diana Raznovich, Sylvia Iparraguirre, Belén Gache, Diana Bellessi, Luisa Futoransky, and María Negroni, adopt a literary form that resembles the characteristics of a postmodern culture. Their works, as those of women of a "double minority," engage "in numerous semiotic transfers in their fictions, gestures of appropriation and deconstruction of the dominant discourse" (Potvin 227). However, women writers still hold a paradoxical position despite their increased visibility in the postmodern cultures of Latin America. As Cynthia Tompkins states, postmodern Latin American women writers "continue to be rendered invisible even though the irruption of Latin- American female and feminist writing has been hailed as the most important phenomenon of the post-Boom era" (1). The poetry of Luisa Futoransky is an excellent example of this complex and paradoxical location of the woman writer within Argentina's postmodernism. In her collection *Prender de gajo* [*Transplant*] (2006), Futoransky reworks the topics of nomadism and global mobility that she had previously explored in her novels *De Pe a Pa o de Pekín a París* [*From Pe to Pa or From Pekín to Paris*] (1986) and *Son cuentos chinos* [*Tall Tales*] (1991). Her works engage in a postmodern aesthetic of collage and artifice; they bring to the fore the role of women and other minorities in the complex scenery of the postmodern metropolis. However, Futoransky's locations are paradoxical, at once unbounded and yet highly constrained; they reveal, through what Masiello calls a "nomad's poetics," the "restless, multivocal, mobile" expressions of those located in the margins of modernization processes in different global geographies. She combines the playfulness of a postmodern aesthetic with a search for memory through a complex set of spatiotemporal relations embodied in connections between memory, mourning, and place. In times of a generalized historic and cultural amnesia and in light of the disappearances caused by the Argentine dictatorship, Futoransky's postmodern aesthetic acquires a distinct feminist perspective. Written from the standpoint of a critical postmodernism, she unveils the domestication of memory and oblivion in contemporary societies and the fragile situation of minorities in the contemporary spatial realities of the globe.

Feminism is, in Raquel Olea's words, "the incomplete project of modernity" in Latin America; the women authors included here address this incomplete, virtual project of constructing a new subject form of woman

(197). The last few decades in Argentina have witnessed the appearance of new social actors as a consequence of the country's transition to democracy: women, young people, union workers, and human rights activists are part of a larger group of informal social movements that are reclaiming public spaces and gaining new levels of political and social representation. Although during the 1970s and 1980s, feminist movements around the world regained importance through international meetings and conventions, feminism has remained a marginal force behind many of the women's movements in Argentina that stayed attached, as Elizabeth Jelin states, to traditional gender roles. In fact, it is through the identities of mothers and housewives that women have slowly begun claiming new rights, something that explains, for instance, the impact of movements such as the mothers and grandmothers of Plaza de Mayo in Argentine society ("Los movimientos" 33). This in part can be explained by the fact that the dictatorships of the 1970s and 1980s reinforced the seclusion of women to a domestic role by defending the family as a site that would protect young people against the "dangers" of leftist ideologies. Women paid a high price for transgressing this domestic ideal: 30 percent of the thirty thousand disappeared by the military juntas were women (Feijóo and Gogna 45). During the democratic transition, the most active women's movement has been the Housewives Union, founded in 1982; these women organized a series of public protests against the government's price adjustments and inflation (62–63). And, as Barrancos states, women have been central protagonists in more recent social protests, such as the *piquetero* movements of the 1990s (172–74). In addition, a number of social and legal reforms, such as the legalization of divorce in 1987, the law for shared legal custody of children in 1985, and the 1991 "ley de cupo" that guarantees that at least 30 percent of senators must be women, are important developments in the advancement of women's rights in the country (176–79). However, the existing poor protection for women victims of domestic violence, the increase in human trafficking, and the penalization of abortion are some of the many facts that still place women in a vulnerable social position (176–91).

This is the complex social scenario where a larger part of the women's literature addressed in this book finds its context. Although not all the works considered here are openly feminist, they engage in a questioning of the historical absence of women from the discursive, social, and political power in Argentina's social and literary cartographies. Discussing the issue of space in literary representations also implies addressing the spatial segregation of women endemic to the country's literary and social landscape. The feminist methodologies employed here intend to shed light on possible sites of social intervention, as described by Olea: "It has been this liminal space that feminism in the last several decades has installed itself as both a theoretical discourse and a social movement with the capacity to intervene in and modify forms of social functioning. Feminism comes from 'no-where' to spaces where its discursivity does not yet have a history, where it does not yet have the capacity even to negotiate or enter into alliances" (197). Néstor Perlongher, the gay activist who died of AIDS, and one of Latin America's most engaging poets and thinkers, describes this social and political potential of marginal spaces in what he calls a "devenir mujer" ("becoming woman"). In "Los devenires minoritarios" ["Becoming Minority"], and borrowing from spatial theories by Deleuze and Guattari and Foucault, he develops the notion of hidden social maps, cartographies of desire where racial and sexual minorities engage in the redefinition of hegemonic image reservoirs. Becoming a minority implies, above all, "becoming woman," because women embody a minority position in relation to men's majority paradigm—*machista,* white, adult, heterosexual, sane, father of a family, the city's dweller (169). By becoming woman, other minorities can intervene in identity discourses and reclaim the role of margins and minor identities in altering social spatialities of power. As Masiello states, Perlongher proposes that "it is precisely from the often invisible margin—the site of the unincorporated, the irreducible, the constantly shifting and mobile—that a theory of democratic practice emerges to fill the blank horizon" (*Art* 39).

As this is written, the city of Buenos Aires witnesses a series of "illegal occupations" of public lands in the neighborhoods of Villa Soldati and Villa Lugano. On the outskirts of a city that has been booming with the presence of international tourists attracted by a favorable currency exchange, a group of thirteen thousand impoverished homeless, the majority of them immigrants from neighboring Bolivia and Paraguay, set precarious tents on the surface of 130 hectares of the "Indo-American Park." Riots and the resultant police repression yielded the deaths of two people, Bernardo Salgueiro, a 22-year-old immigrant from Paraguay, and Rosemarie Churapuña, a 28-year-old immigrant from Bolivia, and the eviction of the entire group, whose living situation remains unresolved. The increased vulnerability of marginalized social groups with no access to their own residence is a chronic problem in Argentina. Some authors link this problem to a series of public building projects that increased dramatically during the dictatorship of the 1970s and caused compulsive evictions of people living on public lands and the liberalization of rent prices, also in the period from 1976 to 1979 (Fara 271–72). Writing about spatializations of power in women's literary representations, I cannot avoid the discussion of the histories behind such violent effects of spatial segregation in the country. How can one forget the military campaigns that in the nineteenth century exterminated thousands of indigenous people in Argentina in the name of conquering a territory for the project of modernizing the country and achieving economic and social development? Or the formation of *villas miseria* in the 1940s when migrants from the provinces settled in the outskirts of Buenos Aires in search of a better life? And the disappearance of thirty thousand people in concentration camps built in the city's subterfuges where street wanderers could completely ignore the torture and illegal detention taking place, in many cases under their feet? And finally, the experiences of Argentina's homeless: entire families suffering from the effects of the compartmentalization of social spaces led by a revived racism and xenophobia and the lack of structural solutions to the problem of housing? It is not my goal to idealize women's literature as the sole place for resistance of such tragic spatial histories in Argentina. In fact, not all women's literature would necessarily yield crucial knowledge about power and inequality. However, the texts included here demonstrate an acute consciousness of place and the material effects of such spatial segregations in the lives of women and other minorities in the country. Within this context, the role of feminist interpretations of space can be instrumental in disclosing the histories and developments of systemic power struggles, as represented in social and literary spatializations. In exposing gendered spatialities, the women writers included here open possibilities for identifying sites of interventions, spaces in which social codifications of gender, race, and social class break down and reveal their unreality. As such, women's literature provides ways in which it is possible to retrace alternative spatial genealogies in the literary and social traditions of the country.

Chapter 1, "Displacing Domesticity: Cosmopolitanisms, Travel Writing and Narratives of the Home," addresses the production of gendered spaces in travel diaries, fiction, and autobiography by Victoria Ocampo and Norah Lange during the period from 1920 to 1950. Compared to the social restrictions women immigrants suffered in the 1910s, these women writers enjoyed a greater spatial mobility. Through international travel and tourism, they reshaped social and literary notions of domesticity that were at the foundation of a division of cultural labor. Home narratives, as depicted in both Ocampo's and Lange's works, demonstrate a transformation of the home into a cultural site from which women authors sought to build their unique literary style. In the narratives and autobiographies considered here, I analyze the conflation of discourses on domesticity and cosmopolitan experiences of international travel that allows Ocampo and Lange to reshape their social position within the culture of the period. In their narratives of the home, these writers create new cosmopolitan representations of domesticity that challenge gendered views on the public and private sphere and their role in literary production.

Chapter 2, "Of Other Spaces: Staging Repression in the Works of Griselda Gambaro and Diana Raznovich," focuses on the role of theater as a genre that offers a critical perspective on the historical realities of the Argentine dictatorship of the 1970s and early 1980s, as well as the democratic transition that followed. Within the context of the artistic innovations of *Teatro Abierto*, Gambaro and Raznovich wrote dramas addressing the connections between authoritarianism, violence, and gender. Although a considerable number of critics studied this relationship in both authors, I propose to focus on the issue of dramatic space in their works. Through what I call the "uncanny" and "specular" uses of theatrical space, both writers question the manipulation of space by the dictatorship and its repressive apparatus. Gambaro's plays address the spatial formations during *La Guerra Sucia* [The Dirty War], whereas Raznovich explores their later effects in the Argentine society of the 1990s. As addressed in the cases of Lange and Ocampo in chapter 1, the domestic is also a predominant setting in Gambaro and Raznovich because one of the main historical conventions in theater has been to identify the home and the stage. We can trace a common feminist genealogy among these authors based on the transformation of the domestic into an unhomely space, as represented for instance in the works of Norah Lange and another author not addressed in this study but who similarly transforms domesticity through the fantastic—Silvina Ocampo. As Hannah Scolnicov demonstrates, the origins of theatrical scene can be found in the *oikos*, the impenetrable space of the home that Greeks associated with women (15). Traditionally, theater has maintained this division between the *oikos* and the *polis*, making the stage the preferred site for exposing the domestic. However, in Gambaro and Raznovich, the domestic is both familiar and recognizable, yet concealing and enigmatic; in the Freudian sense, their works dismantle the association between theater, the oikos, and a domesticated femininity. By using Foucault's notions of heterotopias, chapter 2 addresses the ways in which the stage's "other spaces" represent a way of reflecting upon our role as historical actors and a means to building new places of memory, social awareness, and change.

Chapters 3 and 4 focus on global experiences of space and place during the 1990s and 2000s and how globalization impacts the scope and shape of literary culture and the location women occupy in it. In chapter 3, "Global Patagonia: Rewriting the National Space," I focus on the region of Patagonia and investigate how Sylvia Iparraguirre and Belén Gache describe changes in the territorial identity of Argentina under the influence of global spatial models. In Iparraguirre's uses of historical fiction and Gache's digital literature and art, we can see how both writers depict the possibilities and limitations of cultural artifacts in redefining masculinist notions of territorialism. In the context of a national culture increasingly influenced by global models, their works explore how the region of Patagonia is built as a territorial and symbolic, national and global frontier that women's literature can reinterpret and read anew.

Chapter 4, "Poetic Crossovers: Paradoxical Spaces of Women's Poetry," examines ways in which poetry portrays other forms of global displacement, such as cultural nomadism and diaspora. Authors such as Bellessi, Futoransky, and Negroni contest the spatial constraints of militarized societies and global consumerism. Bellessi writes on ideas of a "global South," whereas Futoransky uses the diasporic experience to deconstruct spatial fictions of patriarchy and authoritarianism. Negroni describes poetry as an archipelago, *Iceland,* where the woman nomad can re-create the oppressive positions they occupy in society. Poetry is, in all of these examples, a way of connecting women's experiences of diaspora and nomadism through different geographies and historical periods into virtual networks of female solidarity.

Returning to the opening reflections on *La cautiva,* one cannot cease to wonder about the last images that María saw during her final days in the desert. What would María's desert look like? Would it have been as violent and infertile as Echeverría represented? We know only that the desert was a textual construction of the abject, the ultimate frontier in the literary imagination of the period, a fantastic geography of barbarism embodying what was left out from the spatial imagination of the nation, the *mestizaje,* barbarism, uncontrol, the sexualized body, the Other (Rotker 84). As Rotker astutely points out, not only the space is a textual construction in the poem, the body of María is completely absent as it acts only as the container of an empty subjectivity included in the poem to brand the fight against barbarism and to legitimize a political project. As such, she is an absolute victim who needs to die almost immediately so that the advances of civilization are not threatened by contamination with the abject. As space needs to be made into a bare landscape, her body is similarly erased lest this contamination will stop the progress of nation-building (97). I like to think of the task of the critic as one that fills in the gaps, ties the loose ends, or simply reads in between the lines of the hidden narratives that shape the literary imagination of a country. Space offers, I believe, a marvelous opportunity to weave together those loose ends in the many histories that intersect in literary texts. The project of *Gendered Spaces in Argentine Women's Literature* is nothing more than a dire attempt to reconstruct the silent perspectives of how certain women experienced space and place as sites of resilience and domination. I cannot ignore in this critical perspective my own struggles with so many social placements and locations. As I migrate from them, as I am able to transform them through my critical inquiries, I hear the echoes of many other women whose whisperings still resonate in the literature I include in my study. This book attests to the many ways in which those voices tell the imaginary intersections shaping the intricate tapestries of space and place.

CHAPTER 1

Displacing Domesticity: Cosmopolitanisms, Travel Writing, and Narratives of the Home

1. Cosmopolitan Reinventions: Negotiating Domesticity

During the first decades of the twentieth century, Argentina witnessed a transformation of its social and cultural landscape due to experiences of travel and immigration. Cosmopolitan travelers had been frequent in the country since the nineteenth century, but it was during the period from the 1920s until the end of World War II that these visitors had a definite impact on its cultural life. In the 1920s, the "avant-garde" traveler helped local literary enclaves to establish symbolic locations within the new world's cultural map (Aguilar 32). The "cultural travelers" of the period from 1928 to 1950 shaped national debates even more deeply. Through conferences and, in many cases, because they relocated and lived in Argentina for many years, these travelers were instrumental in the transformation of Argentina's cultural identity (Aguilar and Siskind 368). The paths of this intellectual traveling were multiple and took different directions. Before this period, Latin American writers traveled to Europe in great numbers in search of a professional space that could consolidate their prestige and international recognition. Between 1900 and 1920, this intellectual diaspora established an extraterritorial "lettered city" in Europe, mainly in Paris, and from this perspective, founded key supranational narratives such as the notion of "Latin Americanism," which shaped intellectual debates for decades to come (Colombi, "Camino" 545).

Within this same period, some women also engaged in this form of intellectual traveling, enjoying a certain level of mobility allowed by their class condition. Many of them, such as Victoria Ocampo and María Rosa Oliver, had traveled with their families to Europe since childhood—a common practice in Argentine aristocracies since the nineteenth century—and they wrote lengthy accounts of such experiences in their autobiographies. However, these international travel experiences also had a definite impact on women's writing and on the formation of an identity for women within Argentinean literary culture, as Mónica Zsurmuk's *Women in Argentina: Early Travel Narratives* demonstrates. In her *Autobiografía* [*Autobiography*], Victoria Ocampo narrates, for instance, her 1912 trip to Europe as a newlywed woman and, in a telling example, describes how, wrapped in an Argentine flag, she entered a party where a crowd of tourists from Argentina, Chile, Brazil, Uruguay, and Peru saluted her. As Masiello explains, aboard the transatlantic vessel, a metaphor of Latin American modernity, Ocampo embodied the symbol of national culture (*Between Civilization* 164). Ocampo frequently employs the image of the transatlantic trip to represent the cultural cosmopolitanism of *Sur* [*South*], the literary journal and publishing house she founded in 1931, when she compares it, for instance, to her great-grandfather's trips to England and the United States as an emissary of the new Argentine nation at the beginning of the nineteenth century.[1] Similarly embarked on a cargo vessel to Norway, the main character of Norah Lange's *45 días y 30 marineros* [*45 Days and 30 Sailors*] also serves as a metaphor for international encounters, where the narrator is a translator playing with gender and language differences. In this fictional travel journal, Lange negotiates the complex role she held as a cultural producer within the Argentine avant-garde as she engaged in a feminist critique of the restrictive social roles women occupied during this period.

Why begin a discussion on domesticity with references to transatlantic trips? In fact, as this chapter contends, both Lange and Ocampo gender the experiences of cultural journeys upon which Latin American intellectuals had embarked since the nineteenth century. Further, such experiences of cosmopolitanism allowed them to "rewrite the text" of domesticity.[2] I propose here that domesticity and cosmopolitanism functioned as complementary discourses in both writers. Although, as I later demonstrate, this association was not present exclusively in women writers, Lange and Ocampo employed it to gender Argentina's modernist culture. The home and abroad, the private and the public are intersecting spheres, for as Alison Blunt and Robyn Dowling discuss, "home is not simply domestic"; "an understanding of what home means, and how it is created and reproduced, requires as much attention to processes of commerce, imperialism and politics, for example, as to household negotiations" (19).

Norah Lange dealt almost obsessively with the home. Her four novels, *Cuadernos de infancia* [*Childhood Notebooks*] (1937), *Antes que mueran* [*Before They Die*] (1944), *Personas en la sala* [*People in the Room*] (1950), and *Los dos retratos* [*The Two Portraits*] (1956), take place in domestic spaces where female protagonists are trapped by windows, doors, and fences they are not allowed to cross. The houses Lange describes are unhomely refuges where female protagonists question a culture that seeks to domesticate them. The distinct contrast she traces between the public and the private can be read against a culture of modernity that was defined as public and masculine—the man of the crowd, the flâneur as its epitome—and that confined women to an antimodern representation and excluded them from the processes of social change (Felski *The Gender* 16). As Vicky Unruh describes, Lange's writing depicts this gender contrast by creating two "disparate worlds—the lively fraternity of the literary avant-garde and a vanishing community of familial women" (74). However, as critics point out, the isolation of private experience in Lange is also projected outward and linked to negotiations between the public and the private, where literary and cultural production is central (Domínguez 32). In fact, her depictions of domestic dynamics complement her almost exhibitionist public role evident in the speeches collected in *Estimados congéneres* [*Speeches*] (published in 1968) and in the early fictional travelogue *45 días y 30 marineros* (1933).

In a similar fashion, Ocampo negotiated national and cosmopolitan tensions by dealing with spatial constructs, such as the home and the city. In her writings, literary locations embody the tensions women faced in a cultural landscape regulated by men. Ocampo wrote extensively in her autobiography about the secluded spaces where she grew up, namely houses that were monitored by a multitude of servants, relatives, and governesses. Her literary project represents an attempt to escape the bounds of this constrictive domesticity. She crafted a cosmopolitan writing that redefined her role as a woman and cultural producer during the first decades of the twentieth century. She designed a number of alternative literary habitats and—to employ the expression of her very good friend Virginia Woolf—"rooms of her own," carefully arranged and decorated to her own taste, that paralleled a literary practice seeking to transform spatial limitations into sites of creative production. Read in the light of her *Autobiografía* (published posthumously between 1979 and 1984), her ten volumes of essays, *Testimonios* [*Testimonies*] (1935–1977), shed light on the intricacies of the mediation between the public and the private in Ocampo's writing and the complexities of her cultural identity.

During the period in which Lange and Ocampo produced their works, a number of important changes in relation to women's rights and their public and private roles took place in Argentina. The first decades of the twentieth century were a period of intense debate about gender roles and their implications for the traditional family structure. In 1926, important reforms of the civil code took place that benefited women's rights in marriage in regard to issues of property, financial independence, and jurisdiction over children.[3] For instance, married women were allowed to practice different professions and use their income freely without reporting it to their husbands (Carlson 167). The perception that women had been denied intellectual and personal freedom informed many of the debates surrounding the new economic role of women, their juridical place within the family, and their participation in the public life of their country (Lavrin 4). An intense debate on gender, prompted by massive immigration and the alteration of a nineteenth-century understanding of national culture, shaped the feminist struggle for rights. Women held the role of mediators between the ideological complexities of the period, modernity and nationalism, as Masiello demonstrates.[4] Such social changes impacted Argentina's literary culture. As depicted in Lange's and Ocampo's works, women had to maneuver changing positions and social roles. Although they had little contact with women's movements, their works portray a shared interest with early twentieth-century feminism in how women negotiate their participation in public life (Unruh 23). And, as Masiello posits, women's writing of the period also questions the gender implications of modernity by challenging the masculine privilege in speaking and controlling literary culture (*Between Civilization* 13).

This chapter explores the intricate dialogue between cosmopolitan and domestic imaginations of place in which women engaged during this period. Although critics have written extensively on the topic of public and private spheres in writers such as Lange and Ocampo, little attention has been paid to cosmopolitanism as a crucial influence on the redefinition of the private.[5] Here, I propose to concentrate on the construct of the home as a symbolic and material site that spatializes the gender conflicts central to a country facing a sweeping modernity brought about by demographic, economic, and cultural changes. An "Argentine Eurocentrism," where "Argentina consumes Europe's view of it, not only in a self-defeating desire to be seen by the metropole and to be its 'other,' but also to establish a visible, viable self in the world" (Kaminsky, *Argentina* 9), was key in redefining local dynamics of sex and gender. Although one could argue that interactions between internally and externally generated notions of Argentina as a culture and a place pervaded the country's history during different time periods, this dialogue was particularly rich in the first decades of the twentieth century, when foreign debates on cultural production strongly influenced discourses on the home and the domestic.[6] Literary culture was the medium where such exchanges took place. In fact, contextualized in the social transformations of the period, Lange's and Ocampo's narratives of the home are metaphors for the changing literary landscape and represent women's efforts to redefine social and cultural roles. Lange actively participated in the activities of the Argentine avant-garde through her involvement in the Martín Fierro group. Although not engaged with avant-garde circles, Ocampo maintained an intense dialogue with European modernism through the literary friendships of Virginia Woolf, Ernst Ansermet, Waldo Frank, Pierre Drieu La Rochelle, and others. Following the nineteenth-century tradition of the literary salon, Lange and Ocampo transformed the domestic space into a site where social and literary gender relations are redefined through the discourse of a literary modernity that challenges existing boundaries between the public and the private.

This chapter also stresses a connection with the autobiography, which as a discourse of identity formation, shapes the domestic narratives analyzed here and establishes alternative social and literary positions for women. I study the autobiography here, not as a transparent rendering of "real" life, but as a complex, performative term that describes textual variations of self-representation. More specifically, autobiographies can be read as dynamic texts wherein individual and collective models of identity establish an ever-changing dialogue. Sidonie Smith and Julia Watson describe the components of memory, experience, identity, embodiment, and agency as central to the autobiographical process and stress that "in effect, autobiographical telling is performative; it enacts the 'self' that it claims has given rise to an 'I'...that is neither unified nor stable—it is fragmented, provisional, multiple, in process" (9). Although autobiographies by women have been undervalued, either for being considered a "personal genre" or because they have been seen as undermining the public role of women, I contend here that it is precisely this use of the personal in autobiographical writing that is key in shaping a distinct genealogy for women's writing during this period. In their autobiographical or semi-autobiographical "self-figurations," Lange and Ocampo mold a narrative of the self that negotiates generic attributions and opens up virtual spaces of literary production. Based on new configurations of personal and collective identities, they propose alternative cosmopolitanisms that express how the internationalization of the public sphere transforms the private. Thus, the autobiography holds a key role in understanding how the public and private intersect, how women negotiate social and literary roles, and how they build new patterns of literary creativity. By displacing narratives of the domestic and the self into the realm of cosmopolitan encounters, Lange and Ocampo balanced difficult social roles. I am not proposing, however, that the private or autobiographical element, as "characteristic" of women's writing, is somehow the revolutionary trait in these fictions. I align my reading with Felski's theories on going "beyond a feminist aesthetics."[7] What I believe is truly distinct in Lange and Ocampo is the novel use of the private and the autobiographical in relation to patterns of textual circulation and dissemination, specifically to the issue of the location women held in the social and literary milieu. The home is then not only an autobiographical construct but also, most importantly, a symbol of the cultural negotiations women writers faced in the midst of a national culture profoundly transformed by cosmopolitan influences. It is in the "performative" realm of the autobiographical fictionalization that Norah Lange and Victoria Ocampo were able to invent new locations for women and redefine the role of gendered spaces in cultural production.

2. Norah Lange's Unhomely Residences

The first edition of *45 días y 30 marineros* begins with the following statement by Fermín Estrella Gutiérrez: "Nora Lange es una alondra de Escandinavia que ha aprendido a cantar en el tala criollo" [Nora Lange is a Scandinavian lark who has learned to sing in the Creole tala tree].[8] And then he adds, "Por su verso corre, a veces, un frío de nieve recién caída y hay una sensación de fuego en el hogar, y de manteles tendidos al viajero que pasa... Pero hay también, criollismo nuevo y gusto de cantar el tango y asomarse a la calle para ver los paraísos del suburbio" [At times the cold of a fresh snowfall runs through her verse, and the sensation of a fire in the hearth and tablecloths laid out for the passing traveler... But there is also a new Creole style, and the pleasure of singing a tango and looking out on the street to see the suburban paradises] (4). Such remarks doubtlessly evidence the close association between women and ideologies of nationalism and cosmopolitanism frequent in the modernist Argentine culture of the early twentieth century. In a cultural milieu where the polarization of the literary scene between the groups of Florida and Boedo embodies this debate, women acquired the role of icons within the transformations of the literary culture and its relation to ideologies of nationalism. Their changing role in the public sphere triggered fears and anxieties around new patterns of literary production. In this section, I explore the refashioning of domesticity by modern discourses on travel writing and cosmopolitanism within the context of the Argentine avant-garde in Lange's novels, *Cuadernos de infancia, Personas en la sala,* and *Los dos retratos,* and her earlier fictional travel journal narrating her trip to Norway, *45 días y 30 marineros*. Gender imagery from discourses on cosmopolitanism and domesticity shape her project of dismantling traditional social roles for women. Although mainly concerned with the literary and, to a certain extent, focused exclusively in the personal and intimate world of her female characters, Lange used her narratives to discuss the highly controversial issue of women within the country's gender relationships, which described them mainly as angels of the home and marginalized them from an active role in the cultural scene of the period.

In Argentina, representations of domesticity had been associated since the nineteenth century with the role of women as mothers, and their bodies were therefore turned into laboratories for the birth of the modern nation. In the 1920s and 1930s, as Marcela Nari contends, women's reproductive systems were under scrutiny; demographic changes brought about by immigration were perceived as a threat to the state's goals of increasing population under the ideal of racial purity. The "naturalization of motherhood" reestablished ideals of the nineteenth-century patriotic motherhood.[9] However, cultural representations of the period also describe women in new public roles that transcended such ideals, for as Unruh explains, women gained recognition in their roles as writers and intellectuals. Struggling with the division of cultural labor that confined them to the realm of the home, women "manifested an emergent feminism for its time: a distinct self-consciousness about gender, a recognition that the rhetoric or realities of modernity posed singular challenges for women, and keen attention to their own anomalous status as women writers" (23). Experiences of travel and immigration also provided a new set of challenges for gendered spatial divisions. The figure of the immigrant was key in destabilizing gender and class conventions, as the journalism of Alfonsina Storni so clearly depicts.[10] Upper-class women ventured outside of the restrictive boundaries of the home and the domestic and began exploring new writing formats. Travel writing, for instance, was vital in helping women to challenge their social roles; it was a genre that "afforded them the possibility of playing against the limits of acceptability while they could still pretend they were simply performing the roles of good women, good mothers, and good teachers" (Szurmuk 12).

Within the context of these changes in women's social roles during this period, the language and imagery of the avant-garde allowed Lange to go a bit further in gender transgressions. Her characters cross many borders through a set of linguistic and visual manipulations, overcoming the traps of the private and disguising the voice of public dissent. The visual, adapted as a textual medium, is a central element in this dynamic. Lange's narrators—all of them identified as women—position themselves in the margins of a scrutinized spatiality where they are able to transform social conventions in a random yet subversive way. Home and abroad, the national and the cosmopolitan, are the sites where such transformative processes take place. This predominance of the visual comes from the culture of modernity, which focuses on the centrality of vision as a resource for aesthetic innovation. Women occupied, however, a complex position within this visual rhetoric. The avant-garde privileged women and the feminine as the object of their representations. Modernity in general has been characterized by a "putting into discourse of 'woman,'" that is, the artistic objectification of the female body as evidenced, for instance, in surrealism (Suleiman 13). However, real women were relegated to a secondary place in the realm of aesthetic production. As Suleiman states, women artists and writers affiliated with this movement were placed into a "double margin": "The avant-garde woman writer is doubly intolerable, seen from the center, because her writing escapes not one but two sets of expectations/categorizations; it corresponds neither to the 'usual revolutionary point of view' nor to the 'woman's point of view'" (15).

As Unruh studies, performance afforded the woman writer the possibility to transgress from her marginal role into the cultural scene during the avant-garde period (4–5). As I examine here, the manipulation of visual constructs allowed Lange to transform and reinvent the domestic realm. The visual rhetoric of photography is central in this endeavor. Following the techniques of artistic doubling, ironic mirroring, and photomontage, Lange employed the aesthetic conventions of the portrait, very much in vogue since the late 1800s in Argentina. As Marcy Schwartz and Mary Beth Tierney-Tello state, "With a growing middle class, portrait photography in nineteenth- and twentieth-century Latin America became not only a mode of self-representation but also a way to tout a family's prosperity and fulfill class aspirations" (4). Photography was first cultivated around the 1840s in Argentina, and it had a central ethnographic role, as the pictures of indigenous people and gauchos in Benito Panunzi's "albums de costumbres" [ways of life albums] attest. However, it also contributed significantly to the establishment of class identities; the "carte de visite," which included different poses of the same individual or group portrait, became very popular at the end of the nineteenth century. Daguerreotypes had previously expanded the domestic uses of portraits, as demonstrated by photo-miniatures used in personal objects, such as in jewels for medallions or rings, and jewelry boxes and porcelains (Niedermaier 36). In Argentina, many portraits also documented the histories and genealogies of literary enclaves, as a browsing of the avant-garde journal *Martín Fierro* and its series of photographs of banquets and conferences reveals.

Lange recycles such domestic uses of photographs by employing the portrait as a site of aesthetic experimentation for the woman writer. She establishes innovative partnerships between photography and writing and transforms images into sites of performance and revision of gender roles associated with notions of domesticity and cosmopolitanism. In addition, the growing perception that women had public visibility explains the visual configurations of Lange's narrative project. In all her works, vision is an iterative and dialogical tool with which the woman writer negotiates and contests gender positions. Moreover, her narrative depicts situations and settings of learning, a noticeable reference to the training of women for domestic roles that is particularly evident in the autobiographical *Cuadernos de infancia*. However, her female protagonists twist this learning process and change it into an apprenticeship of defiance of visual and linguistic conventions. Lange's texts represent this visual apprenticeship as a way of transforming the position for the woman writer in the complex scenario at the beginning of twentieth-century Argentina. As critics such as Domínguez demonstrate, Lange engaged in an astute negotiation of her public role, for instance, through the use of the mask, when such public exposure was deemed dangerous (32). As such, her narratives express a constant fluctuation between visibility and invisibility and transform the home and the domestic into a phantasmagorical, unhomely place.

The home is the main narrative setting in Lange's works, a fact connected to the importance of the family home in her life and literary career. María Elena Legaz identifies two houses as crucial in Lange's career: the first is the house on Tronador Street, where many literary encounters took place, and the second is Suipacha 1444, where she lived with her husband, Oliverio Girondo (13). As described in Leopoldo Marechal's novel *Adán Buenosayres,* they were both central in the meetings of literary enclaves. Lange transforms these biographical sites into places for visual experimentation; she alters domestic ideals of balance and order and the maternal role of women within the "sacred place of the home." As in other literary texts that evoke photographs without actually reproducing images, her novels employ a photographic aesthetic as a "catalyst for the fantastic" (Schwartz and Tierney-Tello 8); fictional interactions with family portraits serve as a mechanism to make present the dead and to examine the formation of literary genealogies. As such, her novels possess some traits of detective fiction, such as the suspension of chronological time, the shadowy and mysterious spatial backgrounds, and the protagonist's psychological confusion between real and fantastic perceptions. The mystery at the heart of these narratives is the conflicting search for a familiar memory, a field that is fiercely contested in a war of visual representations played by different family members. Her narrative project depicts power struggles taking place within the domestic space; as Domínguez states, such representations refer to family identity as a construct in a process of change (31). Further, as I contend here, this ongoing "visual battle" embodied in the family home is also a reference to the struggles of the woman writer to gain a position within the literary family of the avant-garde groups of the period. In addition, the eccentric characterization of the domestic also relates to Lange's critique of the association of family and state and the arbitrary relation between nationhood and language (Masiello, *Between Civilization* 156).

Domestic spaces adopt a labyrinthlike form in Lange's works; they are collages of present and past images, either located in a central position in background descriptions or evoked through the family's collective memories. The autobiographical *Cuadernos de infancia* adopts the form of a textual photomontage; the novel describes a detached life narrative in which the protagonist learns to manipulate and transform self-images in the process of coming of age. Gender expectations are displayed to the reader as different narrative "windows," opening and closing a series of family images—her father's cosmopolitan studio, her mother's sewing room, and the "mysterious" room of her sister Irene, displaying and hiding her voluptuous body to the disconcerted eyes of the child narrator. In another sequence, she narrates an encounter with the "strongest woman in the world," working for a circus near Mendoza, where the family temporarily relocates before her father's death. This house of memories allows the narrator to interact with these different images as if they were old photographs chosen and discarded from an old album. The feeling of aberration imposed by the portraits of a sexualized or anomalous woman's body—the circus performer, the sister—exhibits the narrator's own fears and anxieties about gender roles for women. Familiar images are detached from any emotional connection or involvement; the focus is placed on objects instead of psychological descriptions, a trait that María Elena Legaz associates with Robbe-Grillet's *nouveau roman* (147). Because of its fractured plot and cinematographic style, this narrative adopts the forms of literary cubism (Legaz 139). This detached narrative style is further enhanced by the creation of a gothic ambience of dark shadows, gloomy interiors, and subtle whisperings that transform the family house into an uncanny place.

Cuadernos de infancia demonstrates how Lange investigates the process of identity formation through the genre of autobiography. The narrator manipulates dissimilar self-representations as images and discourses about ideal roles for women. However, even when this fragmentary composition has been studied as characteristic of women's autobiography, I agree with Sylvia Molloy that the novel's form results from ultraist and surrealist literary conventions (176), a format that exposes the complex relationship between ideologies of gender and selfhood. If the generic contract of autobiography engages the autobiographer in a doubled subjectivity,[11] establishing a dialogic relationship between the narrator and the protagonist, this doubling is exasperated in *Cuadernos de infancia* by the use of avant-garde literary conventions. For instance, the novel adopts the form of a visual performance that, exhibiting the genre's reflexive traits, allows for a manipulation of social representations of women as visual constructs. As in the ubiquitous photomontages of the avant-garde, *Cuadernos de infancia* assembles a female subjectivity made of pieces and parts of visual constructs stored in the depths of family imaginaries. The space of the home is thus transformed into a fragmentary and interactive visual structure that the narrator learns to manipulate at the end of the coming-of-age process. The home becomes a metaphor of a female subjectivity in the making, whereas its spatial labyrinths refer to the dismantling and composing of new identities for the protagonist. *Cuadernos de infancia* adopts the form of a visual autobiography in which visibility becomes a tool for self-reflection and for altering gender roles as visual constructions.

The concept of domesticity developed in Europe in the nineteenth century as a direct result of both the division between work and home and the growing separation of the male and female spheres. Gradually, the home became the sphere of the wife and children, which coincided with the cult of motherhood, the feminization of culture, and cultivation of sentimentalism (Heynen 7). As Gülsüm Baydar explains, this notion has had detrimental implications for women because, as a social construction to domesticate, it compartmentalizes sexual identities, solidifies gender roles, and represses the female element (41). In Latin America, such ideals have been at the foundation of national narratives; the home, as the site of heterosexual love, provided a figure for an apparently nonviolent consolidation of the nation-states around the middle of the century (Sommer 6). Domestic romances "go hand in hand with patriotic history in Latin America. The books fueled a desire for domestic happiness that runs over into dreams of national prosperity; and nation-building projects invested private passions with public purpose" (7). The Argentine avant-garde focused on a remaking of the association between the domestic and the national, as Jorge Luis Borges's works from his *ultraísta* period and the debates in the journal *Martín Fierro* demonstrate. In "El escritor Argentino y la tradición" ["The Argentine Writer and Tradition"], Borges engages in a redefinition of Argentine literary nationalism and redefines the country's literary traditions not as local, but as "occidental." He states that "being Argentine" should not limit the topics and techniques of the writer. In fact, Argentine modern traditions should be shaped by European influences, which the local writer could transform, redefine, and even "treat with disrespect" (273). The nineteenth-century landscape of Buenos Aires offered Borges the perfect site to experiment with these ideas of artistic innovation. In fact, as Cristina Grau studies, Borges's early works, especially his poetry, redefined the city's architecture. The home is central in this spatial rhetoric; patios, windows, and narrow corridors are part of this reinvention of Buenos Aires, according to modernist aesthetics. As on the cover of *Fervor de Buenos Aires* [*Fervor of Buenos Aires*], which Norah Borges, his sister and a central artist in the Argentine avant-garde, designed for the first edition in 1923, Buenos Aires became an eclectic space where Borges combined the cosmopolitan and the domestic.

Lange's novels play with similar notions by altering space through techniques such as performance, doubling, and repetition that effectively transform the role of the feminine within the domestic economy of the home. For instance, *Personas en la sala* restructures space through the process of artistic doubling. This novel describes the female narrator's attempts to investigate the identities and activities of three women living across the street. She spends her days spying on them through window blinds, and all of her actions are confined to "la sala," the living room, which is covered with family portraits that silently witness the protagonist's activities. Eventually, we realize the neighbors are only projections of the narrator's imagination, which, throughout the novel, unravels imaginary settings and visualizes them wandering busy streets and venturing out into public places. In fact, the neighbors' house is a fantastic double, the world of fiction that the narrator creates through the manipulation of family images. One of the characters, identified only as "She," acts as the narrator's double, monitoring and regulating the activities of her two younger sisters. The story also tells how the protagonist rearranges the family portraits as she carefully crafts choreographies with the faces of her fantastic beings, her neighbors. Artistic doubling, a technique that had been introduced in *Cuadernos de infancia* through uses of what Paul De Man calls the "autobiographical de-facement," the transformation of the self into a fictional "other," here serves the purpose of manipulating collective family memories, as depicted in family portraits, a skill that the narrator of *Los dos retratos* (1956), Lange's next and final novel, masterfully exploits. These processes of spying and rearranging the family portraits convey notions of a visual, performing learning process that supports the questioning of the family's power dynamics, evidenced in the hierarchical disposition of her doubles. The mystery this fantastic detective fiction seeks to resolve is the construction of the symbolic order of the family embodied in the home's spatial organization. As such, the narrator's new learned skills are perceived as dangerous by her "real" relatives; after questioning her activities at the window, her family sends her outside the city for a few days. Upon her return, the three neighbors have vanished, thus ending her search.

Lange's fantastic fictions draw attention to the underlying anxiety in the production of the home's feminized metaphors; Baydar coins the term the "architectural uncanny" to refer to such representations. Lange's homes are uncanny in the Freudian sense: they depict the recurrence of familiar objects and memories that, as the feminine, have been repressed. They are "unhomely" in that they foreground what has remained hidden in the spatial economy of the domestic—the "unheimlich," to use Freud's German term, both familiar and recognizable, and yet concealing and enigmatic. Lange employs a visual rhetoric to transform the familiar through visual and narrative elisions, the proliferation of image reflections and fantastic duplication, and the fragmentation and estrangement of language. She disrupts the regulations and gender constructs that regulate domesticity by mirroring and yet distorting its scenes' familiarity. Her characters trespass beyond the symbolic markers that establish spatial hierarchies; they disturb the home as a material construct by setting in place new choreographies of gender. A central feature of the uncanny is repetition, Freud states, a trait that is at the foundation of the fantastic duplication taking place in *Personas en la sala*. Photography is closely associated with this recurrence of the uncanny. As Rosalind Krauss discusses, the avant-garde's concept of originality is based on the grounds of repetition, a notion that, as Walter Benjamin states in "The Work of Art in the Age of Mechanical Reproduction," comes from the contact of art with new technologies, such as photography (152–53). *Personas en la sala* demonstrates the influence of these avant-garde ideas on the role of the repetition and the copy as aesthetic strategies. Although a concealed reference in this novel, the manipulation of family photographs and the associated process of artistic doubling are at the core of its narrative project, a technique that will be further developed by Lange in *Los dos retratos*.

This novel is an excellent example of contravening spatial memories through the manipulation of family portraits. As the last stage in the narrative and visual learning process that progresses from *Cuadernos de infancia* and *Personas en la sala*, *Los dos retratos* showcases the skills of an accomplished narrator reorganizing and manipulating family images displayed in the dining room. The novel's title refers to two family portraits hung on a dining room wall opposite a mirror of similar proportions. Each Sunday, the family gathers at the dining table, sitting between the portraits and the mirror. The narrator, a young woman named Marta, comments,

> No bien se entraba al comedor casi podía percibirse un fluir constante, como de delgados hilos, que unía los dos retratos con el espejo. Los domingos a la noche, esos hilos no se cortaban. Más bien parecían fluir

con mayor rapidez hacia el espejo, aunque debieran arrastrar las caras agrupadas alrededor de la mesa.

[Upon entering the dining room, one could almost perceive a continuous flow, as of thin threads, that linked the two portraits with the mirror. On Sunday nights, those threads were not severed. Indeed, they seemed to flow even faster toward the mirror, even as they swept along the faces gathered around the table.] (18–19)

The interactions between the real faces of family members and their iconic representations in the portraits and mirror are masterfully controlled by the family matriarch, the protagonist's grandmother, who determines the shape and form of each of those Sunday "virtual portraits." In the story, Marta, like her grandmother, remains outside these visual interactions in a neutral location that grants her the power to experiment with new scenes and compositions. The story describes family rivalries that try to control the interactions among the photographs and mirrors. For instance, Elena, who used to arrange shop windows during her youth, a profession that not only displays her visual skills but also is perceived as inappropriate by the family, contests the grandmother's power. Teresa, married to one of the youngest sons, is described as the grandmother's main opponent, an ambitious woman who, eager to occupy the role as the family matriarch, distorts family memories. In spite of Elena's and Teresa's ambitions, Marta is designated as the heiress once she occupies the grandmother's seat after her death. In the novel's last scene, Marta applies to her mentor the power-bound mechanism of image reflection and transforms what she perceives to be the sacred image of grandmother by "collecting it" using a hand mirror. Highly aware of this transgression, Marta concludes her narrative by performing what she describes as an act of love and memory preservation: "Esa noche su rostro se quedó dentro de un espejo para siempre" [That night her face remained inside a mirror forever] (196). I interpret Marta's last act as the most loving and yet treacherous act toward family tradition: fascinated by the power of image reflection, Marta hesitates between losing her grandmother's image forever or congealing it into a beloved picture that she can mentally re-create at will in the future.

Los dos retratos evidences that memory is a visual space wherein family narratives are enacted. Although the novel preserves the domestic role of women as the keepers of family traditions, it is significant that such a role acquires modern traits in references to visual manipulation, which links this novel to the avant-garde aesthetics of prisms and mirrors as artistic tools, described by ultraist writers Eduardo González Lanuza and Jorge Luis Borges.[12] Photography is a central tool in the family's visual narrative, skillfully controlled by women, and the dining room the setting where a symbolic battle takes place. Image reflection and active mirroring are strategies of textual productivity that contest the containment of women to the physical confines of domesticity.[13] If the domestic is regulated by what Grosz describes as an "architectural economy" that consists of architectural plans and "the production and distribution of discourses, writings...and its divisions of space, time and movement," *Los dos retratos* distorts the material and symbolic regulations of this economy by mirroring the spatial powers of the domestic (118). The fictional representations in *Los dos retratos* have important links to the manipulation of life narratives that are central to the autobiographical *Cuadernos de infancia*. As visual and linguistic performances, Lange's novels set up a series of self-constructions composed of endless interactions between the real (e.g., the family, the autobiographical element), photographic representations, and mirrors' virtual reflections. Space is fully composed by a set of images that can be duplicated and that question the construction of the personal and literary being as a visual formation. However, space is also a narrative, and Lange's intense reflection on language formation spans from the linguistic games the young child plays in *Cuadernos de infancia* to the role she conducts as a translator in *45 días y 30 marineros*.

An earlier text by Lange published in 1933, *45 días y 30 marineros*, combines fiction and travel writing. Contrary to her later texts located in the space of the home, here the focus is on the transatlantic journey's cosmopolitan scene. As in many examples of women's travel writing, such displacement allows Lange to challenge certain social roles in a more direct way. This fictional travel journal focuses on the perspective of a "female other" (Masiello, *Between Civilization* 152). Narrated in third person, it centers on the protagonist's female subjectivity, a detached yet intimate perspective in which the narrator adopts an "ethnographic position as participant observer" (Unruh 81). Travel writing entails, according to Mónica Szurmuk, this transformation of the writer/narrator into a "stranger"; it is a genre that "requires leaving the comfort zone, as it were, traveling to other places, questioning categories...such as home, landscape, region, language and nation" (8). Lange uses this narrative style of avant-garde influences to explore female eroticism, in particular the construction of the woman's body as an object of visual consumption. As feminist criticism demonstrates, metonymy, referring to the whole body by the handling and exhibition of one part, is a recurring image in surrealist art and photography (Caws, "Ladies Shot" 271). Poems like "Exvoto" ["Devotion"] by Oliverio Girondo similarly play with the notion of women's bodies enticing male desire: "Al atardecer, todas ellas cuelgan sus pechos sin madurar del ramaje de hierro de los balcones,...

y de noche... van a pasearse por la plaza, para que los hombres les eyaculen palabras al oído, y sus pezones fosforecentes se enciendan y apaguen como luciérnagas" [Towards evening, they dangle their still-ripening breasts over the iron lacework of the balcony... and, late at night... they strut through the plaza, so that men may ejaculate words in their ears, and their phosphorescent nipples blink on and off like fireflies] (*Scarecrow* 69). Lange ironically mirrors such aesthetic conventions to reverse the direction and intentionality of men's erotic gaze. As in Claude Cahun's self-portraits, she experiments with the power of mirrors and reflections as a process of self-exploration, her text transforming images of the self into "an other."[14] In the novel, Ingrid dismantles male desire by describing, instead, the male body as "shot" and, quoting Caws, "eaten by the eyes after the camera or the brush," held, in this case, by a female onlooker ("Ladies Shot" 267). In the following example, the male body is cut into pieces and followed by Ingrid's playful gaze: "A la tercera noche, el agua, de repente, le corta su significado de belleza total y se acuerda de los hombres. Las cabezas de los marineros en la popa, parecen unirse a veces. Los oficiales caminan a su lado, por las noches lentas, y poco a poco, sus uniformes blancos se acercan más a ella" [On the third night, the water suddenly cuts into her sense of complete beauty, and she remembers the men. Sometimes, the heads of the sailors on the stern seem to merge. On slow nights, the officers walk alongside her and, little by little, their white uniforms get closer to her] (13).

Photography furnishes key narrative strategies to deconstruct the images of women's bodies as consumed by the avant-garde artist. In a central scene, Karl, the ship's cook, seeks to entice Ingrid's desire by showing her a photograph of his naked lover. While viewing the image, they engage in a long discussion on female eroticism in which Karl advocates for women's increased sexual freedom (93). In another scene, Ingrid mocks the captain's sexual obsession as she imagines him holding a huge imaginary portrait of her: "De pronto se le aparece la visión de su enorme cuerpo acostado encima de su figura en cartulina, y la risa se le sube a la garganta, oponiéndose al escrúpulo, al resentimiento" [Suddenly, she imagines his gigantic body lying on top of a cardboard reproduction of her image, and she cannot contain the laugh that emerges from her throat, in opposition to her doubts, her resentment] (87). Photographs allow Ingrid to destabilize the homosocial order of the ship and men's almost infantile obsession with her body. Ingrid employs photographs' symbolic power, as Susan Sontag describes, "But a photograph is not only like its subject, a homage to the subject. It is part of, and extension of that subject; and a potent means of acquiring it, of gaining control over it" ("The Image World" 351). Through such visual manipulations, Ingrid explores the economy of desire happening on board and the possibilities of women subverting the erotic intentionality of the male gaze. In both examples, the photographs create doubles of Ingrid and the male characters: they mirror eroticism and displace it into the realm of ironic manipulation that Ingrid seeks to accomplish. As Rosalind Krauss demonstrates, surrealist photography employed doubling, or the showing of spacing by a double imprint, in order to produce a sense of difference and to let deferral penetrate the original image (109). In the cultural context of the period, which was profoundly influenced by the visual, the photographic aesthetic of this fictional travel journal explores what Sontag calls the "richly informative deposits" left in such images (367); that is, the complex relations between gender and literary conventions.

Hence, the narrative describes Ingrid's constant play with male eroticism. As in Lange's later novels, the narrator describes a learning process, this time related to the use of the erotic as a means of negotiating the intricate power dynamics surrounding the protagonist. Autobiographical connections are relevant, as this text abounds in examples comparing its fictional setting to the *Martín Fierro* scene. References to banquets and ideological debates taking place on board, the name of "walkyria" that applies to both Ingrid and Norah Lange, and the character of Stevenson with whom Ingrid maintains extended literary discussions are all examples of textual markers establishing an identification between the protagonist and the implied author. Furthermore, *45 días y 30 marineros* is a fictional account of an actual trip that Lange took to Norway in 1928 when she was only 22 years old. In a relevant scene, Ingrid wears the captain's cap and presides over a banquet while she listens to the officers' speeches. The role reversal is quite compelling, as it was Lange who was in charge of delivering the speeches at the literary banquets of *Martín Fierro*. The transatlantic trip is a metaphor of Lange's role in the avant-garde scene. Indeed, Lange refers to *Martín Fierro* as a ship commanded by her husband, Oliverio Girondo.[15] The narrative in *45 días y 30 marineros* thus represents how women negotiated social and gender expectations in Argentine society at the beginning of the twentieth century as well as a metaphor for her initiation as a woman writer in the literary fraternity of *Martín Fierro*.

The trip across the sea is particularly dangerous for such visual experimentations. In her study on gender and travel narrative, Kristi Siegel states that rhetorical constructions warning women of danger abound in women's travel writing since the nineteenth century. Moreover, the culture of modernity transformed travel writing conventions by including specific advice that cautions women from certain ethnic and social groups—in particular, those upper- or middle-class white women who were travel pioneers and whose activities abroad were perceived as disruptions of the social order (61). In this text, mentions of such perils reinforce references to male desire and the pressures of convention serving as the background of Ingrid's experimentation. Within this context, linguistic explorations accompany erotic visual games. Because the port and the transatlantic trip are metaphors for social, linguistic, and gender contacts, the overseas fictional world relates to the role of the woman as a language teacher and translator in a cosmopolitan and multilingual society. Although this function conforms to pedagogical ideals of social motherhood, the novel describes the protagonist in constant attempts to transgress and subvert this role, as the previous discussion on female eroticism makes evident.[16] On a different level, Ingrid's trip also mirrors those journeys of European intellectuals traveling to Latin America during the first decades of the twentieth century. Gonzalo Aguilar explains that the arrival of these visitors to Buenos Aires transformed the cultural scene; they were revered as representatives of new ideological or aesthetic trends, and thus, their presence was exhibited as a trophy against opposing intellectual groups. However, as mere symbols of European culture, they were only "ghosts," projections of new cosmopolitan imaginations (30). Lange's *45 días y 30 marineros* reverses the direction of such itineraries; now the desiring woman is the protagonist, or the "trophy," of such cultural imaginations. As Masiello states, the journey allows for the emergence of female desire within the context of a "no-man's-land where Norwegians, Irish, Argentines, and English are joined in frivolity and passion, distanced from the nations they represent and from the families that remind them of tradition" (*Between Civilization* 152).

This fictional travel journal embodies, as such, a reflection on translation and the role of linguistic tensions within the cosmopolitan scene. Its style is close to a performance text, as the narrator, acting as a playwright, adds notes how the characters should modulate their voices: "todo esto en noruego severísimo" [all this (said) in the sternest Norwegian] (26). Moreover, the narrator states that Ingrid "se hace la políglota" [she acts like a polyglot] (24). The linguistic uses of translation further reinforce the notion that Lange's fiction is a metaphoric site where women question their roles as cultural producers. In fact, the literary genealogy established by Lange through a provocative use of visual and linguistic devices conforms to a redefinition of cosmopolitanism and the avant-garde geopolitical tensions. Lange reimagines the cosmopolitan foundations of *Martín Fierro,* as evidenced by the comparison of this fictional travel journal to other works by avant-garde writers. Take the case of Girondo's *20 poemas para ser leídos en el tranvía* [*Twenty Poems to Be Read on the Streetcar*] (1922), a modernist travelogue wherein a flâneur recounts his cosmopolitan wandering in cities like Río de Janeiro, Buenos Aires, and Venice. Organized as travel vignettes, this text describes the poet's spatial and symbolic mobility through the modern cosmopolis, described as a text assembling different cultural traditions. As Jorge Schwartz explains, the avant-garde cosmopolitanism is a "textual system" in which "the poetic function transforms the *city-cosmopolis* into a *text-cosmopolis*" (emphasis in the original, 21). Moreover, ubiquity, the fragmentation of spatial references, and the representation of the poet as a citizen of the world characterize this cosmopolitan style (19). Indeed, *Martín Fierro*'s international aesthetics reformed literary nationalism.[17] In Lange's novel, ample references to *Martín Fierro*'s cosmopolitanism fictionalize the geopolitical tensions of the literary scene, and Ingrid is particularly aware of them.[18] However, Lange's cosmopolitanism denies the cultural and spatial mobility of the flâneur and proposes instead a female subjectivity the spatial maneuverings of which are depicted as a series of complex gender and linguistic negotiations. Lange crafts a cosmopolitan scene where the private is preserved and shown as the mystery of a bounded and rich female subjectivity. Contrary to the exclusion of women from the modern cosmopolis that Griselda Pollocks studies, her novel suggests a modern "flâneuse" who carefully wanders through the public arena of modernity, a representation that relates to the increasing participation of women in modern cities.[19] However, in her narrative project, the transatlantic ship replaces the city as the site of modern cosmopolitanism, a symbolic location where women are able to craft a literary genealogy in the midst of cultural tensions between the national and the foreign.

Although this novel does not directly address the domestic, the cosmopolitan setting and narratives of the home intersect in a number of crucial scenes. This is particularly evident in the construction of narrative settings and how they connect to gender and literary transformations of female subjectivity. Bare ship interiors substitute, for instance, for the ornate rooms that characterize the nineteenth-century domestic ideal of the home as a refuge of bourgeois subjectivities (Heynen 17). In the scene where Karl and Ingrid hold an open discussion about free love, which is one of the rare feminist statements in Lange's works, the narrator describes in detail the cook's cabin as decorated by scarves, ribbons, and romantic postcards, a depiction that references the construction of the domestic as the realm of sentimentalism. However, traditional gender identifications of the woman as the bearer of such domestic constructs are here inverted, and this scene dismantles the association of woman, home, and sentimentalism that is at the foundation of the links between domesticity and female domestication (Baydar 37). In addition, short narratives of domestic horror further erode the image of the home as a realm of an orderly family structure.[20] This novel mirrors the domestic in the transatlantic scene; it negotiates domestic and cosmopolitan ideals and engenders a project of literary production for women within the complexities of the culture of modernity. It reverses the gender roles that Raquel Olea describes for the modernist project in Latin America:

> Modernity restructured the assignment of the social spaces corresponding to the masculine and the feminine according to the needs of the liberal bourgeoisie and its economic concept of functionality and profitability. Masculine was the open space of the public sphere, of the agora, of individualization, of discursive elaboration, of symbolic and cultural production (of "production" itself in the narrow sense), of the agents of history, of modernization and social and economic progress. Masculine was the space of adventure and discovery—yesterday geographic, today spatial. Masculine was in sum, the space of power that constructs projects of civilization and society. Feminine, by contrast, was the closed space of the private, of unpaid domestic labor performed without a contract, the space of the reproduction of labor and of the species. (194)

Toward 1928, the family home underwent considerable alterations in Buenos Aires. Beatriz Sarlo describes how interiors began to incorporate cubist artwork and furniture of geometric design. The modern home now included places for women's work not related to traditional domestic activities. *Caras y Caretas* [*Faces and Masks*] describes, for instance, the adding of small desks, reading lamps, suspended bookcases, radios, and accessories of abstract design. Sarlo adds that such changes connect to the alteration of the urban landscape—following the architectural projects of Prebish, Vautier, and Wladimiro Acosta—the modernization of the media, and the transformation of social customs (*Buenos Aires* 26). Heynen similarly proposes that, at the beginning of the twentieth century, women conceived of the home as the place where modernity was enacted (12). The debate on social and political maternity and its role in feminist struggles in Argentina is a direct consequence of these revolutionary conceptualizations of the domestic space. Lange's performative domesticity directly responds to the modernization of domestic ideals. Her works displace domesticity to the realm of the uncanny and engage in a process of negotiating the public and the private; her unhomely residences are metaphors for a project of gender and literary displacement that is at the basis of a cultural genealogy of women's writing. Historical limitations most certainly explain the subtle character of her project's transgressions and its confinement to the realm of aesthetic production. However, as virtual habitats for a modern female subjectivity, her works shelter an acute awareness of the material and symbolic power dynamics that shape social relations in the public and private spheres. The association of modernity with homelessness is even more pronounced in the cultural enterprise of *Sur*. Although strongly influenced by social class conventions, Victoria Ocampo furthers Lange's project of a displaced domesticity. She ventures into the world and creates *Sur* as the cultural home of national and cosmopolitan cultural productions.

3. Modern Homelessness: Victoria Ocampo's Architectural Cosmopolitanism

The years of 1928 and 1929 marked the beginning of a significant period in the life of Ocampo. Her marriage to Bernardo de Estrada was coming to an end, and three visitors to Buenos Aires would alter her life dramatically. In 1928, José Ortega y Gasset visited Argentina for the second time. He was already a mentoring figure for Victoria; in 1923, he had published the Spanish translation of *De Francesca a Beatrice* in the second volume of *Revista de Occidente* [*Western Review*]. A year later in 1929, the Swiss architect Charles-Édouard Jeanneret (Le Corbusier) arrived in Buenos Aires, invited by La Asociación Amigos del Arte [The Friends of Art Association]; like many of the intellectual travelers of the period, Le Corbusier came to Buenos Aires to deliver a series of conferences. His lectures on modern architecture and urbanism were later published in French in 1930 under the title *Précisions sur an état present de l'architecture et de l'urbanisme* [*Precisions. On the Present State of Architecture and City Planning*], causing great impact on the local scene. Alberto Prebisch published a review in the first issue of *Sur* in 1931, and Ocampo often referred to the lectures in the essays she wrote during this period.[21] Ocampo consulted with Le Corbusier about a project on which she was embarking: a new home in the wealthy neighborhood of Palermo Chico. Although a local architect, Alejandro Bustillo, would eventually be in charge of the building, Le Corbusier profoundly impressed Ocampo, who was very keen on modernist architecture, as her essays on architecture from the 1920s and early 1930s demonstrate. A third visitor established an important, yet short-lived relationship with Ocampo. The American Waldo Frank arrived a few weeks after Le Corbusier; his lectures on American identity and the need for a Pan-American unity were published in *La Nación* [*The Nation*] and *La Prensa* [*The Press*], and even President Hipólito Yrigoyen put at his service a private plane to fly over the country's provinces (Aguilar and Siskind 6:379).

As Aguilar and Siskind state, the conferences delivered in Buenos Aires by these "cultural travelers" profoundly impacted the ongoing debate about the modern "Argentine character" among local intellectuals. The three figures aforementioned were also instrumental in the creation of *Sur*, the journal Ocampo founded in 1931 and directed until 1971. Frank proposed the idea when he visited Buenos Aires in 1929, and a year later, the details were finalized during Ocampo's visit to New York. Ortega y Gasset also supported Ocampo in this venture and, in a phone conversation, as she acknowledges in *Sur,* he gave her the journal's name. The influence of cultural travelers was important through the years of the publication of *Sur,* and World War II made this collaboration even more fertile; these visits were central to the "bridge to universality" that the journal represented (Aguilar and Siskind 6:369).

In the context of these rich cultural exchanges, the discussion on architecture, urbanism, and home design shaped the debates on a modern national identity for the country. During this period, Ocampo commissioned the construction of two homes that sparked great public controversy in Buenos Aires. The white, three-story house with stucco-covered brick walls and rectangular windows she built on Rufino de Elizalde Street followed architectural principles of European modernism.[22] In the nearby seaside resort of Mar del Plata, a second house of similar characteristics provoked the anger of her neighbors, who complained that its unadorned surfaces and clean lines were incongruent with the European classical architecture prevalent in the neighborhood. The construction of these two residences preceded another project she carefully directed over the 40 years that followed: the journal *Sur* and, later, the publishing house of the same name marking the beginning of her intense public life as a writer and cultural critic. As her *Autobiografía, Testimonios,* and a number of essays she wrote for *Sur* demonstrate, her interests in architecture, urbanism, and home design paralleled her ideas on cultural production. Her project of combining the nationalist ideology of her aristocratic class and a strong fascination with European modernism challenged ideas on the domestic; through her redesigning of the home as a material and symbolic space, Ocampo was able to transform it into a symbol of her modern cultural identity.

In this section, I would like to focus on this redesign of domesticity from the perspective of discourses on architecture, urban planning, and home decor present in Ocampo's works. Alison Blunt and Robyn Dowling maintain that the home is "a spatial imaginary: a set of intersecting and variable ideas and feelings, which are related to context, and which construct places, extend across spaces and scales, and connect places" (2). From this perspective, the home is both a "material dwelling" and "an affective space," relating "material and imaginative realms and processes" (22). Ocampo remakes the home from the perspective of a "homeless" modernism, and as in Lange, such transformations have a metonymic function, for they refer to the remaking of the woman writer's subjectivity and its place within her contemporary cultural scene. Eroticism and female desire populate images of the home and the domestic in Ocampo. Such references are scarce and carefully placed throughout her works, opening and closing doors to the contravention of a normative sexuality for women. For instance, acutely aware of the tenor of her transgressions, Ocampo ordered that her *Autobiografía,* key in disclosing this project, be published only after her death. As the place of both erotic and intellectual passions, the home acquires a different design and challenges its identification with motherhood and sexual procreation, topics prevalent in the Latin American literary imagination of the nineteenth century, as Doris Sommer demonstrates. Space is a text that can be reorganized by different social behaviors and interactions, Henrietta Moore states. Ocampo engages in such redefinition by performing the roles of a desiring subjectivity in the "sacred place of the home" and by crafting a new architecture of cosmopolitan intersections. Ocampo becomes homeless as she erases the ties between her female subjectivity and the social conventions associated with a domestic ideal for women. In her writings, the home is also the place for a modern feminist struggle against class expectations; although she enjoyed many opportunities for international travel because of her social status, she also wrestled with the limitations imposed by her class on her intellectual endeavors. However, it was the home where she was able to paradoxically reinvent herself as a writer; in the realm of the domestic, as depicted in her *Autobiografía,* she reorganizes power cartographies of gender that shaped her life and her career as a writer and cultural critic. As María Cristina Arambel-Guiñazú demonstrates, Ocampo's writing is "architectural," for it assembles and disassembles spaces of the domestic, each new life stage being preceded by the transformations of the homes where she lived (79).

Let's consider the Palermo Chico home on Rufino de Elizalde Street, which currently houses the Fondo Nacional de las Artes [National Endowment for the Arts] (figs. 1.1 and 1.2). As the pictures taken in 1931 during a gathering to celebrate the foundation of *Sur* show, this was the site of important intellectual meetings; it epitomized the journal's project of strengthening the cultural networks connecting America and Europe. Probably the most famous literary image of the period is the one showing, among others, Jorge Luis Borges, Norah Borges, Oliverio Girondo, Ramón Gómez de la Serna, Ernest Ansermet, and María Rosa Oliver (fig. 1.3). Ocampo adored this house because of the simplicity of its architecture, its white walls, and clean style; she purchased its furnishings in Europe and decorated it in a functionalist style.[23] Frank describes it at length in *América Hispana: South of Us,* the book he published in 1940 retelling his experiences of traveling throughout Latin America: "Doña Victoria has borrowed lavishly from Europe. The rugs are by a Frenchman and a Spaniard of

Figure 1.1 Alejandro Leveratto, Victoria Ocampo's House in Rufino de Elizalde y Castilla, Palermo Chico, Buenos Aires (built by Alejandro Bustillo, 1928). Used with permission of Alejandro Leveratto. Fotografía©alejandroleveratto.

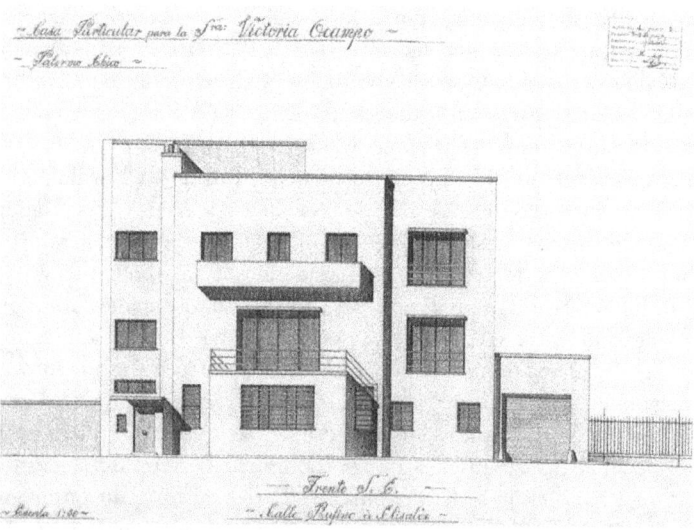

Figure 1.2 Victoria Ocampo's House in Rufino de Elizalde y Castilla (sketch). Used with permission of Architect Martha Levisman, President Asociación Civil ARCA, Archivos de Arquitectura Contemporánea Argentina.

Figure 1.3 Literary Meeting at Victoria Ocampo's house in Rufino de Elizalde y Castilla in 1931. From the top: Francisco Romero, Eduardo Bullrich, Guillermo de Torre, Pedro Henríquez Ureña, Eduardo Mallea, Norah Borges, Victoria Ocampo, Enrique Bulrich, Jorge Luis Borges, Oliverio Girondo, Ramón Gómez de la Serna, Ernest Ansermet, Nenona Padilla and María Rosa Oliver. Used with permission of Fundación Sur.

Figure 1.4 Victoria Ocampo's House in Rufino de Elizalde y Castilla (stairs detail). Used with permission of Architect Martha Levisman, President Asociación Civil ARCA, Archivos de Arquitectura Contemporánea Argentina.

the day; the tables are English; the vast globe in the hall is Renaissance; the architectural lines owe much to schools of Germany and France. But all these details have been transfigured by an Argentinean—an American will" (127) (fig. 1.4). Frank's description exemplifies the overall goals for his book, which, in the climate of President Franklin Roosevelt's Good Neighbor policy, he conceives as a treaty for "understanding" and creating a "closeness of collaboration and exchange (cultural and economic)" between the United States and Latin America. Ocampo's home symbolizes the integration of the essential characteristics of America, embodying the "house emblem... the cactus": "Victoria Ocampo, woman of Argentina and America, in her cult of light, in her work of structure within the chaos of the Pampa motion, has learned that she must clasp the bitter cactus in her hand, clasp it against her breast. She has prophesied for her country" (128). In Frank's example, the house also embodies what he saw as the main goal for *Sur:* establishing north-south connections among the continent's intellectuals. Although the journal maintained a certain eclectic tone and even a Latin American focus until the 1950s, it eventually shifted its orientation to Europe, partly because of the ideological polarization of the war and postwar climates (Fernández Bravo, "Introducción" 12). Many contributors who were more inclined to Latin American literature or who had expressed sympathy for socialism, such as Waldo Frank, María Rosa Oliver, and José Pepe Bianco, later abandoned the publication.

Furniture and home decor were of particular interest to Ocampo and embody *Sur*'s cultural role as mediator between national and cosmopolitan influences. In its first issue, Ocampo's essay, "La aventura del mueble" ["The Adventure of Furniture"], describes her visit to Alfred Stieglitz's apartment in New York City.[24] Perceiving similarities between the home's neutral decoration—"blanco-gris, ningún mueble, espacio, luz" [white-gray, no furniture, space, light]—and her Palermo Chico residence, she comments at length on the modernist style of decoration, as described by Le Corbusier during his conferences in Buenos Aires. Reflecting on how furniture must be kept only for its functional uses, Ocampo focuses on the aesthetic implications of this style, which she sees as the embodiment of a rising Euro-American modernism. Stieglitz's new "American place" makes her feel "at home" at the crossroads where the North and the South intersect:

> Sentí que las palabras que Stieglitz me dijo junto a la ventana podían ser aplicadas a algunos de mis actos. Porque cuando Le Corbusier, al hablar de mi casa, dice gustarle mi manera de resolver 'la aventura del mueble', me aprueba, en suma, por haber puesto en práctica, aquí, en el Sur, lo que

piensa Stieglitz allá en el norte: *Is this beauty? I don't know. I don't care. I don't use the word beauty. This is life.*
[I felt that what Stieglitz said to me by the window might apply to some of my actions. Because when Le Corbusier, in talking about my home, says that he likes my way of resolving the 'adventure of furniture,' he is ultimately expressing his approval of me, for putting into practice, here, in the South, what Stieglitz is thinking there in the North: *Is this beauty? I don't know. I don't care. I don't use the word beauty. This is life.*] (emphasis in the original, 174)

Sur is thus the new "American place"; Argentina can reinvent itself through bare modernist aesthetics of north and south encounters. Numerous articles published during *Sur*'s first years also emphasize the role of architecture, urbanism, and home design in creating this "universal culture." Walter Gropius, in "Arquitectura Funcional" ["Functional Architecture"], also advocates for a simplification of buildings' decorations; for too long, he says, "el arquitecto, el artista, permaneció estancado en un esteticismo académico" [the architect, the artist, stagnated in academic aestheticism] (157). According to Gropius, the new architect finds an abstract code of "colors and forms" modeling the relationship between him and his environment and prepares "la base común sobre la cual una multiplicidad de individualidades puedan luego crear en colaboración una obra unitaria más alta. No es la obra del individuo aislado, sino de muchas generaciones" [the common basis from which a wide variety of individualities can then create, in collaboration, a superior unitary work. This will be not the work of a single individual, but that of many generations] (160). The notion that architecture represents not national but universal traits is at the basis of *Sur*'s cultural project of reinventing Argentine nationalism. Within the context of Argentina's strong cultural industry, its central role as exporter of cultural goods during the years of Nazism and fascism, and the impact of World War II, *Sur* became a central institution in redefining the place of culture within the complex geopolitical relations of the period (Fernández Bravo, "Introducción" 33). Thus, the reflections on architecture, urbanism, and home decor are part of a larger debate on the role of cultural elites in defining a modernist universalism where the intellectual holds a pedagogical role in shaping the country's modern identity. The hosting of exiled intellectuals and the translation of the most representative works of European and American literature will be part of this "democratic role" of educating the masses as perceived by *Sur* (38).

Urbanism was also a topic frequently invoked in *Sur*'s discussions on modernist culture. Ocampo discussed at length the urban maladies of Buenos

Aires, a city corrupted by what she perceived to be the lack of a comprehensive modern design, as evidenced in her essays "Sobre un mal de esta ciudad" ["An Ill Afflicting This City"] and "Dejad en paz a las palomas" ["Leave the Pigeons Alone"]. In "Sobre un mal de esta ciudad" (1935), she narrates from the perspective of a modern *flâneuse* driving around the city and describes the building of entire middle-class neighborhoods that are undermining Buenos Aires's architectural harmony. She concludes by comparing Buenos Aires's urban mishmash to her dreams of modernist perfection, as embodied by the house she built in Mar del Plata in 1927. The irony that unquestionably comes from Ocampo's elitist perspective is more evident in those sections where she describes feelings of being "misunderstood" by the criticisms of neighbors and occasional visitors to the house. She adopts a pedagogical perspective that we very frequently note in her essays and testimonies and concludes with a commentary about the importance of "standardization" in city planning, which she sees as the best solution for Buenos Aires's uneven development:

> Bendita sea la "standardización" que concentra las cualidades esenciales en un tipo, en un modelo, y se hace así sinónimo de unificación, de dignidad. Bendita sea la "estandarización" común denominador de un período, que impedirá al nuevo rico sin cultura y al pequeño burgués presuntuoso materializar su *cursilería* en "el sueño de la casa propia" hecho ladrillo.
>
> [Let us praise "standardization" for it concentrates the essential qualities in a type, a model, becoming a symbol of unification and dignity. Let us praise "standardization," the common denominator of a period that will prevent the uncultured nouveau riche and the arrogant petit bourgeois from actualizing his *bad taste* in "the dream of a home of one's own" made of bricks.] (emphasis added, 103)

In "Dejad en paz a las palomas" (1937), she similarly describes her itineraries for the city and complains about the shameful spectacle of new statues, monuments, and modern homes popping up in massive numbers. She praises the construction of the Rex Theater, which Alberto Prebisch designed in 1937—located across the street from the Opera Theater, which had been rebuilt a year earlier under the direction of Belgian Argentine architect Albert Bourdon—and which represented a symbol of the "good taste" that should guide the city's architectural projects: "Un nuevo cine acaba, por suerte, de abrir sus puertas precisamente frente a ese indescriptible horror que se llama hoy Opera. Por fin puede uno alzar los ojos hacia su fachada sin ponerse colorado. Es sencilla, es limpia, es digna. Da gusto verla en su desnudez y transparencia" [Fortunately, a new theater just opened its doors right in front of that unspeakable horror known today as the Opera. We can finally look upon its façade without embarrassment. It is simple, clean, dignified. It is a pleasure to see its lack of adornment and transparency] (85). In both examples, as in Prebisch's "Una ciudad de América" ["An American City"], another negative commentary on Buenos Aires's urban changes, interests in architecture and urbanism demonstrate close ties to the transformations brought about by immigration in Argentine society. These discussions show, doubtlessly, the perspective of a modern elitism that distrusts the masses and craves for a new form of modern liberalism, all notions at the base of *Sur*'s ideological foundations (King 20).

Similar ideas are present in "Babel," Ocampo's first essay published in *La Nación* in 1920, in which she also describes Buenos Aires as a modern Babylon impacted by the arrival of massive immigration. As Gorica Majstorovic states, this image of Babel represents Ocampo's negative views on immigration and the role of the intellectual as a cosmopolitan translator of dissimilar cultural influences (54). The discourses on architecture and urbanism provide Ocampo a fertile territory for reflecting upon her role as an intellectual; the spatial ideals of harmony and "standardization" that she praises in the Bauhaus and modernist purism are representative of her dreams of a culture where the intellectual blends and regulates the uneven forces of Buenos Aires's modernity. Ocampo's essays also reflect the role of taste in the formation of cultural identities. She uses the term "cursilería" to refer to the new homes built by the new social groups populating the city. The term, which traveled to Latin America around the 1860s, relates not only to "claims or pretensions of quality of anything that tries to be 'artistic' without genuinely being so" (Calinescu 235), but also to pejorative connotations associated with social class. "Cursi" eventually came to refer to the social classification of subaltern groups (Santos 29), and associated with the ideology of the copy, it began to pertain to ways in which concepts and aesthetic practices question social barriers and distinctions. Lydia Santos explains that both the emergent middle classes and other less privileged social groups employed this expression as a form of appropriating notions on "taste" of upper social groups and as a way of imitating or copying social behaviors (134–35). The ending of "Sobre un mal de esta ciudad" is quite compelling in this regard. In a personal tone, Ocampo concludes by addressing the city of Buenos Aires:

Y si no lo has hecho hasta ahora, ciudad mía, comprende mi rencor. Veo tus posibilidades. Líbrate para siempre de la tentación de imitar las viejas

y magníficas ciudades de Europa, o parecerás eternamente una grotesca caricatura. Otro destino te aguarda. Las ciudades que hoy es posible construir, bañadas en follaje y en sol, tienen una belleza que les es propia, peculiar, y que no cambio por ninguna otra. Las viejas ciudades son maravillosas de ver, pero inhabitables como museos.
[And if you have not yet done so, my city, understand my rancor. I see your possibilities. Free yourself forever of the temptation to imitate the old and magnificent cities of Europe, or you will always seem like a grotesque caricature. Another destiny awaits you. The cities that can be constructed today, suffused with foliage and sunlight, have their own particular beauty that I would not change for any other. Old cities are wonderful to see, but as uninhabitable as museums.] (104)

Ocampo engages in a discussion on architectural principles, led by the conviction that the formation of a modern cultural identity lies at the basis of new spatial designs. As her concerns about the aesthetic and social connotations of taste demonstrate, she conceives of the intellectual as a key figure in regulating this process, led by a modernist taste, a "buen gusto" [good taste]. The project of *Sur,* with its considerable attention to book reviews, translations, and the later publications of European and American authors, fulfilled this role for the intellectual elites as architects of good taste, as creators of a modern Argentine identity branded as original and designed on national and cosmopolitan influences.

In a cultural landscape where the influence of the avant-garde was waning, the somber tone of Ocampo's essays also explains the conflictive role that a group of intellectuals occupied within the changing social and cultural scene of 1930 through 1950. As Ricardo Piglia states, *Sur* was a literary journal of the 1880s generation published fifty years late; its project of conceiving Europe as the center of literary influences had become outdated because of the increase of intercultural circulation since the end of the nineteenth century ("Sobre *Sur*" 78–79). Many of Ocampo's works make clear this role of the intellectuals as the heirs to the literary dreams that founded the country's national identity in the 1880s. In the drama that she wrote in her younger years, *Habla el algarrobo* [*The Locust Tree Speaks*], first published in 1959, we can trace the origins of these notions of cultural production. The play describes an ancient locust tree, narrating the history of the house and the developments in the lives of its owners, General Juan Martín de Pueyrredón, a central figure in Argentine independence, and his wife, María Calixta Tellechea y Caviedes. The drama retells main political events of the nineteenth century, such as the liberation of Buenos Aires from the British occupation of 1806 and 1807, historic encounters between Pueyrredón and

José de San Martín while planning the military campaign in Chile, the rise of Juan Manuel de Rosas to power, the exile of Pueyrredón and his family to Europe between 1835 and 1849, and the selling of the estate to Ocampo's maternal great-grandfather, Manuel Hermenegildo de Aguirre. Central in this drama are the private events in the lives of historic characters, with important sections retelling, for instance, the role of María Tellechea in the life of the family. This drama interrelates Ocampo's family life with the country's historical foundations and provides a domestic, intimate version of Argentine history that is at the core of *Sur*'s ideals on cultural production. Ocampo reinstates the literary patriotism of the 1880s when, for instance, in her *Autobiografía*, she describes growing up listening to the national anthem as one of her nursery songs. The home embodies this sense of nationalism; for instance, she later comments that her family home, later the journal's offices, was located at the core of the city's historical center: "Como ya dije, nací frente al convento de las Catalinas, que habían ocupado los ingleses en el momento de las invasiones, desde el 5 al 7 de Julio de 1807. Esta iglesia se encuentra en la esquina de San Martín y Viamonte, frente a la casa donde vivían mis padres y frente a la que ocuparían las oficinas de SUR" [As I said, I was born in front of St. Catherine's, which had been occupied by the English during the invasions, July 5–7, 1807. This church is located at the corner of San Martín and Viamonte, in front of the house where my parents lived, and in front of the house that the offices of SUR would later occupy] (*Autobiografía I* 49). As such, *Autobiografía* marks the space of the family home as the birthplace of Argentina's literary establishment. In fact, familial bonds are at the foundation of *Sur*. John King states that the journal sought to maintain the intimate connections between the members of the 1880s generation in the challenging setting of the 1930s and 1940s. This literary project, bound to the notion of the home as the site of literary genealogies tied to the country's historical origins, as in *Habla el algarrobo*, was thus conceived as the enterprise of a family of equals, which presented, as King describes, particular challenges for Ocampo, who was perceived as an outsider in the predominantly male culture of the period (22). The rise of Peronism and Ocampo's imprisonment in 1953 changed this scenario by presenting an opportunity for the liberal elite to publicly confront the regime, and *Autobiografía*'s preface, written as a public response to Perón, transformed Ocampo into a symbol of the cultural elites associated with *Sur*. A couple years before, Ocampo had been granted an honorary degree from the Sociedad Argentina de Escritores [Argentine Writers Society], acknowledging her passionate defense of traditional liberal values and her rejection of Eva Perón's populism (Iglesia 13). Ocampo embarked upon writing *Autobiografía* under these circumstances, which also explains the role of that book as a public justification, a trait generally recognized for this genre.[25] As a continuation of the national project of the 1880s generation, *Sur* and *Autobiografía* engage in the construction of a critical location for the intellectual during the *Peronista* years, reinventing the notion of Argentine originality within the complex geopolitical exchanges between Europe and America during and after World War II, the rise of socialism and totalitarianism, and the consolidation of a new cultural scene that would become increasingly controlled by other actors, eventually marginalizing *Sur*.[26]

However, this metaphoric reinterpretation of the domestic also addresses a new role for the woman writer according to a feminine imagination (Masiello, *Between Civilization* 164). In fact, as Unruh states, Ocampo focused on the relationship between Argentina and Europe, *Sur* being a place to reinvent genealogies through the practice of a literary feminism involved in public writing (57). She reshaped the position that women held in the national imaginary as the bearers of a patriotic motherhood. As Unruh confirms, her positions on women's rights, as expressed in "La mujer y su expresión" ["Woman and Her Expression"] (1935) and "La mujer, sus derechos y responsabilidades" ["Woman, Her Rights and Responsibilities"] (1936), to some degree "coincided with feminist political discourse that posed special civic roles for women through the social motherhood model" (58). As Rita Felski demonstrates, gendered images of modernity served to redefine motherhood as both a refuge and an empowering site during the conflictive times of the early twentieth century.[27] In Argentina, this debate translated into what Marcela Nari describes as the "naturalization of motherhood," a conscious attempt by the state to identify women as mothers and, as such, key players in the formation of a modern population of citizens. However, Ocampo also challenged this maternal role by transforming the home into the site of literary exchanges and by incorporating the desiring body as a key element of women's empowerment in the domestic sphere. The cosmopolitan culture to which she was exposed in her countless experiences of international travel became central in redefining the space of the home as a site that transcends what Judy Giles calls the "artificial binaries" of home/away, private/public, traditional/modern, and feminine/masculine (141). As in Lange, Ocampo is "at home in the world," displacing experiences and reflections on domesticity to cosmopolitan scenes.

Ocampo creates in her works "unhomely" places that break normative notions of the domestic (Blunt and Dowling 26) and reinvent the home as a cultural location. In fact, the *tertulias* (literary gatherings) and literary encounters portrayed in her Palermo Chico home were alternative locations where the woman intellectual could perform literary roles because other public sites, such as the Buenos Aires cafés, were prohibited to women because of social conventions.[28] Many women in a similar social status were involved in the "making of the modern house" during the period of 1880 to 1920. Using examples of homes built in Europe and the United States, Alice Friedman explains how women, aided by architects such as Frank Lloyd Wright and Le Corbusier, significantly altered nineteenth-century conventions on domesticity and created "hybrid domestic places," including room for different work and leisure activities by the modern woman. These homes shifted the balance between the public and the private, for instance, by transforming the home into a center for intellectual activities open to the community (12). In Friedman's words, these homes highlighted "the importance of spectacle, and of home as a representation (in stylistic as well as spatial terms of the activities and values of its occupants)" (17).

Ocampo's works eventually came to reflect a migration to more eccentric places abroad, such as hotel rooms or small apartments, symbols of a modern homelessness that increases as her redefinition of social expectations and gender roles intensifies. In *Autobiografía,* as in *Testimonios,* references to home design describe the construction of a personal identity, as evidenced in this description of her Palermo Chico home:

> En mi nueva casa tenía una mesa de comedor espléndida (siglo XVIII caoba). La tengo todavía. Algunas cosas de época que me encantaban por la madera y por la forma. Algunas mesitas. Un tapiz de Picasso...una tapicería de Léger. Grandes canapés. Libros. Un piano. Árboles alrededor. Las cosas estaban colocadas estrictamente de acuerdo con el uso al cual estaban destinadas.
>
> [In my new home I had a splendid dining table (eighteenth century mahogany). I still have it. Some period pieces that I loved because of the wood and their shape. Some small tables. A Picasso tapestry...and a Léger. Big couches. Books. A piano. Trees around [the house]. Things were arranged in strict accordance to the use for which they were destined.] (*Autobiografía III* 148)

This house embodies a period of personal fulfillment that she refers to as "una liberación simbólica de los objetos" [a symbolic liberation from objects] when she confesses how, when a fire threatened to destroy the San Isidro estate, Villa Ocampo, she experienced a deep sense of relief (*Autobiografía II* 132). Home decor parallels Ocampo's eclectic and feminist cosmopolitanism; through the process of decorating and remodeling the home, she was able to reinvent literary genealogies in *Sur,* whereas she designed new locations for the modern woman. Translation plays a key role in this process, as Ocampo translated the 1880s generation literary project into a feminist endeavor located in the cosmopolitan scene of the early twentieth century; she displaced and transformed the pedagogical functions of women in early twentieth-century Argentine culture, which until then had been considered their sole respectable role in public culture (Unruh 69).

As Beatriz Sarlo contends, Ocampo cultivated genres associated with linguistic and cultural displacements (*La máquina* 127). This allowed Ocampo to build alternative locations for a more open discussion of gender roles. Translation is thus a gender-based activity, paralleled by a transformation and relocation of literary settings, as evidenced in "Costumbres" ["Customs"]. This essay is a book review that possesses the traits of a performance text, a characteristic that Unruh identifies in the majority of Ocampo's works but that is particularly evident in her *Testimonios,* wherein she combines "the tactics of the actor assuming a role with those of an experienced spectator attuned to the interplay of spatial, bodily, and verbal cues and to the sites of convergence between stage and audience" (60). In this interactive travelogue, the reader is first introduced to *The Arab Mind* by Raphael Patai from within the cosmopolitan setting of New York:

> Me volví al hotel (estaba en la Quinta Avenida) con *La mentalidad árabe* en una bolsita de celofán. Vamos a ver qué nos dice este señor Patai y qué novedades nos trae su obra sobre la mujer árabe...Me instalé en la cama-biblioteca (uso dos camas en los hoteles: una para mí, otra para mis libros, sistema que no deja espacio ni para un sillón); saqué de su bolsita *La mentalidad árabe* y me puse a escudriñar el índice.
>
> [I went back to my hotel (on Fifth Avenue) carrying *The Arab Mind* in a small cellophane bag. Let's see what this Mr. Patai has to say about Arab women...I sat on my library-bed (when staying at a hotel I use two beds: one for me, the other for my books, a system that doesn't even leave room, for an armchair); I took *The Arab Mind* out of its bag and began to scan the table of contents.] ("Costumbres" 48)

We are then invited to a discussion on gender conventions from the Arab perspective, which Ocampo counterbalances with her own experiences of growing up in the restrictive social scene of Buenos Aires: "Este balconear, para mirar al paseante, era un acto reprobable" [This "balconear" (looking from the balcony) in order to see the person strolling by, was a reprehensible act]. And later, "Desde luego, mirarse a diez o doce metros de distancia era un escándalo" [Of course (for two people), to look at each other from a distance of ten or twelve meters was scandalous] (52). Ocampo's writing is multilayered and serves multiple functions: it is foremost pedagogical, as it translates and comments a foreign text for a local audience; it also adopts the form of a travel journal, describing the experiences of the woman writer in the modern metropolis; and finally, it deconstructs social conventions by comparing two sets of cultural constructs on gender and by unveiling the force of regulatory discourses on sex. As Unruh demonstrates, Ocampo's texts reproduce the "performative quality" of Latin America's early twentieth-century literary culture (6). In what Judith Butler describes as the exclusionary matrix of sex and gender, Ocampo engages here in a "gender performativity" as a "reiterative and citational practice" (2), thus establishing a dialogue on gender ideals with women from different locations. "Costumbres" thus exemplifies the versatile form of Ocampo's literary criticism where reading becomes a complex activity of citing and addressing multiple social conventions. As such, as Sylvia Molloy states, Ocampo's texts are multifaceted, combining "*lo vivido*" and "*lo leído*," or "body" and "writing" (84).

The complex relation among gender, location, and translation is evident in *De Francesca a Beatrice*. Ocampo first wrote this text in French, and Ortega y Gasset published it in Spanish in the second volume of *Revista de Occidente* in 1923. As in "Costumbres," the cosmopolitan scene allows Ocampo to displace her feminist discussions by using French, the proper language for a woman of her class and for the confession of private feelings, as Sarlo states (*La máquina* 122–23). This text also adopts conventions of travel literature; Ocampo calls it her "Baedeker" of *The Divine Comedy* (*II* 83). Following the rules of travel guides of the period, she invites her "tourist readers" to accompany her as if they were visiting a museum (25). Written after her two trips as an adult woman to Europe, in 1908 with her family and as a married woman in 1912, *De Francesca a Beatrice* transgresses a number of literary conventions. First, she adopts the eclectic format of the Baedeker travel guide to engage in an exercise of literary criticism, to which she adds a ciphered personal confession of her love for Julián Martínez.[29] This text is a model of feminist engagement and critical passion wherein Ocampo defends reading and translation as ways of gaining a legitimate space within the literary culture of the period. As Elizabeth Marchant explains, Ocampo's literary criticism is deliberately subjective, as she approaches textual commentary from the belief that "one's 'self' is always inextricable from one's 'object' of study" (48). Although Ocampo's text is about Dante, it truly addresses the role of the woman critic who, like the fearful reader forced to stand back by obsessive and cerebral critics, is impeded from crossing the gates of the precious hidden inferno of *The Divine Comedy* (15). Returning to the metaphor of furniture, she tells an anecdote about an antique dealer who years ago had forbidden her to open the drawers of a piece of furniture she intended to buy. Her commentary, she confesses with a defiant tone, will look into all those "secret small drawers" that others have disregarded (17). Ocampo asked Paul Groussac and Ángel de Estrada to read *De Francesca a Beatrice* and write commentaries. The two responses—Groussac considered it too pretentious, Estrada as exhibitionist—clearly refer to the contraventions of Ocampo's approach (Molloy 97). The text embodies the struggles in finding a location and a language for the woman writer; through a metonymical displacement, Ocampo addresses both her literary and personal situations and her struggles with gender conventions in both areas. The genre of travel writing, which as Sarlo states, is central to the operations of cultural importation and translation in Ocampo's cosmopolitan style (*La máquina* 127), allows the woman writer to imagine alternative cultural places and practices for women.

We cannot fully comprehend the domestic in Ocampo without addressing the distinctive sense of cosmopolitanism that gave her class a collective sense of selfhood. The project of *Sur* reflects the role of the European trip in the complex exchange of commodities and services of the period; in fact, as Ocampo states in her *Autobiografía*, it paralleled the intellectual importation of trends and ideas (*III* 148). As Rudy Koshar states, patterns of leisure shape collective identities of national communities, which, in the case of Argentina, were linked to notions of cultural identity (6). Beatriz Colombi describes the period between 1880 and 1915 as particularly rich for the experiences of "intellectual travelers," writers who represent themselves as cultural agents and actors of a foreign public scene (*Viaje* 16). Ocampo challenges class and gender expectations when she ventures into travel writing as a way of consolidating a personal and public image and redefining the association between woman and home. She genders the experience of the intellectual traveler; in *De Francesca a Beatrice*, as later in *Autobiografía* and *Testimonios*, she defies spatial limitations for women and uses the cosmopolitan scene to create a personal style of cultural criticism. Through the genre of travel writing, she establishes a tacit dialogue with preconceived cultural norms present in the Baedeker guides and with the structures and beliefs shared by members of her class, the intended audience for this publication (Palmowski 111). By adopting this genre, Ocampo not only seeks to insert herself in the tradition of combining travel and intellectual exploration, but also constructs a projected audience, the "tourist readers," members of her class and the intellectual elites of Buenos Aires accustomed to the tradition of reading guidebooks such as the Baedekers. Ocampo's gesture is highly symbolic of her attempt to enter the masculine literary culture of the period by engaging in discourses on nationalism and cosmopolitanism. In fact, her cosmopolitanism has been interpreted in many different ways. Gorica Majstorovic describes it as a cosmetic attempt to recast old national models of the nineteenth century as revealed in "Babel" (57). Sarlo connects it to linguistic displacements seeking "common places" in different cultural traditions (*La máquina* 129). Equally important is understanding her cosmopolitanism as a hybrid construction that establishes spatial dialogues, as a "discrepant cosmopolitanism," as a productive site for cultural crossing, and in Ocampo's case, as a way of locating herself within a literary culture that registers both national and foreign influences.[30] As evidenced in her discussions on architecture and urbanism, Ocampo's cosmopolitanism is also architectural; it recasts the role of the feminine in a newly built modern home, the symbol of a universal culture that she conceived as more open toward and tolerant of women. Gender and class restrictions certainly limited the feminist undertones of this endeavor. However, literary relationships with writers and intellectuals such as Virginia Woolf, María de Maetzu, and Gabriela Mistral further enabled Ocampo to publicly discuss women's rights. Even when her feminism adopted certain conventional gender roles, as Unruh demonstrates, the displacement of domesticity to the cosmopolitan realm reinforced new possibilities for critical gender roles and opened new spaces for women's cultural criticism.

The reconfiguration of feminist genealogies is particularly evident in her later *Testimonios*. In the acceptance speech to the Argentine Academy of Letters in 1977, she describes herself as the heiress of a legacy represented by Virginia Woolf, Gabriela Mistral, and Águeda, the Guarani woman, mistress of one of Pedro de Mendoza's captains, Domingo Martínez de Irala, to whom she admits to being related: "Traigo conmigo a este lugar a tres mujeres porque les debo algo que ha contado en mi vida. A una, parte de mi existir; a las otras, en parte, el no haberme contentado con existir" [I bring with me to this place these three women because I owe to them something that mattered in my life. To one (I owe) part of my existence; (to) the others, in part, my refusal to simply exist] ("Mujeres" 23). Ocampo stresses that other forms of conquering have taken place in her life—as she compares herself with Irala—namely the conquest of a place within the literary institutions of the country: "También habré trabajado y servido piloto de otro navegar, en estos parajes no siempre apacibles. Han hecho falta cuatro siglos y medio, desde Irala, para que me permitieran, para que nos permitieran a nosotras pisar el césped de las universidades" [I will also have worked and served as the navigator of a different voyage, in these not always hospitable places. It has taken four and a half centuries, since Irala, for me to be allowed, for all of us women to be allowed to set foot on university lawns] (23). Ocampo's acceptance to the Argentine Academy of Letters is a symbolic moment in her engagement in the arena of women's rights, as is her creation, with María Rosa

Oliver, of the Unión de Mujeres Argentinas (Argentine Women's Union) in 1936 to stop changes in the civil code that would have negatively affected the social position of women in the country. In "La mujer y su expresión," a radio speech Ocampo gave to women in Spain and Argentina in 1936, she stresses the importance of cosmopolitan bonds among women. By using the metaphor of the ocean as a source of interconnectedness, she states that women need to "navegar este océano para superar nuestras diferencias" [sail this ocean to overcome our differences] (10). Further, she proposes the notion of a global sisterhood where local struggles affect women's rights as a whole:

> Por lo tanto, tal como los sucesos se presentan hoy, la suerte que corre la mujer en China o en Alemania, en Rusia o en los Estados Unidos, en fin, no importa en qué rincón del mundo, es cosa extremadamente grave para todas nosotras, pues sufriremos su repercusión. Así, pues, la suerte de la mujer sudamericana concierne vitalmente a la española y a la de todos los otros países.
>
> [Therefore, in light of the current situation, the fate of women in China, Germany, Russia or the United States, in whatever corner of the world, it is extremely serious for all of us (women), because we all will suffer the repercussions. Thus, the fate of women in South America is of vital importance to women in Spain and in every other country of the world.] ("La mujer" 27)

Ocampo's cosmopolitanism is profoundly gendered, as it creates spatial connections among literary and cultural landscapes involving many women across different cultures. It is architectural, for it defines the building of new spatial forms linking gender to cultural production. In Christopher Larkosh's words, "It is possible to view the literary landscape Victoria Ocampo creates not merely metaphorically but as an actual physical network, a series of communications that connects radically different spaces and points of literary reference, both national and foreign" (107). Ocampo's very close friend, María Rosa Oliver, coined the perfect expression to define this feminist cosmopolitanism, "Mundo, mi casa" [The World, My Home]: a house built on collective national and international legacies that Ocampo sought to redesign and transform.

The *Autobiografía* is a major contribution to this project. Ocampo's feminist use of that genre enables her to question how ideologies of gender shape ideologies of selfhood (Smith 15). She asks how sex and class form self-representations and reinvents literary genealogies bound to national and cosmopolitan narratives. Thus, *Autobiografía* retells Ocampo's complex affiliation to social and cultural conventions. As such, *Autobiografía* and *Sur*, the life narrative and the intellectual project, are associated, as the concluding words of her *Autobiografía* attest: "En el verano de 1931 nació SUR. A partir de ese momento mi historia personal se confunde con la historia de la revista. Todo lo que dije e hice (y escribí) está en SUR y seguirá apareciendo mientras dure la revista" [SUR was born in the summer of 1931. From that moment on, my personal history merges with that of the journal. Everything I said and did (and wrote) is in SUR, and will continue to appear there as long as the journal lasts] (*III* 204).

As in Lange, *Autobiografía* depicts the family home as a highly regulated space. Ocampo describes its intricate configurations in great detail:

> La casa de las tías era mucho más grande que la nuestra. En el piso de abajo las salas, el fumoir, los comedores (uno chico y otro grande), tenían cortinas de terciopelo y de seda floreada. La escalera principal, con escalones anchísimos y bajos, era especial para bajar por ella a la disparada... Arriba estaban los dormitorios, baños, cuartos de vestir, sala y jardín de invierno con espejos que tomaban toda la pared, el cuarto de los armarios y nuestro cuarto de estudio. En el último piso (el que más me gustaba) vivían los sirvientes y había un enorme cuarto de plancha (como lo llamaban): el reinado de Felisa, la planchadora.
>
> [My aunt's house was bigger than ours. On the first floor the sitting rooms, the smoking room, the dining rooms (a small one and a large one), had velvet and flower-print silk drapes. The main staircase, with very wide and low steps, was especially good for running down the stairs... Upstairs were the bedrooms, bathrooms, dressing rooms, a sitting room, and a winter garden with mirrors that covered the entire wall, closets, and our study room. On the top floor (my favorite), lived the servants, and there was an enormous ironing room (that's how it was called): the kingdom of Felisa, the woman in charge of the ironing.] (*I* 110–11)

The home displays networks of social power that *Autobiografía* deconstructs through a carefully crafted self-narrative. It additionally represents Ocampo's search for an identity within the culture of modernity where women saw themselves as both agents of change—as embodied in the image of the New Woman—and as the keepers of continuity and tradition. This ambivalent role is best described by *Autobiografía*'s redefinitions of the family home. As Ocampo lays bare the social and linguistic constraints of a domestic ideal associated with motherhood, she questions the home as a symbolic construction of a model of femininity that she perceives as antimodern.[31] She downsizes domestic ideals of femininity by transforming the house, aided by the principles of modernist architecture, into a place where modernity was enacted. In addition, she modifies social uses of the domestic. As an accomplished *salonniére*, as Masiello describes Ocampo, she reinvents the tradition of the literary salon in a modernist fashion where categories of gender and their association with social and literary conventions are placed into question.

Domestic transgressions pervade the narrative of *Autobiografía;* Ocampo comments, for instance, how she enjoyed spying in deserted living rooms, or how she would sneak into the highly controlled terrace to see the open skies and acquire a full view of the neighborhood (*I* 80). Her first adolescent love takes place at the forbidden iron gate of the San Isidro estate and at the balcony of the Buenos Aires house on Florida and Viamonte Streets. Because of family restrictions against seeing the boy, she defiantly redecorates her room with pictures of Joan of Arc and Napoleon that remind her of her secret love. Once her marriage ends in a definite separation, the transgressions adopt new forms during her affair with Julián Martínez, as they dangerously defy social regulations of the public space. The city became the setting of a reformulation of daily life and domesticity, for instance, when they pretend to be husband and wife while sitting at a small restaurant in Retiro's train station (*II* 60). Through this relationship, Ocampo plays with gender conventions associated with women's domestic roles by repossessing the home and transforming it into the site of erotic love, as in the encounters in Julián's family house in Rodríguez Peña that deeply trouble Ocampo: "Las garçonnières, los 'románticos bulincitos', como dice el tango, están para eso. Las casas de familia no se profanan. El hogar es sagrado. Yo he cometido un sacrilegio. Yo estoy al margen de la sociedad, vos no, porque se les perdona a los hombres que tengan queridas" [The *garçonnières,* the "romantic love nests," as the tango goes, are meant for this. One should not desecrate the family home. The home is sacred. I have committed sacrilege. I am at the margins of society, not you, because men who have lovers are pardoned] (*II* 37). The lovers eventually build a house in Belgrano, the entire design and floor plans of which Ocampo supervises (68).

One of the most compelling narratives in *Autobiografía* tells of her love affair with French writer Pierre Drieu La Rochelle. This relationship allows Ocampo to fashion herself into a cosmopolitan persona apart from the social conventions that regulate her life and contrast the domestic roles she assumes in her affair with Martínez (*III* 81–82). This is particularly evident in the sequence describing her visits to luxury stores in London where she buys home décor and stationery for the house she is building in Palermo Chico, visits that annoy La Rochelle because they represent the "stable side" of Ocampo's life (84). Autobiographies imply a role reversal, an "autobiographical de-facement," as Paul De Man states, reading being central in this "alignment between the two subjects" in which they determine each other by mutual reflexive substitution." Autobiography's "specular structure is interiorized in a text in which the author declares himself the subject of his own understanding" (De Man 921–22). Ocampo accomplishes, at the end of her text, such defacement, a critical reading of gendered constructions of selfhood by exploring her domestic and cosmopolitan selves as the two sides of a mirror. *Autobiografía* embodies the abandonment of the home, the transformation of her personal and literary identity through a modern homelessness, and an architectural cosmopolitanism that took her to further places where she could reinvent herself as a woman and a cultural producer. Reading has many meanings in Ocampo. As Molloy states, reading has the effects of a performance, for the writer employs it as an "act" that gives meaning to life narration (28). Such is the deliberate reading in which Ocampo engages: the reading of the spatial to transform its materiality, the reading of gender to question its complex effects on women's lives, and the reading of a literary culture and the positions it assigned for them. Reading unlocked many possibilities in Ocampo's writing and in her life, for it allowed her to migrate and reinvent the home and to find her place in a new "world," where she designed new social and literary locations for the woman writer.

To conclude, thinking about domesticity in terms of modernity allows for new understandings of the women writers' search for a place within the literary culture of the first decades of the twentieth century in Argentina. Domesticity is, as this chapter demonstrates, a gendered field through which women writers imagine themselves as modern actors. When read in the light of home narratives, the cosmopolitan discourse of Argentine modern culture discloses important facts about the links between gender, space, and subjectivity. Through travel writing and cosmopolitanism—genres and concepts coded as masculine in the culture of the period—Lange and Ocampo transform the understanding of the home as a site of gender and cultural production. By depicting it as a ghostly realm, or as the site of cosmopolitan encounters, both writers negotiate their complex social and literary locations in the culture of the period. Lange and Ocampo transform the home into a set of cosmopolitan and domestic narratives which women are able to challenge and modify. Their works build virtual residences where women can shift restrictive social and literary locations. Fiction, autobiography, and literary criticism are part of a modernist project that interrelates the fluid binaries of home and abroad, public and private, and national and cosmopolitan. By displacing domesticity, both writers rethink the ways in which literature integrates tradition with modernity, our need for continuity and comfort with our equally powerful desires for autonomy and change.

CHAPTER 2

"Of Other Spaces": Staging Repression in the Works of Griselda Gambaro and Diana Raznovich

My memories as a child growing up in the Argentina of the 1970s do not evoke the violent events that history revealed to me years later. For years I will remember, for instance, the opening ceremony of the 1978 World Cup. The clear precision of the choreography, the army of children and adolescents forming the phrases "Argentina 78," "Mundial FIFA," and the competition logo, two Argentine flags embracing the ball, left my family and me with a feeling of astonishment that we will remember for years to come. After watching it again years later, the images stirred resemblances and identifications between my childhood and that of the protagonists walking on the field: the wearing of patriotic colors and androgynous clothes, the marching (an obligatory activity in my school during major holidays), the tidy hair adorned with blue and white ribbons, the sense of pride and patriotism. The brilliance of that day I will never forget: a bright sky and the field as a clear reflection of our orderly lives where everybody was where he or she belonged and where everything and everybody was contained by an invisible net, holding us tightly night and day. For many Argentines of my generation, that harmonic field on a cold, June morning became the bond of common memories, a mirror of our nationhood, but most importantly, the reflection of a social climate that years later, when the tumultuous years of the young democracy came, we tried to reconstruct as a country.

Ten blocks away, in the Navy Mechanics School (ESMA), operated one of the biggest clandestine detention centers, where thousands were tortured, killed, or "transferred" to the infamous *vuelos de la muerte* [death flights], in which the victims were first drugged into stupor, hustled aboard fixed-wing aircraft or helicopters, stripped naked, and pushed into the Río de la Plata or the Atlantic Ocean to drown. During the 1978 World Cup, the basement of the ESMA, which had previously operated as a torture chamber, was transformed into a dressing room for the players (Feitlowitz, *Lexicon* 172). The dictatorship spent 700 million dollars in the organization of the World Cup and created the Argentine Color Television (ATC) to televise the event to the country and the rest of the world (Malharro and López Gijsberts 146). The production of a common place of belonging and mutual identification—a national space as a shimmering spectacle, an "abstract or conceptual space" defining the country's perceptions and world views (Lefebvre 46)—was without a doubt one of the key pieces in the way the Argentine dictatorship (1976–1983) mastered political control and created a sense of social homogeneity. This illusion dominated the perceptual and lived space shared by the majority of the population, whereby space became a lethal "tool of domination," dissolving internal differences and imposing an "abstract hegemony" (Lefebvre 370). The "Night and Fog" of Argentina, as Marguerite Feitlowitz defines it, was made possible through this manipulation of space; a world of political violence was kept from the eyes of common citizens even as corpses surfaced in rivers and abandoned fields and denunciations from relatives emerged in the news. "I was there; I saw it; I couldn't have known a thing" was the most frequent excuse of casual observers to the abductions of their fellow citizens taking place at times in broad light right before their eyes (Feitlowitz, *Lexicon* 151). The regime managed to create a mirage whereby social space resembled a split screen simultaneously showing peace and order alongside brief glimpses of violence: "As official rhetoric worked to conquer the mental space of Argentine citizens, in shared physical space, a coercive discourse was also brought into play, one that could turn a 'normal' setting into a bizarre, and disorienting, theatrical. The performance of normal daily actions, like riding a bus, could make one impotent player in a deadly spectacle" (Feitlowitz, *Lexicon* 151). As space became an ambiguous place of both harmony and horror, euphemisms populated common language. Argentines lived in an undifferentiated space where ghosts coexisted with them. "Fueron hallados los cadáveres de siete personas muertas a balazos," "Presentáronse en los tribunals 159 recursos de habeas corpus," "En un basural fueron hallados tres cadavers" ["Seven gunshot victims found," "159 writs of habeas corpus presented in the courts," "Three bodies found in dump"] are some examples of the headlines at the major dailies

La Nación, Clarín, and *La Prensa* (Malharro and López Gijsberts 93). Under the grip of fear, and ignoring what they had seen, most Argentines would simply say, "por algo será" [There must be a reason].[1]

Geographers have long demonstrated how the spatial and the social are closely related. Edward Soja calls this relation "spatiality," "a socially produced space" where physical and psychological spaces are intertwined (*Postmodern* 121–22). Theater's aesthetic space reflects, more than any other literary genre, this complex relationship. In many traditions of Latin American drama, the stage is a location that is considered to restore vitality to social practices and to question processes of domination and colonization in the continent (Taylor, *Theatre* 23). In the case of Argentina, this rich tradition began in the 1880s with Juan Moreira and continued with the *grotesco criollo* [creole grotesque] (1923–1924) and the independent theater from the 1930s through the 1960s (Pelletieri, *Historia* 20–21). In the early 1980s, *Teatro Abierto* [Open Theater] embodied the cultural-didactic dimension of the endeavors of *Teatro del Pueblo* [People's Theater], a movement led by Leónidas Barletta that in the 1930s sought to restore critical consciousness in the people (Giella 28–29). In fact, *Teatro Abierto* began from the necessity of many dramatists to restore the capital place of theater in society and included not only the staging of many dramas but also the development of seminars and classes open to the general public (Giella 42–43). Historically, the stage has been a mirror reflecting the intersections between what Lefebvre calls the abstract, perceived, and lived qualities of space. In fact, theorists such as Augusto Boal gave theatrical space predominance in drama's effects on social transformations; he conceived of the stage as a "space of transitive learning in which people are actively engaged in multiple ways of problem solving" (Popen 125). From the perspective of both identification and distance, theater organizes space in a way that is qualitatively different from everyday space in a highly symbolic and meaningful manner through aesthetic conventions such as the "fourth wall." The distance between the stage and reality, traditionally organized around the perspective system from the Renaissance, has been transformed in twentieth-century theater by changes that unsettle this frontal and illusionary spatial relation, such as the shortening of the distance between actors and spectators, the incorporation of multiple stages, and the use of "non-theatrical" spaces (De Marinis 76–77). Boal conceived of, for instance, theatrical space as "transitive," for it allows an acute way of learning society's hopes and fears, a "mirror" giving spectators the capacity to observe themselves and modify certain social images (Popen 126).

Within the context of the artistic innovations of *Teatro Abierto*, Griselda Gambaro and Diana Raznovich wrote dramas addressing the connections between authoritarianism, violence, and gender. Although a considerable number of critics have studied this relationship in both authors, I focus on the issue of dramatic space in their works. Through what I call the "uncanny" and "specular" uses of theatrical space, both writers question the manipulation of space by the dictatorship and its repressive apparatus. Gambaro's plays address the spatial formations during *La Guerra Sucia* [the Dirty War], whereas Raznovich explores their later effects in the Argentine society of the 1990s. As in the cases of Lange and Ocampo addressed in the previous chapter, the domestic is also a dominant setting in Gambaro and Raznovich because one of the main historical conventions in theater is to identify the home and the stage. We can trace a common feminist genealogy among these authors based on the transformation of the domestic into an unhomely space, as represented for instance in the works of Norah Lange and another author not addressed in this study but who similarly transforms domesticity through the fantastic—Silvina Ocampo. As Hannah Scolnicov demonstrates, the origins of the theatrical scene can be found in the *oikos,* the impenetrable space of the home that Greeks associated with women (15), and traditionally, theater has maintained this division between the oikos and the *polis,* making the stage the preferred site for exposing the domestic. However, in Gambaro and Raznovich, the domestic is both familiar and recognizable, yet also concealing and enigmatic; in the Freudian sense, their works dismantle the associations among theater, the oikos, and a domesticated femininity.

Gambaro's and Raznovich's dramas explore gendered configurations of public and private spaces through feminist lenses that enable a critical examination of the broader effects of authoritarianism in society. As such, theatrical space acts as a "heterotopia," or a "counter-site," "a kind of effectively enacted utopia in which the real sites, all the other real sites that can be found within the culture, are simultaneously represented, contested and inverted" (Foucault "Of Other Spaces" 24). Although heterotopias are "real places"—in fact, Foucault considers the examples of the cemetery, the boarding school, and the honeymoon hotel to be heterotopias—they are endowed with an imaginary or virtual quality that locates them "outside of all places" (24–25). Rather than being only a background or setting, theatrical space in Gambaro and Raznovich performs many dramatic functions demonstrating the effects of multiple axes of power over women. As Foucault's heterotopias, the stage mirrors social referents by inversion while it creates "other spaces" that compensate for whatever is found unsatisfactory in certain social locations (27). Through a relationship of both identification and distance between the oikos and the polis, these "uncanny" or "specular" spaces make possible a critical examination of the spatial divide that ruled over Argentina in these last decades. In my conceptualization of theatrical space, I utilize the notions on both space and domination from Foucault's and Freud's ideas of the uncanny. As demonstrated in the previous chapter, Freud's theories have been particularly productive in feminist critiques of gendered domestic space. What I would like to highlight here is the connection between space and vision present in the theories of Foucault and Freud. Theater enables such a relation. Through an aesthetic practice that seeks to create new levels of social consciousness, "uncanny" or "specular" theatrical spaces mimic or duplicate the complex mechanisms of the scopic regime that forms collective perceptions of space. As Diana Taylor states, "Individual and state formation take place, in part, in the visual sphere through a complicated play of looks: looking, being looked at, identification, recognition, mimicry" (*Disappearing* 30). In the works by Gambaro and Raznovich, we detect the potential for critical forms of spectatorship in a society where the repressive apparatus of the state and delusions of the media and consumerism have fogged social perceptions. Theater offers the possibility of rebuilding the broken spatial and linguistic bonds through the creation of "other spaces."

Griselda Gambaro's prolific writing career of over forty years, including novels, short stories, and plays, deals with issues relating to the oppressive political and social environment of Argentina. A world-renowned writer, her works offer a social commentary about not only Argentina but also about universal power dynamics and the role of women in society. Taylor classifies Gambaro's plays into three periods. Her dramas of the 1960s depict a chaotic and menacing world that announces the violent turn in Argentine society to fascism and authoritarianism, whereas the works from the 1970s and 1980s portray the issue of disappearances—of people, values, and judicial and moral frameworks—and the causes and effects of the crisis in Argentine society (*Theatre* 97–98). The plays discussed here delve into the recurrent theme of the disappeared: *La malasangre* [*Bad Blood*] (1981), *Del sol naciente* [*From the Rising Sun*] (1984), and *Antígona furiosa* [*Furious Antigone*] (1986). They address the building of an abstract and highly allegorical space in a "spatial un-differentiation" that is common in her early plays, such as *Las paredes* [*The Walls*] (1963) and *El campo* [*The Camp*] (1967) (Taylor, *Theatre* 99). Set in situations seemingly detached from any close references to Argentine history, with the exception of *La malasangre,* where the colors and political language are clear indications of the violence that ruled the country during the regime of Juan Manuel de Rosas, the election of an "orientalist" setting in *Del sol naciente* and the classical scene in *Antígona furiosa* stresses the uses of an allegorical space to convey the effects of violence and authoritarianism in society. Space highlights a relationship of identification and rejection that characterizes Gambaro's drama, influenced by the *grotesco criollo*'s techniques of alienation or estrangement. As a broken mirror, this "uncanny spatiality" in Gambaro displays a deformed image of a country where society can see its reflection in the grasp of endemic forms of despotism in Argentina.

Diana Raznovich's plays *Jardín de otoño* [*Inner Gardens*] (1983). *Casa matriz* [*MaTRIX, Inc.*] (1988). *De atrás para adelante* [*Rear Entry*] (1993). and *De la cintura para abajo* [*From the Waist Down*] (1999) are all situated in domestic spaces dramatically transformed by other experiences of authoritarianism coming from the influences of the media and consumerism. Like Gambaro, who in 1977 was exiled to Spain for three years after the military junta banned her novel *Ganarse la muerte* [*Earning Your Death*], Raznovich also suffered political persecution during the 1970s. She was exiled to Spain until 1983 and returned to Argentina upon the restoration of democracy. A prolific playwright and cartoonist, she also maintains a blog where she explores the dark sides of gender conventions, heterosexuality, and the effects of violence and materialism on the lives of women (dianaraznovich. blogspot.com). Her plays have been staged in Argentina, in various countries in Latin America, Europe, and in the United States. In the four plays considered here, intersections with the media alter dramatic space and prompt reflection on the connections between visuality, space, and power. In *Jardín de otoño,* for instance, the living room with a gigantic TV that Griselda and Rosalía tend to daily changes into a television set where the protagonists enact love scenes of their favorite soap opera with the star of the show, Mariano Rivas, or "Marcelo the Mechanic," whom they had kidnapped in order to protect him from an imaginary, life-threatening danger. In *De la cintura para abajo,* the bedroom becomes a studio set where the national and international media come to photograph a fictional, sadistic performance by a couple who otherwise can never have sex because of the lack of desire of the male protagonist, Antonio. Dramatic space conveys the fluctuations of the characters' sensibility while exploring the role of different media— theater, television, newspapers, and magazines—in visualizing relations of power and domination. The issue of desire and sexuality as commodities of a market culture brings to the fore another form of "disappearance" in Raznovich, that of a true sense of community and a shared space that bonds people beyond the relationships artificially produced by the media. Whereas Gambaro addresses the immediate effects of violence and authoritarianism in the Argentine society of the 1980s, Raznovich goes one step further to explore the long-term obliteration of human relationships affected by violence and repression. As Gambaro's plays prophesied the aberrations that took place in detention centers during the Dirty War, Raznovich acutely addresses the sinister connections between historical amnesia and the media-ridden Argentine society of the 1990s, as expressed both in the slow justice for the victims of political violence and their relatives and in the rebuilding of a collective memory.

When referring to the effects of exile on our sense of space and place, Amy Kaminsky stresses that the exile has lost a sense of a familiar place (*After Exile* 40). In her works, Gambaro explores at length the effects of this loss through the ways in which authoritarianism transforms our spatial perceptions, where women and other disempowered subjects are displaced, not only physically, but also at their emotional and perceptual levels. In her plays, theatrical space becomes "uncanny" in the Freudian sense of being both a familiar and yet unrecognizable place where her protagonists find themselves like in a dream, or better yet a nightmare, invaded by feelings and sensations they cannot fully recognize.

1. Bloody Legacies: Trapped in the Allegorical Crypt

The early plays *Las Paredes* [*The Walls*] (1963) and *Información para extranjeros* [*Information for Foreigners*] (1972) are two excellent examples of the centrality of space in Gambaro's theatrical productions. In *Las Paredes*, the protagonist, a young man, is placed in a prison cell transformed by an artificial decor resembling a luxurious bedroom in the style of the 1850s. As the room becomes considerably smaller and it becomes stripped of its decorations and furniture, the protagonist progressively loses his ability to respond critically to the absurd and increasingly threatening games the usher and the functionary play with him. The walls, this play suggests, not only represent the sense of confinement and the gradual loss of freedom by the protagonist, they also embody the alienation of his perception and the disappearance of his will and, eventually, of his own life. "*The Walls* illustrates that the things that disappear from consciousness (the painting, the shrinking social space, logic, coherent language) must be understood in relation to the disappearance of humans, of consciousness, from the world" (Taylor, *Theatre* 105). At the end, we do not really know what is going to happen to the character. It truly does not matter, for his keepers have attained their goals: he has been reduced to a servile condition in which the crumbling of the walls mimics the absurd and yet indisputable reality of his alienation. His situation is also a powerful mirror reflecting that of the audience. Gambaro's play is a commentary on the dormant condition of citizens entrapped by the deceptions of sophisticated, repressive systems. Blinded by these illusions, they, like the protagonist, live enmeshed in separate compartments, surrounded by walls forcefully separating them.

Gambaro's most experimental play in its uses of dramatic space, *Información para extranjeros* is also highly ironic about how distorted perceptions that dominate a society bound by authoritarianism take the form of spatial constraints and divisions. In the play, the spectators' position is unsettled from the very beginning as they are invited to have a first-hand experience of the effects of political violence through a nontraditional theatrical setting: "El ambiente teatral puede ser una casa amplia, preferentemente de dos pisos con corredores y habitaciones vacías, algunas de las cuales se comunican entre sí" (69) ["The theater space can be spacious, residential house, preferably two stories, with corridors and empty rooms, some of which interconnect"] (Feitlowitz, *Lexicon* 69). A series of "guides" lead the audience through the labyrinthine structure of the stage; they occupy, like the "joker" in the Theater of the Oppressed, the polyvalent role of directors, interviewers, and narrators performing a commentary on the performance within the performance and forcing spectators to achieve an active participation in the play.[2] By enacting interventions and interjecting disorientation and incongruity into the small sequences they "show" to the audience, the guides prompt reflections about the role of art and theater in a society ruled by violence and authoritarianism. *Información para extranjeros* brings together the street and the stage; the play is based on excerpts from Argentine newspapers from 1971 and 1972, an effect of reality that is further emphasized by the subtitle, "crónica en 20 escenas" ["A Chronicle in Twenty Scenes"]. Through the transformative mirror of drama, spectators are shown the hidden violent realities happening in society: the abductions in broad daylight, the torture in clandestine centers, the public assassinations, the ubiquitous presence of violence both in the streets and the private home. Gambaro's play also erases the distinctions between the oikos and the polis: stage directions indicate that the house's different rooms need to be interconnected, thus allowing us to see secret corridors interconnecting the violence taking place in both. The play also targets the notion of innocence and its relationship to authoritarianism through references to word games, puns, children's rhymes, and the presence of a child-monster harming other children playing with him. Such uses of games and play have been linked to ritualistic uses of violence and to the interrelationship of dominance and subjugation within the political context of Argentina (Larson 92). They undoubtedly reflect the victimized condition of characters participating in such rituals without fully comprehending the depth of the physical and psychological manipulations they suffer. However, they are also references to the loss of our innocence as passive spectators, our childish perceptions shattered by a physical world where we are able to perceive the depths of the roots of brutality in social realities. As Feitlowitz explains, Gambaro's writing is "prismatic," for it adopts the structure of collages characterized by a "deep embedding of cultural codes" (*Information* 3). By shortening the distance between the stage and the spectator in *Información para extranjeros,* Gambaro urges us to reflect on the place we occupy in the scene of violence we are witnessing, a scene that is highly referential, as the direct quotes from newspapers make us believe. This erasure of the boundaries between onstage and offstage creates in the spectator what Feitlowitz describes as the "great anxiety... of not being able to move through space" as we envision the victims' imprisonment and torture (3). We are now in the house of horror that we desperately sought to ignore in our lives outside the theater. What are we going to do? Are we going to applaud? Scream for help? This is the profound paradox of Gambaro's "theatre of crisis," as Diana Taylor calls it. As readers and as spectators, we are now trapped in this violent and ambivalent space that theater displays for us; we are enmeshed in the rituals of violence, and we cannot run away or escape into oblivion. We can neither fold the newspaper and stop reading nor can we hide behind doors and windows. Is this the spectacle we were waiting for? The final words of *Información para extranjeros* ironically invite us to applaud:

> El teatro imita la vida
> Si no aplauden
> Es que la vida es jodida
> Vayamos a la salida. (128)
> [Theater imitates life
> If you don't clap
> It means that life is rotten to the core
> And we may as well just head for the door.] (Feitlowitz, *Information* 130)

The spatial divide that characterizes Argentine society during *La Guerra Sucia* is broken down by what Ana Elena Puga calls the uses of concealment and "abstract allegories" in Gambaro's theater. Allegory is an aesthetic form common in literature dealing with political violence in Latin America. Driven by grief, this is a trope that voices mourning in an "untimely past" that "takes distance from the present, estranges itself from it by carrying and caring for the seeds of time" (Avelar 20). As such, allegory conveys the ambiguities of presence and absence that characterize spatial and temporal experiences during times of political violence; it allows for the recognition of what has disappeared, and it brings to the fore the invisibilities corroding the social fabric. Allegory involves active forms of readership and spectatorship. The "abstract allegories" in Gambaro's theater "lead the spectator *away* from the most superficial interpretation(s) in order to signal just as plausible, and more compelling, hidden meanings" (emphasis in the original, Puga 145). As a means of expression that has both discursive and ethical functions, Mary Beth Tierney-Tello emphasizes the feminist possibilities that allegorical expression furnishes women writers: "...as allegories of sexuality *and* politics, these texts show us simultaneously the *political* nature of sexuality as well as the *gender-based* nature of authoritarianism...they make a traditionally private sphere into a public and political matter, transgressing and blurring the very boundaries between public and private spheres that authoritarianism attempts to portray as rigid and impenetrable" (emphasis in the original, 18).

As the examples of *Las paredes* and *Información para extranjeros* make evident, dramatic space has a key role in the construction of this allegorical function in Gambaro's theater. Space is a "performed relationality," Gillian Rose states, a "doing," "a matrix of play, dynamic and iterative, its forms and shapes produced through the citational performance of self-other relations," and most importantly, a "strategy of power," machinery in the way Foucault conceived it in *Discipline and Punish* ("Performing" 248). The plays analyzed here, *La malasangre, Del sol naciente,* and *Antígona furiosa*, demonstrate the ways in which the stage becomes a plastic mirror, enacting memories of disengaged social relationships and possibilities of new communal spaces of memory and mourning. In all cases, spatial constructions can be described as "uncanny" in the Freudian sense, as the setting shows the discrepancy between the familiar and the strange, the emergence of which "is secretly familiar, which has undergone repression and then returned from it" (245). Estrangement and spatial and temporal distance characterize these plays. The settings set them apart from what could be recognizable as an ordinary experience for the spectator: *La malasangre* takes place in an unidentified location in the 1840s; *Del sol naciente,* in a Japanese setting; and *Antígona furiosa*, in a coffee shop where a dead woman comes back to life. I call this spatial estrangement "uncanny," for it reflects the spatial incongruities of a society ridden by authoritarianism. As in the situations happening on the streets where casual spectators doubt about the reality of abductions and public violence, the uncanny space in Gambaro's plays presents us with events that seem to be unfamiliar, out of place, and yet possessing fully recognizable traits that relate to the Argentine historical context. This contradiction, central to Gambaro's allegorical expression, questions the ethical dimensions of spectatorship, for it forces readers and spectators to observe historical reality through a new perspective. As a "performed relationality," the uncanny space in Gambaro's plays trains us in visualizing new perceptual fields by enabling hidden comparisons and similarities where the stage becomes full of specular possibilities. In addition, the plays bring to the fore the uncertainties and the delicate balance of societies undergoing a democratic transition. The plays considered here were all written in the early 1980s as the country was awakening to the horrors of *La Guerra Sucia*. Most important, the uses of the uncanny, in connection with techniques coming from traditions of the Grotesque and the Gothic, enable a historical revision of the role of collective spectacles as sources of memory and social justice. In all three cases, women are the bearers of this important role as the leaders of a necessary change in perspective about the horrific events that took place. Dolores, Suki, and Antígona, although limited in their attempts at feminist resistance, offer a model for new forms of democratic awareness in the country. Even though gender is only one of the many variables in Gambaro's critique of the risks and possibilities of democracy, it certainly occupies a central role, for her plays unveil the complicities between the maintenance of sexual difference and authoritarianism in Argentina.

Michel Foucault's *Discipline and Power* discusses the connections between spatiality and power based on disciplinary systems and spatial orderings taking place in different penal systems during the modern age. He refers to Bentham's Panopticon—a prison shaped as an annular building with a control tower in its center—as a "house of certainty," for it guarantees an automatic power and "a real subjection...from a ficticious relation" of domination (202). "Visibility is a trap," Foucault states (200). The inmates do not know with certainty when they are being looked at, but the ubiquitous presence of the central tower creates a permanent consciousness of being seen: "The Panopticon is a machine for dissociating the see/being seen dyad: in the peripheric ring, one is totally seen, without ever seeing; in the central tower, one sees everything without ever being seen" (202). One important effect of this scopic regime is the internal division it creates; the inmates cannot see one another, and in a "sequestered and observed solitude," they remain numbered and supervised (201).

Written in 1981, a couple years before the restoration of democracy in Argentina, *La malasangre* addresses the continuities of authoritarianism in the country. The piece is set in the 1850s, in clear reference to the power struggles of the nineteenth century, and its protagonists are members of a family ruled with an iron fist by a despotic father. The play's spatial organization bears striking similarities to Foucault's description of the Panopticon. The invisible yet ubiquitous father's rule is evident in the opening scene. Standing at the curtained window, he looks down at a long line of applicants for the position of private tutor for his daughter Dolores. According to stage directions, the window is not in a prominent position but rather located upstage and covered with heavy curtains hiding the father's presence, thus guaranteeing his invisibility. No one is allowed to share the privileges of seeing from the hierarchical position the father enjoys; when he briefly invites the mother to see through the window, she is quickly forced to leave after a scene of jealousy and rage. While twisting her arm, a sign of the subdued violence dominating their relationship, he says: "¡Sólo mi cara tenés que mirar, puta!" (60) ["Mine is the only face you're allowed to look at!"] (Feitlowitz, *Bad Blood* 6). Contrary to the father, the mother's capacity to see is fully domesticated to the point that she is blind to the clear and present dangers posed by both her husband and later, Juan Pedro De los Campos Floridos, her daughter's fiancée, who makes open sexual advances to her right before her eyes. Like the sadistic servant, Fermín, she also acts as the father's surrogate, spying on Dolores and the teacher, Rafael, and later spoiling their plans to escape together. The house is thus ruled by the father's ominous presence who, as an invisible eye present on- and offstage, enacts a system of vigilance similar to Foucault's "disciplinary mechanism" where each family member is constantly being located and relocated in a "fixed place" (*Discipline* 197).

This scopic regime is possible because of the fact that the house is hermetically sealed from the exterior. Only Benigno, the father, and Fermín have unrestricted access to the outside. The relationship between the on- and offstage spaces is monitored by the domineering position of Benigno, granting access only to those elements that will not disturb his inflexible rule. He chooses Rafael as a tutor after long consideration and with great care, a hunchback who poses no threat to the domination he exerts over his wife and daughter. This orderly space, however, is pointedly interrupted by the ugliness of the exterior world, its physical impurity represented by Rafael's hunch, and the heads that Fermín brings in bags and shows to Dolores repeatedly are signs of the horror that the protagonists, just as the readers and spectators, cannot fully see. As in the strategies of the military junta that allowed certain scenes of horror to be seen by casual spectators in the street, the father allows the intermittent appearances of the ugliness occurring in the city in order to secure the maintenance of a fierce and yet subtle domination by fear. This "house of certainty" is thus built upon a complex visual dynamic of seeing, being seen, and the unseen that seeks to regulate, above all, the two women's desires. As Puga states, "the play's structure allows for the image of the tormented family to connect to the domestic abuses of patriarchy with both the nineteenth- and twentieth-century regimes, showing how history repeats itself in domestic and public spheres" (169). In the tradition of the "national romances" that characterize the nineteenth-century narrative in Latin America that Doris Sommer describes in her *Foundational Fictions,* the home is an allegory for a nation confronting centuries of internal political division where the sexual is associated with the political. This complex dynamics of desire and fear is also evident in the relationship of Benigno and Rafael as antagonists. Rafael can be interpreted as the political adversary who is invited home to tame any form of political confrontation. Although the power struggle is unequal, as Rafael is dispossessed of any form of strength or agency, Benigno seeks to humiliate him and reduce him to an even more servile position. The opening scene demonstrates toying with Rafael's body as a fetish for the father's political benefit. Benigno requests repeatedly that he get naked with the excuse that he only wants to see his bare hunch. In this process, Rafael is feminized, echoing Juan Manuel de Rosas—a consistent implied reference in the text—and his attempts to degrade political opponents. The maintenance of sexual difference is at the foundation of political binaries at the core of authoritarian regimes that historically have taken shape in Argentina. Following examples from the Rosas' regime, Diana Taylor states:

> Society, historically organized around the recognition of sexual difference, continued to ground divisions along gender lines—but now the line was drawn between the political insiders and their male opponents, who were feminized and marginalized as others. As men came to occupy the degraded status of historical women, women were erased as historical subjects. Nonetheless, the idealized realm of the abstract "feminine" (as in Motherland or *Patria*, or Liberty, or Independence) was elevated to the higher plane of male bonding and moral resistance to a brutal dictatorship. (Emphasis in the original, *Disappearing* 36)

This abiding misogyny is at the center of the spatial organization of the house. The father erects himself as its protector, an allegory of the motherland, blaming his political opponents as "wild, filthy, disgusting" beings trying to alter its order. As allegories of the political opposition between Federals and Unitarians during the nineteenth century, the father and Rafael demonstrate the impossibilities of any form of conciliatory encounter between political enemies and the failed political promise of a democracy in a country divided by hatred. As a representation of the body politic, the images of mutilated or imperfect bodies describe the endemic attempts to "cleanse" the country of that which is perceived as anomalous or deviant (Puga 170).

Sharon Magnarelli explains that the limitation of the field of vision by the despot evokes the issue of censorship and how the perspective of women, as well as their bodies, is controlled by different regimes of power (59). Although the mother lacks any possibility of visual empowerment,

Dolores offers interesting possibilities of a feminist form of spectatorship. Initially she can only "see" from her father's perspective; she humiliates Rafael repeatedly and ignores him as she initially considers him to be a representation of her father's attempts to control her will. When she starts paying attention to him, she enacts her father's behavior: she seeks to domesticate him by forcing him to look at her and dominate his "furious eyes." "Te amo con tus ojos furiosos" (80) ["I love the rage in your eyes"] (Feitlowitz, *Bad Blood* 31), Dolores admits after the father has effectively punished Rafael for the first time. Rafael maintains a submissive position throughout these visual games played by Dolores, not daring to raise his eyes, cautious of the chance that he will be beheaded for his transgression. However, Dolores's capacity to "see" gradually develops as she becomes able to distinguish the falsity of the binaries that dominate the reality around her. She starts to question the epithet of "wild, filthy, disgusting," that her father repeats, referring to those on the outside: "¿Quién no es salvaje? ¿Quién no es asqueroso? ¿Quién no es inmundo? Sólo el poder otorga una pureza que nada toca" (99) ["Who isn't wild? Who isn't disgusting? Who isn't filthy? Only those in power are clean and pure"] (Feitlowitz, *Bad Blood* 55). Ironically, it is her own father who enables this awareness by bringing Rafael to the house and allowing him to "impart an education" that challenges the boundaries between beauty and ugliness, order and chaos: "Que nada es tan simple como uno cree. Y nada tampoco tan complicado. Que lo derecho puede ser torcido y lo giboso plano como un campo dorado" (101) ["That nothing is as simple as one might think. Nor as complicated. That which is twisted may in truth be straight, and paradise can signify hell"] (Feitlowitz, *Bad Blood* 57). In her words, Dolores unveils the intricacies of power and its fallacies: what seems to be a "straight" and "uncomplicated" spatial order, the regulated field of the domestic, the imagination of a national space as an open and golden field, reveals to her, for the first time, a convoluted fiction set in place by her father. The capacity to recognize this mirage is instrumental in the critical spectatorship that Dolores acquires in the play, a powerful skill for revealing the darker side of the Panopticon, where the walls imprisoning her imagination crumble before her eyes. Although critics such as Magnarelli downplay the importance of a feminist resistance in the character of Dolores—in fact, Magnarelli calls Dolores's rebellions "mini conversions" without any lasting impact—I believe the play, although not completely destabilizing the patriarchal order, opens up new possibilities for women as agents of change. The most compelling example of this destabilization is the final scene when she is allowed to see Rafael's corpse. In a clear reference to the common denial and passivity that abounds in the Argentina of the last decades and the disappeared during the many periods of Argentina's political violence, Dolores sees, in bright light, Rafael's disfigured corpse:

> Entonces, uno finge que no pasó nada y todo el mundo duerme en buena oscuridad, y como el sol no se cae, al día siguiente uno dice: no pasó nada. E ignora su propia fealdad (*Con una sonrisa crispada*) Y para colmo encendí las luces (*La madre tiende la mano para apagar una*) ¡No te atrevas! ¡Necesito ver el castigo! ¡Necesito que no me quiten eso, el cuerpo castigado! (108)
> [We pretend that nothing happened, and all go to sleep in the dark. And the next day, as though the sun never set, we say nothing happened. And we don't even know how ugly we are. Touch yourself! (*With a tight smile.*) As if that weren't enough, I've lit all the lights! (*MOTHER reaches to extinguish one of the candles.*) Don't you dare! I need to see his punishment! I won't be spared his tortured body.] (Feitlowitz, *Bad Blood* 66)

At the end, Dolores is sent to sleep, but she refuses to close her eyes as she reverses the direction of her father's hateful look: "¡Jamás cerraré los ojos! Si me dejás viva, ¡jamás cerraré los ojos! ¡Voy a mirarte siempre despierta, con tanta furia, con tanto asco!" (108) ["I will never close my eyes! Never! For as long as you let me live! I will stay awake, I will always be watching you. Quick with rage and loathing!"] (Feitlowitz, *Bad Blood* 68).

In her essay on abjection, Julia Kristeva posits the contemplation of the corpse as one of the instances where the abject shatters the wall of representation and its judgments, for "it takes the ego back to its source on the abominable limits from which, in order to be, the ego has broken away—it assigns it a source of non-ego, drive, and death. Abjection is a resurrection that has gone through death (of the ego). It is an alchemy that transforms death drive into a start of life, of new significance" (15). In Artaud's theater, Kristeva states, the contemplation of the abject, the corpse, provokes horror as the "I" witnesses the truth of its own decomposition (25). Dolores's final transgression comes from the contemplation of this horror, the dissolution of an order finally coming to an end. In her "permanent state of awakening," Dolores embraces the difficult task of mourning, understood to be a political duty; Rafael's body is transformed into a mirror for collective recognition of that which disappeared in order to produce the spatial illusion of symmetry and order of the nation. As Walter Benjamin states, allegory brings to light the "*facies hippocratica* of history," an "allegorical way of seeing" that reveals "everything about history that, from the very beginning has been untimely, sorrowful, unsuccessful" (emphasis in the original, *Origin* 166). Dolores's awakening reveals the contradictions of a society awakened by death, by the contemplation of its ruin and the fragility of its democratic order. The ending conveys this uneasy resolution in the Argentina of the 1980s, whereby Dolores is now being sucked up, *chupada,* and disappears into the invisibilities of a perverse cartography of power that Gambaro simultaneously reflects and temporarily distorts.[3] Society, the play suggests in its closing, is not ready to make peace with the bloody legacies of history; rather, it prefers to remain in the dark, in the illusion of order and stability that the rulers have maintained for centuries.

In 1839 Esteban Echeverría wrote another political allegory, *El matadero* [*The Slaughterhouse*], a short story that remained unpublished until 1871. A gruesome depiction of the activities in the climate of authoritarianism and violence during Juan Manuel de Rosas's regime, *El matadero* indirectly refers to the Mazorca, Rosas's secret police, and its activities of imposing order through fear and coercion. The country has become a "slaughterhouse," Echeverría suggests, where political assassination is the order of the day. As in *La malasangre,* the image of blood, represented by the color red that *Federales* such as Rosas forced the population to wear, becomes a symbol of a country fragmented from the visceral, fratricidal fights endemic in Argentina's history. References to beheadings and torture by the father and heads in a bag as gifts to Dolores that Fermín brings are a couple of examples of the correlations between Rosas's regime and the father's authoritarianism. "Fui a hacer las compras al matadero" (71) ["I was going to the abattoir to do some shopping"] (Feitlowitz, *Bad Blood* 20), Fermín says in one scene. Contrary to Echeverría's story, *La malasangre* is set in the orderly space of the house that, as the play proposes, is only possible because of the existence of *mataderos* on the outside. However, the boundaries between the interior and exterior orders have collapsed and we are, as in *El matadero,* at the center of a perverse space where violence threatens to erupt any minute. In *El matadero,* details such as groups of grotesque women removing the intestines of slaughtered animals and the lifeless head of a child rolling on the streets of the slaughterhouse, beheaded by accident by one of Matasiete's men trying to trap a bull that is on the loose, compose a gory picture for the reader. Matasiete, the butcher in charge, rules the place from his *casilla,* a booth where at the end he attempts to torture a political adversary. In *La malasangre,* we are confronted with the remains of political violence intermittently threatening the premises of a false social order, the foundations of the "house of certainty," a symbol of the authoritarian state.

Critics have commented at length on Gambaro's cultivation of the *grotesco criollo* style. And, as Walter Benjamin states, there is a close relation between allegory and the grotesque (*Origin* 166–67). The word "grotesque," according to Benjamin, "seems to have been associated with its subterraneanly mysterious origin in buried ruins and catacombs. The word is derived from *grotta* in the literal sense, but from the 'burial'—in the sense of concealment—which the cave or grotto expresses..." (*Origin* 171). Allegory thus interrupts the narrative of history through the persistence of nature, embodied by that which has been concealed through a historical dialectic of presence and absence; they reveal what society displaced to the crypts of collective consciousness, and in an indirect and yet powerful way, they act as mirrors distorting the transparent face of history. Allegorical dramas such as *El matadero* and *La malasangre* reveal the hidden foundations of a decrepit social order by pointing to those grotesque aspects that have remained invisible. Spatially, allegories work as Foucault's heterotopies, as narrations taking place in society's "counter-sites" where certain cartographies of power are simultaneously represented and inverted. Allegorical space has the dialectical quality to which Gillian Rose refers as "performed relationality," whereby order presupposes chaos; beauty, the hidden face of the grotesque; and the clean and transparent fictions of government, the sites of political repression and murder. *La malasangre* ironically depicts Argentina's bloody lineage in the image of the hunchback as a powerful trope of a deformed, dysfunctional cartography of power. What the play "brings to the light," both literary and metaphorically, are those buried places of history that the political imagination seeks to deny, the obscure corners of a broken collective consciousness affected by authoritarianism and violence.

2. Gambaro's Creative Ruinations: Del sol naciente *and* Antígona furiosa

In *Del sol naciente* and *Antígona furiosa,* we are brought into the allegorical crypt first envisioned in *La malasangre.* Gambaro highlights in both cases the role of the spectral in the formation of a national consciousness and its implications for the frail democratic transition of the 1980s. The gendered spaces of the oikos and the polis become central in this process, as Gambaro investigates the possibilities of women's agency within the misogynist traditions at the core of Argentine authoritarianism. In *Del sol naciente,* the house and the woman's body are allegories of a national space branded as feminine and described as "unguarded" territory, a place for communication between the citizen and the exile, the historical present and the past, and the living and the death. Similar to *La malasangre,* space is depicted as a dialogical entity whereby the intermittent apparitions of the victims of a senseless war destabilize the space of the nation-state. The protagonist is a Japanese prostitute, Suki, who has the attributes of a goddess; she plays the biwa, a Japanese flute used in narrative storytelling that is a symbol of music, eloquence, poetry, and education. In *Antígona furiosa*, we witness, on the contrary, the presence of a woman ghost coming back from death, her spectral presence invading a coffee shop, a site traditionally gendered as masculine. The character of Antígona has been compared to the Madres de Plaza de Mayo, and as this comparison suggests, the polis is a key location in the enactment of different forms of female agency where women destabilize the imaginary geographies of the nation-state. In both plays, Gambaro employs the trope of the invasion, a common motif in Argentine literature, for instance, as depicted in the literature of Peronism and in the figure of the *cabecita negra* [little dark head].[4] She also exploits the uncanny effects of the invasion, as her plays create a sense of disturbance in the spectator, also accomplished by Cortázar's fantastic short story "Casa Tomada" ["A House Taken Over"]. However, Gambaro genders this trope as she demonstrates the profound connections between the erotic and the political from the perspective of what is missing, what has been disappeared, and the specters that haunt Argentina's national imagination. The ghosts in *Del sol naciente* are clear references to those lives lost during the *Guerra de Malvinas* [Falklands War] in 1982.[5] In *Antígona furiosa*, we hear the voice of the people who disappeared during the dictatorship in a moment when the first testimonies of survivors and relatives are being heard as part of the 1985 trials of military leaders for human rights violations during the democratically elected government of Raúl Alfonsín. As such, both plays are "creative ruinations," to use the term coined by Francine Masiello ("Scribbling" 29), for they articulate a reflection on the transformative possibilities of literature in a society collapsed by violence, the stage transformed into a place in ruins, a powerful allegory of the frail situation of Argentina in the 1980s. As they offer a space for changing historical trauma into actions of solidarity and memory, both plays can be read from the perspective of the testimonial genre in Latin America and its claims of an "ethical solidarity" and the creation of an "epic narrator" (Beverly 27–31) and also within the tradition of testimonial writings produced by survivors of the dictatorship in Argentina, such as Alicia Kozameh, Alicia Partnoy, and Nora Strejilevich.[6]

Del sol naciente evokes dreamlike visions: armies of beggars and wounded and moaning men marching incessantly, their presence increasingly invasive, eventually taking over Suki's house. In a country where authoritarianism has controlled society's perceptual field and has maintained the effects of political violence in the shadows, Gambaro exploits the dramatic tensions between what Scolnicov calls the "theatrical space within and without," the onstage and offstage spaces that are traditionally being kept apart, to show the spectral faces of history. Scolnicov describes theater's "space without" as "negative," for it traditionally lacks dramatic significance. Contrary to the "space within" that spectators directly perceive, the offstage space is rather "conceived"; it forces spectators to imagine and re-create actions and situations that remain hidden from them (4–5). As in many examples of Gothic literature, *Del sol naciente* engages the spectators through the fear of what remains unseen, hidden in the "space without," and leads our imagination to reconstruct that which we can only hear. "Se oye, afuera, el ruido monótono de una cuchara golpeando contra un plato de lata" [One can hear the sound of a spoon hitting a metallic plate coming from the outside] (142). As a permanent chant, these words resonate throughout the play as the ghosts of history gradually invade the space of the house. In this "house of the blind," as Feitlowitz describes a country unable to see the horror happening in the shadows, sounds haunt the illusions of cohesion and complete vision that theater as a genre has traditionally built. In other words, the fictional distance between spectator and stage, embodied by dramatic conventions such as the fourth wall, is broken as we are uncertain about the spectral intrusions present in the play. *Del sol naciente* recreates the feeling of the uncanny, haunting our certainty as spectators and introducing doubt as a form of critical spectatorship. Beyond the aesthetic effects of the uncanny in the play, it re-creates the sense of uncertainty and horror shared by many Argentines during the Dirty War. In the words of one witness living near a clandestine detention center:

> They built an enormous dividing wall there, erected a barbed wired surround, and put gratings in the windows. There was the constant sound of people coming and going. At night the searchlights were beamed in all directions. Firing could be heard from morning to night, as though they were practicing shooting or trying out weapons. Heart-rending cries could also be heard, leading one to assume that the prisoners there were undergoing torture. (*Nunca Más*, 152, qtd. in Feitlowitz, *Lexicon* 167)

Gambaro's play describes this "house of the blind" as an anomalous space, and vulnerable to the invasion of burglars and criminals. The house, states Obán, the warrior who takes on the unrequested role of its defender, lacks "solemnidad, reverencia" [solemnity, reverence] (119). Stage directions indicate that the house is open to the exterior, by the presence of both sliding doors and a transparent back wall that allows the spectators to see a tree and the bright daylight. Eager for praise and attention, Obán quickly proposes to replace the house's emptiness with wealth. He declares a war without any apparent reason. The motives are unimportant, he states, for "siempre hay alguno que nos ofende, que nos quita lo nuestro. Lo tuyo" [there is always someone who offends us, who takes away what belongs to us, what belongs to you] (119). Obán's claims of protecting the "unguarded space" of the house are allegorical references to how the military engaged in a series of territorial claims during the period of the dictatorship. The most compelling example is the Falklands War, led by the last president of the military juntas, Leopoldo Fortunato Galtieri. In April 1982, he initiated the war as a way of increasing the popularity of the government.[7] Along with the Beagle conflict, a dispute over the possession of a group of islands in the Beagle Channel that brought Argentina and Chile to the brink of war in 1978, these events indicate a confluence of territorialism and militarization in the country during these years in a dangerous formula that reflects the eagerness of the military both to gain control over territorial borders and to reawaken Argentine nationalism. The anomalous space of the nation, as well as the social body, needed to be restored, the landscape of the motherland usurped by foreign interests trying to "steal what belongs to us." A song that became popular during the time of the Falkland War, "La hermanita perdida" [The missing little sister] by Atahualpa Yupanki and Ariel Ramírez, embodies these ideals of territorial restitution by "bringing home" those areas that for too long had been missing: "Ay, hermanita perdida. / Hermanita: vuelve a casa" [Ay, lost little sister. / Little sister: come home].

The image of a steak in the shape of a map of Argentina being eaten by voracious enemies was made popular in the years of the Falklands War through a series of commercials promoting the military operations in the islands. A voiceover repeated a few verses from *Martín Fierro*, the epic poem written in 1872 by José Hernández, "Los hermanos sean unidos...porque si entre ellos se pelean, / los devoran los de ajuera" [Brothers should stick together...because if they fight, / they will be eaten by those from outside]. The ads stated that a "brotherhood of heroes" had come to protect the defenseless motherland as part of their patriotic duty to guard its territories. Gambaro's play deconstructs such nationalist rhetoric and the identification of territory and gender through Suki's critical performance of gender roles. "La tierra no existe" [The land does not exist], she claims in a key scene after Obán keeps repeating obsessively, "La tierra es nuestra" [The land is ours] (135). She also welcomes those coming back from a senseless war and transforms the house into a site of memory away from Obán's territorial claims. As the play suggests, memory needs to be housed somewhere, for "memory takes root in the concrete, in spaces, gestures, images, and objects" (Nora 286). In this *lieu de memoire*, in Pierre Nora's terms, the power cartographies of the nation are reshaped as Suki alters her role to become the "motherland" for those returning from death. The play destabilizes theatrical space, which traditionally is sealed into a coherent dramatic narrative. It introduces those elements located in the "off-space." Strange sensations, sounds, and smells are soon occupying the silent house, weakening its foundations and opening doors and secret compartments that have remained for too long shut down. "¡Esta casa es la que huele!" [It's the house that smells], exclaims Obán. "A muerto" [Of death], Suki responds (155).

Such spatial rearrangements imply the disruption of what Gillian Rose calls the "territory of the master subject": "a territory is a kind of property won, historically, often by violence and conquest, imagined as fortresses both for the protection of the self and the exclusion of others" (*Feminism* 148). As Obán seeks to conquer both the house and Suki as the embodiment of the nation, the play proposes instead Suki's escape to a "paradoxical space" where she engages with those who have been excluded, like her, from the imaginary geographies of the nation. Suki occupies the position of being both a prisoner and exile, within and without the confines of the masculine territories of the nation. In Rose's words, such "paradoxical geographies are political projects" (158), spaces of resistance through which we can think about power, knowledge, space, and identity in critical ways (159). The military regime strove to define the contours of the nation. However, in Gambaro's plays, that material geography is now unbound, open, and uncertain. The fact that Suki is a prostitute is highly relevant, for historically, Argentina linked fears and anxieties about female sexuality to family, class, and nation, as the study on prostitution in the country by Donna Guy demonstrates. The desire to domesticate the uncontrolled desires of both men and women was key in certain historical moments in Argentina; for instance, in fears about prostitutes and anarchists at the turn of the twentieth century or about the legalization of brothels during the Peronista years (Guy). While Obán seeks to bring under control not only the house's spatiality but also Suki's sexuality, the play ends by transforming both spaces into fertile and unbounded territories for the remaking of the nation through the process of memory and the construction of a collective testimonial about the dark effects of authoritarianism in the country. As such, memory takes root "elsewhere," in what Teresa De Lauretis calls the "blind spots" of male-centered gender representations "in the margins of hegemonic discourses, social spaces carved in the interstices of institutions and in the chinks and cracks of the power-knowledge apparati" (25). As a countersite of authoritarianism, the stage becomes an uncanny and unstable location, a place for the fragile encounter between the living and the dead, history's present and its ghosts.

The play also challenges Obán's desires of spatial ordering by using humor to erode his authority and the solemnity of his goals. Whereas in *La malasangre* the father had an overreaching power that no one seemed to be able to contest, Obán is almost a tragicomic character, a victim of his own blindness and excessive hunger for power and veneration. The space of the motherland is reconfigured as an empty off-space where women occupy a central role of healers and keepers of the common memories. The last scene reveals Suki sitting at the table with those coming back from the dead, sharing her meals and listening to the testimonies that keep coming in a chorus of endless voices: "Compartiré y entonces podrán morir en paz. La memoria es esto: un gran compartir" [I will share and then they will be able to die in peace. That is what memory is: a great sharing] (162). We can claim that Suki is still, quoting Taylor, "trapped in a bad script," for she remains encaged in the matrix of sexual difference that is at the basis of the masculinist project of a nation.[8] However, Suki is constantly mocking the masculine/feminine binary by using her parodic double, Ama. Suki manipulates her looks, words, and actions in a series of carefully staged performances whereby she uses her not only as a "shield" against Obán's advances but also as a parody of gender expectations that place her in a position of servitude and subordination. We can also add that Suki acts as the double of the woman playwright, at once enacting gender expectations and mocking them, laughing at the situation of servitude of women on the stage, a topic that abounds in many of Gambaro's plays, such as *El despojamiento* [*Stripped*] where an old actress is subjected to different humiliations by an invisible director and his assistant. The theatrical space becomes a complex site where the tradition of the stage as the site of the oikos, the "woman's theatrical space" is plagued by mocking voices, echoes, and disturbing sounds that cloud its traditional identification with a domesticated feminine. The stage is a transformed space where the feminine is both represented and destabilized, an "imaginary space" where the subject is both "doubled and split" (Rose, "Performing" 257). As Rose explains, spatial relations articulate the connections between body, fantasy, and discourse (258). And in Gambaro's case, theater is a embodied space that "does not entail solid shape, boundaries, fixity, property and possession whether of the self or of others;" rather, theatrical space allows a different kind of "betweenness" that challenges the spatialization of gender as the foundation of the nation and the role of women within that spatial economy (254). Gambaro seems to suggest, in a paradoxical ending, that this is possible only by displacing the female subject to an anomalous space occupied by the specters of history.

Gambaro's play builds its house of memory in the ruins of history, in a fragmented collective space of crumbling walls. Ruins have many meanings in the play: the remains of a social structure weakened by fear and violence where all forms of physical shelter are gone, the bodies in ruin, the victims' remains claiming a grave. But *Del sol naciente* also exposes the ruins of a dramatic language in crisis and invites reflection on the effects of a wounded social body in art. Much has been said about Gambaro's close relation to *grotesco criollo*. Dianne Marie Zandstra explains, for instance, that the grotesque is a way to "embody resistance" in Gambaro, where the reader is confronted by the "unresolved nature of the contradictory elements" (20). Gambaro's uses of such grotesque iconography reveal this "unmaking of the world" and our positions as spectators in a dramatic realm filled with uncertainty. In Elaine Scarry's words, "to have pain is to have *certainty;* to hear about pain is to have *doubt*" (13). As a "creative ruination," *Del sol naciente* invites us to hear those voices coming back from the grave and to question our role as spectators of the collective wounds of history.[9] By visiting the crumbling house of history, our imaginations are dragged back and forth in time, forcing conventional beliefs and our sense of certainty to "remote and undecipherable sensations" (Masiello, "Scribbling" 29). Located in a double time and in a liminal and spectral space between the "then" and "now," dramatic language transforms into a fragile diglossia, "a grammar of double voicing, loaded with double meaning" (30). "Haunting belongs to the structure of every hegemony," Derrida states (37), and in this play, Gambaro exploits the political potentials of the uncanny within the context of decades of authoritarianism. Specters are "neither soul nor body, and both one and the other," Derrida says (6). The allegory of the decomposing body in Gambaro is a powerful instrument for unsettling the fictions of a shared history. "Venían silenciosos. Y a algunos les faltaba la quijada, y a otros las piernas. Se sentaron en la calle, algunos...acostados. Y uno entró en la taberna y pidió de beber" [They came in silence. Some were missing a jaw, some their legs. They sat down in the street, some...laying down. And one went into the bar and asked for a drink"] (139). A specter is always a "revenant," Derrida states, for "one cannot control its comings and goings because it begins by *coming back*" (emphasis in the original, 11). Can this endless intromission of the spectral into our shared social space ever finish? *Del sol naciente* seems to suggest that no door can contain its influence. "Señora, pondré trabas en la puerta" [Ma'am, I will lock the door], the Ama says (139). However, in this "unmaking of the world," to borrow Scarry's expression, we can conjure the ghosts only by talking to them, thus the significance of Suki's final words: "Sostenido en la calle, caminando conmigo, poniéndome palabras en la boca. Revelado. No te negaré. Ni la tierra ni el fuego los negarán. Ni el futuro los negará" [Held up in the street, walking with me, putting words in my mouth. Revealed. I will not deny you. Neither the land nor the fire will deny you. Nor will the future deny you] (163).

As Gambaro's plays suggest, theater is a process of spatial reconstruction of a society broken into fragments, the building of an "alphabet of survival, of marks to be recycled via the precarious economies of the fragmentary and of the trace [del trozo y la traza]" (Richard 2). Allegorical dramas such as *Del sol naciente* embody the "insubordination of signs" happening in the literature of postdictatorial societies, the wounded zone of memory as a "zone of tensions and schisms," challenging instrumental realism and its communicational logic. Gambaro's plays allow us to "re-enable" the word as a field of plural and divergent forces (Richard 6). Writers such as Alicia Kozameh, Tununa Mercado, and Reina Roffé have also explored the force of spatial allegories in reflecting the wounds of social trauma. *En estado de memoria* [*In a State of Memory*] (1990) by Tununa Mercado suggests the exile lives in a "small cell," in a fragmented, confined, state of memory, her consciousness split in a way that challenges the possibilities of communication in literary language. In *259 saltos, uno inmortal* [*259 Leaps, the Last Immortal*] (2001), Alicia Kozameh conceives of the body of the exiled as plagued by hundreds of fantastic eyes that observe reality with new senses and new experiences. Space becomes a kaleidoscope of antagonistic views about the past. In her novel *La rompiente* [*The Reef*] (1987), Reina Roffé employs images of the sea as metaphors of an exiled female subjectivity characterized by internal division and the figure of the double. Narrations "out of place," these books embody the difficult task of the woman writer as a double exile, in relation both to gender expectations in society and to Argentina's intellectual field. Roffé describes her position as one of a "ghost writer" in a servile position where the woman writer is always seeking another's approval and borrowing someone else's voice ("Versos" 17). Through new creative directions, however, she is able to devise unexpected paths: "La necesidad de responder a las expectativas y exigencias de los que yo creía eran mis interlocutores...suscitó un fenómeno extraño: me desvió de mi camino" [The need to respond to the expectations and demands of those who I believed were my interlocutors...provoked a strange phenomenom: it diverted me from my path] (56–57). This twisted, fragmentary, antirealist mode of writing has been considered a trait of women working under the legacies of authoritarianism. Feeling the pressures of at least two sets of expectations, that of the authoritarian state's gender codes and the "gen(d)eric authority of literary history," women writers employ experimental and allegorical writing as a critique of past and present forms of gendering. They both transgress authority and seek symbolic transformation by the "re-casting of dominant scripts, plots, and representational models, with re-writing and transforming discursive modes" (Tierney-Tello 13).

Like Suki, the character of Antígona embodies the transformation of gender roles and the questioning of the connections between meaning, identity, and power embedded in spatial structures. She is under the despotic rule of Coryphaeus, the chorus director in ancient Greek drama who, in Gambaro's play, also represents the polis's authoritarian ruler, Creon: "Una carcasa representa a Creonte. Cuando el Corifeo se introduce en ella, asume obviamente el trono y el poder" (196) [Creon is represented by a movable shell. When Coryphaeus puts on the shell, obviously he is assuming the power and the throne] (Feitlowitz, *Information* 135). As one of the few examples in which Gambaro places the dramatic action outside the home, this play exposes women's complex locations in the public sphere, here understood not only as a place of political participation, the polis, but also as the stage, a site of cultural circulation and exchange also ruled by despotic men. Catherine Boyle calls Gambaro the "audacious trespasser," for she has broken many barriers that hinder women's roles as protagonists in the field of Latin American theater: "For the dramatist, the common problems of publication, production, audience, and the actual size and access to theater combine with more specific and localized problems such as censorship and persecution" (146). Gambaro also explains the difficulties women writers face when approaching the "immodest" and "aggressive" genre of theater (Interview 193). *Antígona furiosa* is an excellent example of how women confront the expectations of docility and obedience in both society and art. As noted by critics such as Diana Taylor, Gambaro gives Antígona a more central and human role than in Sophocles' *Antigone*; the play rewrites the traditional roles of women mourning and burying their relative's bodies into the context of the disappeared and the task of the Madres in memorializing death (*Disappearing* 216). Ana Elena Puga additionally proposes Antígona's disobedience as a critique of the Law of Due Obedience passed by the Argentine congress in 1987, which allowed mid- and low-level military officers to defend themselves on the grounds that they were following legitimate orders (184). Antígona's disobedience goes beyond the fact that she claims her brother's body and actually buries it in front of the despot. She performs his memory in front of the despotic eyes of Coryphaeus and the coward, Antinous, by reenacting the fratricidal battle that killed him:

> La batalla. Irrumpe entrechocar metálico de espadas, piafar de caballos, gritos y ayes imprecisos. Antígona se aparta. Mira desde el palacio. Cae al suelo, golpean sus piernas, de un lado y de otro, con un ritmo que se acrecienta al paroxismo, como si padeciera la batalla en carne propia. (199)
>
> [The battle. An eruption of metallic clanging of swords, stamping of horses, screams and cries. Antígona moves away. Watches from the palace. She falls to the ground, hitting her legs, rolling from one side to the other, in a rhythm that builds to a paroxysm crescendo, as though she endures the suffering of battle in her own flesh.] (Feitlowitz, *Information* 139)

As in *De el sol naciente,* woman and national space become one, the motherland a site of conflict among men. "As with the image of the *Patria,* Antígona occupies a space of mediation between men," Taylor states (217). However, Antígona reenacts this relationship from a critical perspective, her body transformed into a *lieu de mémoire*. Aware that living implies the necessary companionship of and communication with history's ghosts, Antígona engages in a dramatic performance that connects the present and the past. This is the paradox of Antígona's role and its most important symbolic function: it shows the "mixed, hybrid, mutant, bound intimately with life and death," characteristic of places of memory "enveloped in a Möbius strip of the collective and the individual, the sacred and the profane, the immutable and the mobile" (Nora 295). Antígona's performance demonstrates the dialogical and almost plastic quality of the places of memory described by Pierre Nora. The play also challenges the notion of space as a passive, static, and depoliticized entity traditionally gendered as feminine (Massey 6–7). As many cultural geographers state, places are relational entities whereby relations of power and privilege can be contested.[10] Antígona's body, as a powerful place of memory, challenges the spatial divisions that lie at the foundation of the authoritarian regime and shows the fundamental quality of social interdependence at the heart of civil society. This, I believe, is one of the most important contributions of Gambaro's play: as a memento mori for the living, it shows the importance of communal spaces in reconstructing social bonds that have been broken by violence and political repression. Gambaro gives women a central role in the process of mediation between memory and history and in the creation of such powerful places of memory. In a society where citizens are bound to empty carcasses, enacting robotic roles and giving formulaic speeches without any depth, as demonstrated by Coryphaeus's dissonant words, Antígona's performance also allows for the healing power of language as a vehicle for building new forms of communication in Argentina's incipient democracy. Compared to the characters of Dolores and Suki, whose frail language shows only incipient forms of agency, Antígona has a clear voice that she articulates against Coryphaeus's cacophonic words. Although the play, as in *La malasangre,* ends "in silence," Antígona's speech creates vital interruptions that challenge the discursive homogeneity imposed by authoritarian regimes. At the end, we hear Antígona's rage, and as she is forced by Coryphaeus once again into her cave, we witness her furious speech, addressed against the state of invisibility that has condemned her to an endless victimization. Her last words are, however, a testimony that, like her subjugation, her transgression is also timeless, for as a ghost she will keep coming back from the grave: "'Siempre' querré enterrar a Polinices. Aunque nazca mil veces y él muera mil veces" (217) ["I will always want to bury Polynices. Though I a thousand times will live, and he a thousand times will die"] (Feitlowitz, *Information* 158).

Marguerite Feitlowitz characterizes the language used by the perpetrators of the Dirty War as a "lexicon of terror:" "Perversions of the language contribute to the sinister, indeed surreal, quality of life in Buenos Aires" (*A Lexicon* 48). Words, Feitlowitz states, become abstract tools of violence and repression. The most compelling example of this "lexicon of terror" is the word *desaparecido*, describing individuals who were made to vanish by the junta, a strategy also employed by the Nazis as part of their doctrine of Night and Fog (Feitlowitz 51). Gambaro's play also engages in a reflection on how language is corrupted during periods of violence. The dialogues are structured as a series of replicas with Coryphaeus and Antinous sarcastically echoing every word Antígona says. "¿No terminará nunca la burla?" (217) ["Will there never be an end to this mockery?"] (Feitlowitz 159), Antígona asks at the end. Through this dramatic play with language, Gambaro demonstrates the ways in which the constant attempts by Coryphaeus and Antinous to erase Antígona are, in fact, proof of her visibility. Her character shows that, contrary to the domestic and public invisibility experienced by women in Latin American societies, women are in fact key political actors in the democratic transition of the 1980s. Further, *Antígona furiosa* claims that such invisibility is orchestrated, not only spatially but also linguistically, by the deceptions crafted by those in power. Because as spectators we see Antígona coming back from the dead, and we know this is an endless process that will take place once again in a near future, the play shows that "her sacrifice is an artifice, as temporary and illusory as performance itself" (Puga 182). As an example of what Nelly Richard calls the "aesthetic of the discard," *Antígona furiosa* uses dramatic language as an art of recollection and interpretation, which stages "the decomposition of general perspectives, centered visions, and finished portraits" (14). Antígona's language is thus intermittent, periodically and cyclically able to interrupt dominant discourses. "History's continuity is that of the oppressors," while "the history of the oppressed is discontinuous," Richard states, citing Walter Benjamin. And, as Gambaro's play makes evident, the disappeared's "creative ruinations" are an unfinished succession of loose fragments, unleashed during the spectral moments of history.

The spatial and linguistic structures in the play demonstrate a dialectic between the places seen and unseen, the words spoken and silenced. Contrary to the artificial order predominant in a society regimented by fear, Gambaro shows us the remains of that which we do not want to see or hear: corpses everywhere, ghosts speaking with rage, their screams on the streets. Within the context of how women in Latin America are condemned to invisibility in the public sphere and how the Madres de Plaza de Mayo defiantly challenged these assumptions in order to seek truth about and justice for their children's disappearance, Taylor explains that Antígona's claims of visibility are a call for "responsible witnessing," contrary to the "dangerous seeing" happening when fearful spectators attempt to negate the reality of violence (*Disappearing* 212–13). They are also a call for women to regain visibility both in the public sphere and, in a field of representation, on the stage, where women traditionally occupy a marginal or invisible role. Antígona enacts an artistic and political performance of ways in which women can destabilize cartographies of power. She challenges the tyrant, Creon, and the spectator to see and to hear: "¿Me ves, Creonte? Yo lo sepultaré, ¡Con estos brazos, con estas manos! ¡Polinices!" (201) [Do you see me, Creon? I will bury him, with these arms, with these hands! Polynices!] (Feitlowitz, *Information* 141). Visibility is thus the fundamental tool of democracy, the play suggests: "Oh, ciudadanos afortunados, sean testigos de que nadie me acompaña con sus lágrimas..." (210) ["Oh, fortunate citizens, bear witness that no one wept with me..."] (Feitlowitz, *Information* 152). The fact that the play takes place in a bar, a site traditionally gendered as masculine, is also significant, for it highlights the links between a gendered gaze and the construction of a spec(tac)ular public space where women traditionally have remained images or reflections of men's desires or fears. In her essay on female *flânerie*, Anke Gleber states that women's confinement is not only spatial, for women also have internalized their image as objects of a public male gaze and have become unavailable to the critical way of seeing that characterizes modern flânerie, their perceptions domesticated through limited and controlled forms of looking (74). *Antígona furiosa* reworks this domesticated flânerie by deepening the visual field and enabling us to see what has remained invisible in the polis: we are placed in the perspective of the ghost, and we are invited to share what Derrida calls a "visor effect," an asymmetry by which we do not see that the specter is looking at us (7). This critical form of spectatorship implies a visual decentering, for we are now engaged in a peripheral, spectral view where we simultaneously see that which has been erased from the polis, the disappeared, and the tyrant's operations to conceal it. Antígona's main challenge to Creon lies in the power of this destabilizing gaze and its capacity to uncover the spatial invisibilities Creon's spec(tac)ular view creates.

"La ciudad pertenece a quien la gobierna" (208) ["The city belongs to him who rules"] (Feitlowitz, *Information* 149), states the Choryphaeus. "Solo, podrías mandar en una tierra desierta," (208) ["One can rule a desert beautifully alone"] (Feitlowitz, *Information* 149) is Antígona's response. Antígona's critical words refer to the creation of a deserted yet immaculate public space, the city epitomizing the attempts at beautification of a national space that was considered to be "mutilated" and "dismembered." As the city became an empty, unrecognizable text that was difficult to decipher, what Marcy Schwartz calls the "urban space semiotics" was dramatically altered (*Invenciones* 51). The eradication of poverty and different manifestations of what the junta considered "filth" was a commonly used strategy:

> "Cleansing," a key word in the official lexicon, entailed first of all the erasure of recent history. Murals, posters, graffiti—any evidence of prior political life—was considered filth and washed away. Popular expression was a "nightmare," "tribal frenzy"—either way, a rampage on the bastion of thought. The environment had to be bright, beautiful, and soigné: a setting for, and mirror of, the exalted virtue ("inherent grace") of the Process. (Feitlowitz, *A Lexicon* 154)

In this process of transforming urban space into a "shining mirror," society experienced what Kathleen Newman calls "de-territorialization" as an effect of political violence in the hands of the state. Spaces and people that had previously been protected by the state were now placed "outside" of the state's territorial protection and therefore became the Other, the enemy, the legitimate targets of extermination (22). Those singled out became dispossessed of space; they first were disappeared as citizens and later became "de-territorialized," a gendered process according to Newman (23). *Antígona furiosa* thus implies a re-territorialization through the cultivation of critical forms of spectatorship and a profound reflection on the role language plays in the establishment of spatial experiences and perceptions. Although she goes back to the grave, Antígona takes us with her, to the depths of an allegorical crypt from which we cannot easily escape. In the Argentine society of the 1980s, the play seems to suggest, the possibilities of democracy are in fact tied to the endless "chain of the living and the death," where we are all paying the price of historical wrongdoings and where those disappeared by the regime cannot be so easily forgotten.[11]

In the case of Diana Raznovich, similar issues of critical spectatorship are brought forward in the context of the Argentine democracy of the 1990s. Her works point to the perverse similarities between democratic governments' uses of visual culture and the media as a continuation of the junta's scopic regime of invisibilities. We are not yet ready for the spectral spectatorship proposed by Gambaro, Raznovich seems to suggest; we are still sleeping in the realm of the spectacle, trapped in the visual constructs of a democracy and its limitations to giving testimony of the abuses of history.

3. Misplaced Views: Diana Raznovich's Fun House Mirror

As a visitor of the Navy Mechanical School's building (ESMA), the site gave me, at first, the impression of solemnity. The ESMA is a large complex, located on the Avenida Libertador, one of the busiest and most elegant boulevards in Buenos Aires. Its main building, the elegant Casino de Oficiales, was built in the 1950s following a neoclassical style. Columned and immaculately white, it projects the image of the elite training institution that was intended at its creation. After stepping inside, however, I experienced a stark contrast. The small windows did not allow in much of the bare light of the cold, June morning. Images and sounds of Liliana Hecker's *El fin de la historia* [*The End of History*] kept coming to mind. I was, after all, in the same place where an estimated five thousand people were tortured, killed, or transferred to the infamous death flights. As I was standing in what seemed to be an endless darkness, I had the strange feeling of being at the edge of time, so well described by Diana Taylor in her article "Performing Ruins." "Walking the ruins"—states Taylor—is a durational performance where we "can summon up visceral connections to lives lived and lost, even to lives about which the visitors know little. But as we conjure them up, we know that they're gone, and remain there forever as gone. They allow us to forget that we too are present and absent at the same time" ("Fighting" 14).

The guide led us next to the "Gold Room," with its still impeccable hardwood floors, and later to the basement, where the prisoners were first sent and where multiple torture chambers operated. "Between 1977 and 1978, they added six more torture chambers here," he explained. "In the basement they also had a dark room to prepare audiovisual materials for propaganda that the junta sent to the national and international press." "*La huevera* (the egg box), they called it," he added. "And in this same room they also conducted torture sessions beginning in 1978."[12] Upstairs was the officers' bedrooms along with a clandestine maternity ward, where women gave birth in captivity. Pregnant women were treated under the same conditions as other prisoners until the seventh month of their pregnancy, when they were provided with better care. They usually were given a lethal injection, and their babies were "adopted" by families associated with the regime; the grandmothers of Plaza de Mayo estimate that four hundred babies were born in clandestine centers during the dictatorship. In the attic, we stood up in *La pecera* [the fish bowl], an area fully covered with glass doors where some prisoners wrote news reports for the junta. Some of them read and summarized books for the commander of the navy, Emilio Eduardo Massera. Standing there, I felt as if I were looking at the place through the eyes of

Liliana Heker's protagonist, Leonora, who, according to *El fin de la historia,* was detained and confined in this same attic. In my memory, I can reconstruct her cell; I can see her sitting in the *capucha*, the section of the attic in the ESMA where prisoners were held in complete isolation.[13]

Places of memory are a form of "territorialized memory." Through them, we seek to make sense of historical trauma; they are paradoxical sites that demonstrate the many layers of social memory and its struggles, its gaps, and the unavoidable presence of oblivion (Jelin and Langland 1). The spatial complexity of the ESMA demonstrates, more than any other icon of the dictatorship, this intricate mechanism of memory. In this site, the many realities of the Dirty War coexisted in a macabre routine: life and death, pride and humiliation, the making and unmaking of a social order. When studying similar complexities in colonial space formations, Sara Mills describes them "not as given, but as a set of superimposed spatial frameworks, as many social spaces negotiated within one geographical place and time" ("Gender" 693). As a torture center, a clandestine maternity hospital, and an intelligence site for the creation and distribution of data and information, the ESMA included them all under the same white façade of solemnity. For decades, no one really knew what went on behind this looking glass. Spaces, Mills reminds us, are not only what we physically see; they imply a position from which they are erected as a representation. Spatial relations are built through viewing and knowing positions (700). The dictatorship's success in concealing this place is astonishing. During the 1990s, certain sectors of society still believed in the persistence of this mirage. Upon the return of democracy, the playing fields of the ESMA were used by prestigious private schools from Buenos Aires for gym classes and, in 1995, its pool was selected as the site for a city-wide high school swim competition (Feitlowitz, *A Lexicon* 173–74). A member of the sports program declared, "The ESMA is as much a state entity as the School of Exact Sciences. We do not believe in opening up the wounds of a sinister past; we should rather look forward, all Argentines united in peace and tolerance."[14] After decades of debate, the city of Buenos Aires reclaimed the complex in 2000, and it is currently in the process of being transformed into a museum for the defense of historical memory, as are many other clandestine detention centers in the country.[15]

Diana Raznovich's works considered in this section, although not directly referring to the atrocities of the Dirty War, echo in a parodic, humoristic way the ways in which scopic regimes produce spatialities of power and domination. Like Gambaro, Raznovich chose the domestic as the site for exploring how spaces are produced through different positions of viewing and knowing. Whereas Gambaro's plays lead us into a spectral realm, in Raznovich we are placed into a glass cage, lost in an endless series of mirages and false reflections. Theatrical spectacle becomes a looking glass that we traverse as spectators in strange, distorting ways. Her plays deal with apparently frivolous topics: two women's love for soap opera, the incurable diarrhea of a father, a couple's intimacy problems. But underneath this thin veneer of superficiality, Raznovich reveals the fabrication and manipulation of images as the roots of authoritarian regimes. In her apparently innocent and humorous plays, we find ourselves trapped in a fun-house mirror, the actions on the stage resembling in strange and unexpected ways the tragicomic life of Argentina's timid return to democracy.

The connections between performance and visuality are at the foundation of Raznovich's specular theatrical spaces. "Space is practiced, a matrix of play, dynamic and iterative, its forms and shapes produced through the citational performance of self-other relations," Gillian Rose states ("Performing" 248). As in Foucault's observations on the Panopticon, Raznovich's plays also engage in a reflection on these "self-other" relationships in visual and spatial terms. However, whereas in the prison described by Foucault, space was conceived as a hierarchical structure produced by an omnipresent eye, its central surveillance organizing the scene from a central projection, Raznovich's specular space is fragmented into a series of distorted views. Power has a kaleidoscopic force where the eyes of those involved in the spectacle look in many different directions and rarely meet. These illusory effects are not only produced on the stage; Raznovich showcases many examples coming from different visual technologies that seek to domesticate our desires and perceptions of reality. Taylor has coined a term that effectively defines this theater—"percepticide." As a mirage, theatrical space becomes a place of false visions and delusion. The series of miscommunications and double entendre that fill Raznovich's dramatic situations are nothing but direct references to how Argentine citizens are blinded and unable to see one another in a period of historical transition where capitalism and globalization have replaced political authoritarianism as the creator of social mirages. As critical references to the frivolity and historical amnesia that predominates in the media-ridden Argentine culture of the 1990s, works such as *Jardín de otoño* and *De la cintura para abajo* shed light on the creative intersections between media and theater, an interest present in Raznovich's theater from the beginning. In 1971, for instance, she staged in Buenos Aires a musical comedy for children, *Texas en carretilla* [*Texas by Weelbarrow*], a satire of the classic plot of American westerns (Martínez 41). Through the combined perspective of the media and theater, Raznovich invites us to walk through the looking glass to see our role as accomplices in the consumption of illusory spectacles as we watch the wondrous views of our daily lives enlarged by the stage's fantastic lenses.

Laura Mulvey states that there is a gendered visual dynamics in film whereby the woman is the icon displayed for men's gaze and enjoyment. Camera movements reflect either desire, the building up of the woman's physical beauty ("fetishistic scopophilia"), or fear; they assert control over guilt associated with the castration her image produces ("voyeurism") (438). This visual process of fear and desire conceals an imaginary threat that constantly endangers the unity of filmic illusion (441). At the core of visual production there is an underlying absence, which in the case of Raznovich's theater, highlights the connections between spectacle and the repression or commercialization of desire. Classic film narratives, Mulvey states, erase the material existence of the recording process and the critical reading of the spectator in order to achieve narrative cohesion and obviousness and truth (441). Spectacles are thus a complex fabrication of a visual illusion, and Raznovich, by including other technologies such as television and photography, invites the spectator to pay attention to the artificial quality of theater and the role of spectatorship in the consumption of a visual economy of desire. She "fights fire with frivolity," we can say using Taylor's words, her works gendering the dynamics of the theatrical look and showing how various systems create and manipulate desire as they seek to control desiring bodies ("Fighting" 23).

Raznovich's specular theatrical space embodies a series of mechanisms of visual identification and rejection. In *Jardín de otoño,* we see the two protagonists, Griselda and Rosalía, trapped in a series of misplaced views, that of themselves and that of the soap opera star, Marcelo the Mechanic, or Mariano Rivas, the actor. The desire of the heterosexual couple projected by the gigantic TV in the center of their living room masks their underlying lesbian desire. The play depicts a series of missed encounters and a story of an impossible love as we witness the characters' eyes seeing and not really seeing each other in the scene. The play centers on the two women's perspectives. We are placed in front of their TV and invited to see what they see, the daily show of their favorite soap opera. However, we are also located in front of a split screen. In the second act, the two women create their own show, forcing Marcelo-Mariano, whom they have kidnapped, to perform a private spectacle for them, where they are now the leading actresses and where they can, for the first time, openly express their desire. This complex visual dynamics of desire and repression is best described by Raznovich's innovative use of theatrical space:

> La sala tiene anexado un jardín vidriado lleno de plantas, ubicado al fondo del escenario. Esta cristalera da transparencia y profundidad al espacio escénico.

A través de este jardín se filtra la luz de la luna, se ve el golpeteo del agua cuando llueve y se perciben los virajes violáceos del crepúsculo. Estos ventanales vidriados redimensionan el lugar, permitiendo una iluminación a veces fantasmal otras a contraluz que acompaña la irrealidad de sus vidas. (13)
[There is a solarium, full of plants, open to the living room at the back of the scene. This glass room adds transparency and dimension to the scene. Throughout the play, different light filters in through the glass, moonlight, rain, and the violet lights of dawn, and times phantasmal, a light that reflects the illusory nature of their lives.] (Raznovich, *Inner* 53)

The play establishes the stage as a set of reflecting mirrors, representing the glass room full of plants and the TV, which embodies Rosalía's and Griselda's incapacities to truly overcome their boring, uneventful lives. In the autumn of their lives, they live in a glass cage of conflicting images of themselves, unable to breathe (as Rosalía), looking to see into the future (as Griselda), but remaining painfully trapped in false perceptions that do not allow them to act or move.

The play's scenography challenges traditional uses of theatrical space and the perspective system introduced in the early fifteenth century in Italy and its notions of central projection. As Stephen Heath explains, the production of this deceptive illusion centered on an implied spectator positioned at a window, seeing the world framed according to a central point of perspective (28). This involves the illusion that the eye will operate according to this central perspective, and in classical cinema, Heath explains, this central perspective has been key in achieving an impression of reality by containing the "mobility of the eye" within a contained and delimited visual field (31). Contrary to film, theater cannot control what the spectator chooses to see, thus the importance of theatrical spatial conventions in creating a visual frame that mimics this "perfect eye" in a steady and ubiquitous control of the scene. *Jardín de otoño* dismantles this framing process; in this performance within a performance, this kaleidoscopic space entices the spectator's imagination by adding different layers of perception through a series of mirroring devices, thereby transforming the central perspective traditionally organizing the scene.

Issues of female spectatorship are at the core of this rearrangement of theatrical space. How women's gaze is either constrained by visual and economic systems or able to engage in forms of fetishism and voyeurism, subverting the position of the male ideal spectator, are key questions in Raznovich's play. The TV's presence as on and off in central scenes is a powerful agent materializing and, at times, misplacing the two protagonists' desires. Undoubtedly, it represents the domestication of female desire as it engages the viewers emotionally but disengages them ideologically (Taylor and Constantio, "What" 82). This is most evident at the end of the play when, after having kidnapped the actor playing Marcelo the Mechanic and having forced him to perform scenes of the series for them, they feel disillusioned and allow him to leave as they go back to watching the soap opera where he is the protagonist. The soap opera reinforces stereotypical gender roles through the creation of a visual simulacrum that bears more reality in the two women's minds than the actual actor with whom they are "in love." Also, in this sequence of misplaced views, they are unable to see the passion that truly exists between the two of them. However, Raznovich seems to also suggest that theater, contrary to the domesticated view of television, is a powerful mirroring space, the "other space" destabilizing self-images, identity processes, and conventional forms of spectatorship. Rosalía re-fashions herself away from the confining space where she lives after watching a scene where Valeria and Marcelo first kiss, their passion as a powerful mechanism for imagining herself as a new Alfonsina Storni with a new life of self-autonomy near the ocean. Although the scene has undeniable humoristic undertones, especially in how Rosalía fashions herself as a tragic woman poet, the soap opera provides her the opportunity to imagine herself living outside the crystal cage where she is currently trapped.

In the second act, the two women perform soap opera scenes, aided by Marcelo-Mariano while forcing him to undress and act sequences they find more enticing, such as the ones in which he bites an apple. They toy with him, kiss him, force him to undress, and even push him to have sex, although he repeatedly demonstrates his incapacity or unwillingness to meet their demands. They finally discover the artificiality of his looks. Disillusioned, Rosalía says, "No son rulos naturales..." [His curls are not natural]; "Tiene maquillaje..." [He's wearing makeup] (74) (*Inner* 92, 93). "Usted no existe. Pero nosotras sí...Nosotras estamos vivas..." (75) [You don't exist. But we do. We are alive] (*Inner* 93), she finally concludes. In these scenes, by parodying Mariano-Marcelo's conventionalized TV performance, the protagonists invert what De Lauretis calls the "looking glass held up to the man," the role of woman as a specular image, the ground of representation depicted as the spectacle-fetish or specular-image and located in an obscene position (*Alice* 15). This process of dismantling the image of the soap opera star makes evident the potential powers of women's critical gaze. Mariano's last words are a compelling example of how his masculinity has been threatened and dismantled by the mirror held by Griselda and Rosalía: "Yo soy un hombre, voy a mostrarles que soy un hombre...¡Yo soy ese, yo soy ese! ¡Ese soy yo, yo! ¡Soy yo! ¡Soy yo!" (77) ["That's me! I'm him, I'm him, I'm him.

It's me, it's me!] (*Inner* 95). Through this desperate cry at the end, Mariano demonstrates that he is only the image of a man. As in Gambaro, Raznovich explores the complex connections between imaging processes and power, her characters seemingly unable to go through the looking glass standing in front of them. And, although Griselda and Rosalía are able to successfully dismantle the illusion that traps them every day in front of the TV, they are unable (or maybe unwilling) to walk away from it. At the end, they choose to keep watching the soap opera while Marcelo bites the apple, "the apple of happiness," an ironic reference to the powerful temptation of the media enticing us every day to walk into the fun-house mirror offered to us.

At first, Raznovich's play seems to repeat certain stereotypes of identifying women and media culture predominant in twentieth-century literature and art, as Andreas Huyssen demonstrates.[16] However, her work also entails seeking out the contradictions, heterogeneity, and ruptures in the fabric of representation so thinly stretched so as to contain excess, division, difference, and resistance. Her plays, although unable to dismantle the gender matrix operating through the media and theater, open up critical spaces in the seamless narrative space constructed by dominant discourses. Instead of thinking in the binary once again, for instance, in terms of "good or bad" images of women in the media and theater, Raznovich proposes that images are potentially productive sites of contradictions in the formation of social processes. Rosalía and Griselda act as doubles. Rosalía is the performer enacting a burlesque representation of femininity. She is the woman poet, the innocent girlfriend for Marcelo-Mariano, the housekeeper bound to ideals of a domesticated femininity. Griselda, on the contrary, acts as an authoritarian and critical director, arranging scenes including Rosalía and Marcelo-Mariano but also laughing at the stiff conventionality of some of their performances. When, at the end of an episode, the women conclude that Mariano is under a mortal threat and Rosalía decides to "pray for him," as if she had caused Mariano's downfall, Griselda comments, "¿Perdón? Si nunca hemos pecado," (43) ["Forgiveness? But we haven't done anything wrong"]. Without even listening to her, Rosalía prays,

> Perdón por lo que no hice.
> Perdón por lo que no tuve.
> Perdón por lo que no tomé.
> Perdón por lo que no sentí.
> Perdón por no haberme reído bastante.
> Perdón por no haber usado mis lágrimas.
> [Forgive me for what I haven't done
> Forgive me for what I haven't had.

Forgive me for what I haven't taken.
Forgive me for what I haven't felt.
Forgive me for not laughing enough.
Forgive me for not using my tears.] (*Inner* 73)

Jardín de otoño reverses the imaging process of fetishism and voyeurism, as described by Mulvey and De Lauretis, by transforming women into agents of a desiring gaze. The issue of women's critical spectatorship is central in this play. Traditionally, as De Lauretis explains, "The female viewer is also positioned in the films of classical cinema as spectator-subject; she is thus doubly bound to that very representation which calls on her directly, engages her desire, elicits her pleasure, frames her identification, and makes her complicit in the production of (her) woman-ness" (*Alice* 15). Raznovich's theater highlights the artificiality of gender constructions—they are, after all, a creation of the media, as the play shows—and invites critical forms of spectatorship by pointing to the repeated trap of gender performance. Although the "production of woman-ness" is only temporarily suspended and examined in this play, Raznovich opens up interstices of critical spectatorship in line with other manifestations of feminist theater that explore the role of the feminist spectator as critic. In Jill Dolan's words, these plays demystify the dominant ideology masked by conventional theater: "Rather than being seduced by the narrative that offers a comfortable gender position, the spectator is asked to pay critical attention to the gender ideology the representational process historically produces and the oppressive social relations it legitimizes" (14).

The role of the media in the production of specular images is central in Raznovich's gender critique. *Jardín de otoño* examines what Walter Benjamin describes as the loss of the artistic aura, a sense of authenticity and uniqueness rapidly disappearing because technical reproduction erases the spectator's temporal and spatial coexistence with the object of art ("Work" 220). Modern technologies such as film and photography enable a different form of perception characterized by distance and "apperception" (240). Mechanical reproduction, which he sees in negative terms for its connections to the rise of the masses and experiences of European totalitarianism, has dislodged this "sacred connection" between art and spectator (223). Raznovich's theater similarly employs the media, in this case television, to deconstruct theatrical illusion. Through the confluence of different visual technologies, she challenges the idea of an "authentic" dramatic experience and invites a disengaged form of spectatorship through a series of parodies and self-referential performances. Her characters demonstrate what Taylor calls "percepticide": they are caught in the active production of social fictions that, within the context of Argentina's recent history, have proven fatal as they demonstrate the role of collective delusion in the instauration of authoritarian regimes ("Theatre" 114). As a powerful reflecting mirror, the actions on the stage enable us to see critically how we are also trapped in the creation of collective spectacles that corrupt our ability to build shared relationships of communication and trust. Raznovich's protagonists, however, are aware of the inauthentic character of the images they consume, and yet they painfully end up choosing to remain trapped in the illusion: "¿Usted sabe qué significa para nosotras tenerlo hoy aquí? ¿Nunca leyó sobre los espejismos en el desierto? Mirarlo todos los días por esa pantalla es un espejismo y esta casa era un desierto hasta que entró usted..." (50). ["Have you ever read 'Mirages in the Desert'? Looking at you everyday on screen was a mirage and this house was a desert, and now you are here..."] (*Inner* 78). *Jardín de otoño* ironically mirrors the situation of an entire society consumed by its desire to believe in false collective mirages. The inauthentic quality of the images on the stage is, Raznovich seems to suggest, a painful reflection of the broken social connections in a society obsessed with the simulacrum of the media.

Although the political implications of her theater are not as openly evident as in Gambaro, Raznovich's attempts to cultivate critical forms of spectatorship are, in fact, a form of raising social consciousness in the public. After her exile in 1975, she returned to Argentina in 1981 to participate in the *Teatro Abierto* [Open Theater] with her play *El desconcierto* [*Disconcerted*], although the theater that housed the event was burned to the ground the same day her play was staged. As Taylor suggests, Raznovich's theatrical style, characterized by disruption and inversion, differs from the critical realisms of other dramatists participating in *Teatro Abierto* ("Theatre" 114). However, in light of the rise of neoliberalism and the consolidation of a presence of a global media in Argentina during the democratic transition of the 1980s and 1990s, Raznovich's ironic references to the media bear new meanings about the role of this new force in the social and political life of the country. Beginning in the 1980s, the emergence of video-politics, combined with new forms of advertisement and marketing, transformed the way social and political life was conducted, not only in Argentina but also in a region awakening to democracy (Quevedo 203). The importance of television proved critical, for instance, during the presidency of Carlos Saúl Menem (1989–1999). Going against Peronista traditions of political activities conducted on the streets in front of massive crowds, Menem chose the safe refuge of television as traditional political scenes were rapidly dismantled through a new articulation of the relationship between the media and politics (216–17). Market deregulation and privatization also impacted different areas of the social field as cultural products, such as literature, weakened due to a decrease in the demand for books as print culture lost its importance in the new primacy of image-centered products (Hortiguera and Rocha 25).[17] Hugo Hortiguera points to the co-optation of the visual for political aims during the Menem years, as politicians became actors in television programs or variety shows. In the 1990s, the concentration of the media in the hands of economic and financial groups close to the government also influenced the homogenization of public opinion and the loss of a plurality of voices and perspectives within the communication system in Argentina. The deregulation of telecommunication during Menem's first presidency created new forms of monopoly in radio and TV. *Jardín de otoño*, like other works by Raznovich, ironically refers to the erasure of the limits between fiction and reality and the creation of a "spectacle world" that privileges the notion of feelings over the importance of informing the citizen (Hortiguera). Argentine life in the 1990s is characterized by a continuum of artifices and disorders escaping any rational explanation, the crossing of fiction and the language of the state. As Hugo Hortiguera explains, the state is a melodrama, and Argentine reality a constant imbalance, an experience of chaos and excess.

The effects of this melodrama on Argentine life are clearly exposed in Raznovich's play through the critical lens of gendered spaces. *Jardín de otoño* depicts the home, an allegory of the nation-state, as in Gambaro's works, as a glass cage where characters are trapped by their incapacity to see one another, and human relationships are ruled by missed encounters and deformed reflections. What is significant in this play is how theatrical space is transformed by the superimposition of different spatial frameworks coming from theater and television. In Rosalía and Griselda's house, the panoptic gaze that we saw operating in *La malasangre* has been fragmented and broken into a series of out-of-focus views. Rather than a monolithic site regimented by heterosexual desire, *Jardín de otoño* demonstrates the transformation of the nation-state by bringing to the fore the desire of those traditionally excluded from it. It also shows how women, rather than being in a position of subjugation, critically intervene, though in intermittent, paradoxical ways, and challenge the social order through a genre traditionally associated with the feminine: the melodrama. The expelling of Mariano-Marcelo at the end of his failed performance can also be interpreted within this context, as women's roles as new protagonists in a social landscape where traditional forms of governability, based on a heterosexual matrix, are being corroded by a culture centered on images of masculinity that are fading away. Although the play depicts the nation-state as a fun-house mirror, where no image seems to have real depth or content, and as a society obsessed with the consumption of media images that only favors the persistence of national fictions, *Jardín de otoño* also opens up spaces for women's critical interventions in the social landscape of the democratic transition of the 1980s and 1990s.

Raznovich addresses the debate on the negative or positive effects of the media and the role of technology in creating social awareness. Although traditionally, cultural critics considered technology as a tool of capitalism, as in notions of "cultural industry" described by the Frankfurt School, Jesús Martín-Barbero demonstrates, however, that the connections between technology, media, and culture are rather complex and have undergone a history of changes in the social meanings attributed to them. In the case of Argentina, Martín-Barbero explains that soap operas, which originated in the radio drama of the 1930s, represented for the masses a way of expressing a social sensibility otherwise excluded. The fact that, in 1947, Peronism created a "cultural recognition" of radio drama by equating it to other literary forms through a series of prizes from the National Commission of Culture is an excellent example of the political importance of the genre (Martín-Barbero 183). Similarly, Francine Masiello studies the role of melodrama in depicting the subjectivity of social groups such as Afro-Argentines and women in nineteenth-century Argentina. Melodrama presents a way for those excluded groups to confront the homogeneity of official discourses by exposing the social realities of those living in the margins ("Estado" 144).[18] In Raznovich, melodrama depicts the broken social relationships during Argentina's democratic transition and the realities of privatization and the transformation of the welfare state into a weak, collapsed entity, whereby the media's simulations have corrupted social and political consciousness. However, in this state of things where the idea of originality seems to be collapsing, Raznovich brings to the fore the powerful effects of media genres, such as melodrama, in the creation of a social consciousness. The origins of melodrama in Argentina are also tied to popular forms of theater, such as *circo criollo,* Martín-Barbero states (182). And Raznovich goes back to those roots by using the stage in humoristic ways to parody a social order being transformed by the overreaching effects of the media. De Lauretis calls film a "memory spectacle," for it shows those areas of our consciousness reflecting desires that are only available to us through the imaginary; women are usually the objects of this memory, and film embodies the image of a woman "desired *as* remembered" (*Alice* 27). Raznovich similarly stages the social order of patriarchy as desired *and* remembered, attractive and yet impossible to materialize. We see Rosalía and Griselda trapped in this memory spectacle, and yet the play also ironically suggests that it is the man's spectacle that is impossible. The key issue of the construction of a female spectatorship, or how to reconstruct what De Lauretis calls the "impossible place of female desire" existing between the historical place of the female spectator and the look of the camera and the image on the screen, is crucial in Raznovich (69). And mass media products, such as the soap opera, clearly highlight the contradictory possibilities of such a project.

In *Casa Matriz,* Raznovich depicts the "memory spectacle" of motherhood and deconstructs another powerful myth in Argentina's national imagination. As in *Jardín de otoño,* this play depicts women's voracious search for emotional relief in the consumption of visual commodities, but this time the mother's performance of love is made according to the customer's demands. The title of the play refers to how home and mother have become one, with the matrix as a powerful metaphor to describe a sociospatial dynamic whereby the cultural and political significance of domesticity is, once again, critically revised and challenged. Allison Blunt reminds us that ideas and lived experiences of home invoke a sense of place that is intimately tied to a sense of self. From this perspective, "the contested sites of home and domesticity [are] critically important not only in the social reproduction of nation and empire, but also in revealing the interplay of power relations that both underpin and undermine such processes of social reproduction" (7). *Casa Matriz* depicts the matrix as a bodily and social space, the site of collective dreams and fantasies where fictions of personal and national identity are produced. Different performances of motherhood not only show the artificiality of gender roles, but they also point to a nation's voracious need for fictions of social belonging and for a communal space that seems to have vanished during the postdictatorship years. Steven Pile describes the bodily and social spaces as "geographies of meaning, identity and power." In *Casa Matriz,* the body and the home are examples of these mobile and conflictive cartographies; they "are mapped through citation of one another" (181). In Argentina, there is a long history of the production of motherhood through the instrumentalization of women's bodies as laboratories for the nation. For instance, Marcela Nari studies how, at the beginning of the twentieth century, public policies sought to regulate the body and the mind of the modern mother. Motherhood was "naturalized" in order to reestablish ideals of a patriotic motherhood that, since the nineteenth century, had impacted the formation of a civic role for women. Education played a key role in defining this "naturalized motherhood." The idea that the environment decisively intervened and transformed innate characteristics led many believers in positive eugenics to stress the importance of the mother's education. In this area, medicine played the role of defining a script for modern mothers through the reinforcement of state policies that focused on strengthening the mother-child bond and transforming beliefs and habits of motherhood through aggressive education campaigns.[19]

In the context of the Dirty War, discourses on motherhood acquired new meanings as the image of a "motherland" was framed within a patriarchal discourse. The mother had the imaginary function of community building, and the feminine remained an entity without any form of real agency (Taylor, "Theatre" 118). As depicted in Raznovich's play *El desconcierto,* the dictatorship erased the feminine and transformed it into the dead center of nation building (119). In *Casa Matriz,* Raznovich gives new meaning to this image of the feminine. The maternal body becomes the site of national and global imaginations of place and belonging, an artifact produced in different centers around the world: "Casa Matriz tiene una sucursal en cada uno de los centros principales del mundo entero. Viaje tranquilo, sabiendo que ante cualquier eventualidad usted puede encontrar una Madre Sustituta." [MaTRIX, Inc. has branches in all major cities worldwide. Travel worry-free, with the knowledge that should any contingency arise you will be able to meet with a Substitute Mother] (82). Although the performances of motherhood shown in this play have undeniable ties to the realities of Argentina—the "Italian mother" of an immigrant's slum, the suffering mother of the tango lyrics—motherhood has become a global product. At the end of the play, the mother becomes a nipple of enormous proportions that Barbara, the protagonist, sucks with great pleasure. As if it were manufactured in a production line, the role of motherhood has become a global commodity, feeding needy costumers around the world. Because of its standard qualities—the performance needs to be as far-fetched as possible, the mother states—the merchandise of motherhood can be sold anywhere:

> Estamos instruídas para eso. Nuestra formación exige un cierto plus. Si no nadie contrataría una Madre Sustituta. El cliente se quedaría con su madre naturalista real. No podemos, no debemos caer en el realismo de las madres que nuestros clientes ya tienen (107)
>
> [We are instructed to do that. Make it extra special. Otherwise no one would contract a Substitute Mother. The client would stick to her own mother. We cannot, we must not try to be like the real mothers of our clients.] (*MaTRIX 119*)

An allegory of the nation entering the neoliberal order, motherhood also represents the need for the human contact that is evasive to a population of global citizens lost in the market's impersonal qualities. Raznovich's disillusioned message is quite compelling: as we lose this precious sense of intimacy, we can only buy a mother's love. But the protagonist's desperate words begging for more love are also a sign that this search is pointless, for this mother-machine will give us only a fleeting fantasy, and we will always need more.

De Atrás para adelante is a grim parody of the family as a hollow structure wherein human relationships, as in *Casa Matriz*, are commodities for sale. In this play, Javier, the son who eventually becomes Dolly after surgery and a change of sexual identity in Miami, challenges the foundations of the heterosexual family. As a powerful allegory of a nation transformed by external influences, Dolly/Javier destabilizes imaginary cartographies based on the idea of the feminine body as a powerful force for community building. Scenes of cross-dressing and the acting of different gender roles demonstrate the instability of gender categories, a concept common to many women playwrights, according to Kirsten Nigro (20). Following the format of a comedy of errors, gender instability indicates that "there is no immutable real that engenders a series of acts—but a series of acts that construct the real" (Taylor and Constantio, "What" 87). *De atrás para adelante* depicts the transsexual Javier/Dolly as a burlesque representation of the absence of the feminine in Argentine culture or, better yet, the construction of the feminine as a national fiction. Javier/Dolly is the intruder in the matrimonial bed in central scenes, when he/she first seduces Mariana's fiancé, Nacho Bergman, two weeks before their wedding, and later, when Simon thinks he/she is his dead wife, Dorita, and almost forces him/her to have sex with his/her own father. As the ghost of femininity coming back from the grave, he/she emerges with increasing force into a family narrative that had formerly kept him/her in the shadows. And as part of a series of humorous exchanges about the connections between the motherland and the citizens' rear end, the play stages that which is obscene and left outside the spectator's views, the abject as a symbol of a country obsessed with hollow images of femininity and masculinity. In the context of Raznovich's interest in the intersections between the media and theater, *De atrás para adelante* additionally foregrounds the role of specular images as replicas destabilizing the role of the real in social constructions. The simulacrum has replaced the original and, whereas the dictatorship resorted to a fabricated image of femininity as the source for a common motherland, the artificially created body of Javier/Dolly points to the uses of this simulated femininity for the purposes of a market economy. The play's humorous ending, where Javier-Dolly saves his/her father's business by convincing Argentines that they love colored toilet paper and that buying it is a proof of patriotism, mocks the role of gender identities in the formation of discourses of nationhood. Theatrical space represents the irruption of the abject with the presence of Javier/Dolly as a powerful signifier destabilizing the home, an allegory of the national space. Julia Kristeva describes the space of abjection not as homogeneous, nor as totalizable, "but essentially divisible, foldable, catastrophic" (8). And Josefina Ludmer states that the fragmented space of the nation-state was, at the turn of the century, a site of experiences of displacement and proliferation of internal frontiers, where the new subjectivities of women, gays, and indigenous people gained new importance (10). *De atrás para adelante* thus depicts those happenings taking place at the rear of the national stage. As a "performed relationality," the stage becomes, using Gillian Rose's words, a matrix of play where self-other relations are examined through the ironic lenses of theater.

In *Manifiesto 2000 del humor femenino* [*Manifesto 2000 of Feminine Humor*], Raznovich explores the endless possibilities of feminine laughter. Written as a series of vignettes that comment on how women are forced by society to stay in silence and repression, this manifesto looks at the corrosive possibilities of humor from a feminist perspective. Raznovich's *De la cintura para abajo,* published in 1999, stages the powers of this feminist laughter and points to repression as a problem affecting the entire Argentine society. Centered around a couple's intimacy problems, the missed encounters in the bedroom symbolize the unmaking of social bonds during the postdictatorial period. This work condenses the paradoxes of a country living at the verge of its disintegration, with Antonio and Eleonora as allegories of the painful realities of the 1990s: a society consumed by its obsession with visual products, appearances, and the media and unable to establish common bonds based on trust and communication. Paulina, the mother, and later a sexologist are called for help. Paulina gives Antonio a basic sexual education, but her attempts fail when he is unable to put into practice what he had learned. Mr. Troncoso, an ex-torturer making a living through this new profession after the fall of the dictatorship, provides lessons to the couple on to how to act in the traditional roles of the male as the master and the woman as a slave, resulting in a sadomasochistic performance that yields terrible results for the couple, for they end up in casts with several broken bones. Eventually, Paulina, who is a successful writer of bestsellers, decides to profit from the couple's pretend violent relationship and transforms their bedroom into a photography studio where journalists from around the world come to photograph them in different sadistic poses. At the end, Eleonora finally resigns to celibacy, while she, Antonio, and Paulina celebrate their new business's success.

Taylor posits that *De la cintura para abajo* shows the continuities between the dictatorship's politics of repression and the internalized violence of authoritarian domination in Argentine society (Taylor and Costantio, "What" 89). The play explores these connections through the role of images, tortured and injured bodies as visual commodities for the consumption of the local and global market. As in her previous plays, Raznovich uses visual technologies, in this case photography, to enlarge theater's role in questioning the connections between image-making, spectatorship, and visual domination. Photography is a form of acquisition, Susan Sontag explains, for it involves the creation of an impersonal, automatic relation to events and people.[20] Following a tradition of interpreting photography as a technique that creates a hollow impression of reality, Sontag proposes that as an automatic image-making process, photography establishes a new, more objective relationship between image and reality: "This image-making process has powers that no other image-system has ever enjoyed because, unlike earlier ones, it is *not* dependent on an image maker" (352). Like the television set in *Jardín de otoño*, photography is a tool for exploring the intricate connections between the real and its theatrical double. In the tradition of Antonin Artaud's notions of theater as a genre that should awaken the spectators' sensibilities and critical reactions, photography shows the artificiality of both theatrical and social performances. The process of transforming the couple into photographic commodities is shown through their burlesque depiction as puppets of the national and foreign markets' demands for sadomasochistic images. Theater reveals the production of Eleonora and Antonio as broken, distorted images of masculinity and femininity in a photographic set regulated by a tyrannical mother who is interested only in the economic benefits of their broken relationship. Paulina, the mother in the role of an assistant stage director, translates the foreign photographer's demands and arranges dramatic poses for Eleonora's and Antonio's bodies, which are covered with fake red makeup mimicking the scars and wounds of their sadomasochistic exchange.

Space, Mary Louis Pratt states, is a projection of fears and desires, a social landscape embodying the perspective of a "hypothetical traveler-seer" (*Imperial* 125). *De la cintura para abajo* shows how this form of spectatorship has gone global, Eleonora and Antonio's staged relationship embodies the construction of a landscape for the eyes of an international consumer. The space thereby depicted is that of a nation as a body covered with artificially created wounds, a photographic fetish to be observed by the eyes of an impersonal spectator. "I've traveled to this unknown and undiscovered country, and we paid dollars cash to ensure a true South American grief," states the American photographer (118). Grief and intimacy have become commodities in a world where the historical memory of pain and human rights abuses is now vanishing. As Andreas Huyssen states, issues of memory and amnesia are further exacerbated by the development of media technologies that affect politics in culture in fundamental ways, as demonstrated by members of the Frankfurt School like Theodor Adorno and Walter Benjamin (*Twilight* 4). The media transforms the ways in which we think and live historical memory and leads us to a contradictory situation where we experience both the waning of history and historical consciousness, best expressed by notions of *posthistoire* and an increased consciousness about the needs of historical memory (5). Although Huyssen considers the paradox of memory and amnesia mainly from the perspective of historical time, his ideas on the role of "twilight memories" in contemporary society also describe the absence of a shared experience of space:

> Memory is no longer primarily a vital and energizing antidote to capitalist reification via the commodity form, a rejection of the iron cage homogeneity of an earlier culture industry and its consumer markets. It rather represents the attempt to slow down information processing, to resist the dissolution of time in the synchronicity of the archive, to recover *a mode of contemplation* outside the universe of simulation and fast-speed information and cable networks, to claim some *anchoring space* in a world of puzzling and often threatening heterogeneity, non-synchronicity, and information overload. (emphasis added, 7)

Memory is both a "mode of contemplation" and the experience of an "anchoring space," Huyssen states. What then are the possibilities that theater offers for this living and experiencing of memory? The contemplation of cruelty, even when it is fabricated, as in the case of this play, poses new questions about the role of spectatorship in a culture of amnesia. Paraphrasing Susan Sontag, one can dream that by regarding the pain of others, we could stop such violence, as if we could be taken away from the atrocities that happened during Argentina's Dirty War (*Regarding* 11). Raznovich's plays address the ambivalence of such spectatorship: we can either become awakened by the cruel imagery her theater displays or, yet, become the detached, consumerist spectator, the American photographer craving for more of this "authentic South American grief." As in *Jardín de otoño*, the play superimposes the realities of the media and theater. Whereas the first has transformed pain and grief into commodities, Raznovich's theater seeks to engage the spectator in a critical contemplation of the tragicomic realities of our recent history. Photographs hold a double-edged power, for they produce an either detached or intimate sense of co-presence with the visual constructs they depict.[21] In the context of Argentina, Raznovich's theater provides opportunities for a face-to-face memory. Whereas Gambaro takes spectators to the roots of violence and authoritarianism through uses of the spectral and uncanny in theatrical performance, Raznovich accomplishes a similar goal by reflecting on spectacles as instruments of visual manipulation. The American photographer embodies, like the ex-torturer sexologist, Troncoso, the powers of the traveler-seer described by Pratt, as both are builders of a spectacular space where vision is a tool for domination. As the "other space" of the national scene, the bedroom reflects how a society's voracious visual needs feed into contemporary oblivion. As an allegory of a social space fragmented, disseminated by the scars of an inveterate violence, the bedroom shows the impossibility of communication and the artificial quality of human relationships in a media-ridden culture.

The construction of reality into a fetish is well described by Sontag's words: "Photographs are a way of imprisoning reality, understood as recalcitrant, inaccessible; of making it stand still. Or they enlarge a reality that is felt to be shrunk, hollowed out, perishable, remote" ("The Image" 356). And we can think of the many ways in which a culture of images built by both the media and the Internet depicts this need for suppressing the fleeting realities of time and space: the obsession with other people's intimacy expressed by reality shows such as *Big Brother,* or the emergence of social networks such as Facebook or Twitter that give us the impression of a permanent co-presence with others through the Web. In the context of Argentina, this obsession with visual products shows the profound cracks in the postdictatorship culture and its claims of surpassing history and denying the claims for human rights restitution. The image of the country as a photographic set producing a performance for international audiences is a compelling metaphor for the ways in which the culture of the Menem years covered up the legacies of the dictatorship through the use of media products that pushed crucial debates on justice and memory to the side. Raznovich's theater enters this debate within the context of the Argentine theater of the crisis, defined by Osvaldo Pelletieri as a theater that shows social disintegration and the questioning of history's totalizing narratives. Since the 1980s, Argentine theater has demonstrated a different kind of political commitment and transformed the role of realism on the stage. These plays adopt an antirealist aesthetic that challenges the role of the spectator by altering the familiar through the technique of estrangement and defamiliarization ("Teatro" 21–22). The incorporation of different visual technologies in Diana Raznovich's theater enables such critical spectatorship, for it is through the complex dynamic among different kinds of images that we are able to see the role of visual commodities in domesticating historical perceptions.

As in *De atrás para adelante,* images possess a spectral side, showing the disruption of theatrical illusion. This fluctuation is best described by the recurrence of Antonio's nightmares of a country besieged by hunger and social instability. Following the tradition of Antonin Artaud's theater of cruelty as a spectacle shaped by dreams,[22] Raznovich exposes the series of ethereal images haunting the collective consciousness that exists underneath the mirages created first by authoritarianism and later by the demands of a neoliberal order:

> Entraba una población de ollas populares, me pedía arroz blanco. Yo solamente tenía arroz integral. La mujer del frasquito en la mano derramaba su contenido que, de inmediato, se transformaba en una revista de gran tirada. (87)
> [Desperate people from a shantytown entered and asked me for white rice. I only had brown rice. A woman with a jar in her hand spilled out its contents which immediately transformed into a magazine with a large readership.] (*From the Waist down* 50)

Raznovich's theater places us in front of a split screen where images that appear onstage are carefully dismantled by their specular double. By means of this complex visual dynamics, Raznovich deconstructs the perverse social mechanisms that transform poverty into an illusion, torture and murder into a disappearance, and social revolts into a nightmare that needs to be repressed. Although centered on sexual repression, Raznovich's work also shows the intricate play between wealth and poverty in a neoliberal economy where the effects of capitalism are hidden in the shadows of a global order. *De la cintura para abajo* describes global capitalism's psychotic space where dreams of development are hallucinations coexisting with the crude realities of a society fragmented by the economic and political wounds of the dictatorship. Jean Franco describes the transformations of the nation-state under these global influences through the metaphor of a house being taken over, where territorial boundaries have been trespassed and the walls protecting the nation are filled with holes. The masculine body, as an allegory of this collapsed space, is no longer an inviolate receptacle of a pure identity; the rigidity of the male identity at the center of the national order has been replaced by an amniotic flux that places us in the situation of feeling lost in space ("Marcar" 35–36). And whereas *De atrás para adelante* shows a rear-ended masculinity, *De la cintura para abajo* describes the masculine body as impotent and paralyzed. Antonio, trapped in his own fantasies and hallucinations, is a powerful metaphor for the unmaking of masculinity in the changing realities of the turn of the century in Argentina. As expressed by the endless photographs of his artificially wounded body, mechanical reproduction lessens the monumentality of Antonio's body, now transformed into a body corrupted and paralyzed by the effects of a profound social crisis.[23]

De la cintura para abajo represents the paradoxical absence of sexuality in a society where it has become a violent, self-destructive aspect of relationships in which women are particularly vulnerable. Although Eleonora is a passionate and intelligent woman, she is the victim of a broken, heterosexual matrix that cannot channel her desire. De Lauretis explains how pornography reflects in a crude and direct manner the construction of the woman as a signifier through the fragmentation and fabrication of the female body that replicates, inside the erotic scene, "the operations and techniques of the apparatus: fragmentation of the scene by camera movements, construction of the representational space by depth of field, diffraction of light, and color effects—in short, the process of fabrication of the film from découpage to montage" (*Alice* 26). The play is a burlesque depiction of how woman, in the phallic order, is at once "the mirror and the screen—image, ground, and support—of this subject's projection and identification" (28). *De la cintura para abajo* shows the role of desire in establishing modes of representation that continue to perform the absence of woman, as in her production as an empty signifier in a sadomasochistic scene where Antonio is the master and Eleonora the slave with no will. However, the play also parodies Antonio's overstated masculinity as embodying a complete absence of desire. As in *Jardín de otoño*, both masculinity and femininity are hollow performances that demonstrate the frail realities of human relationships in a society dominated by the media. Eleonora embodies the contradictory search for a new role in a social landscape damaged by fear and the scars of authoritarianism. And as the play deconstructs the patriarchal order as a fiction, it painfully shows the absence of new locations for women in the democratic transition of the 1990s.

As evidenced in the plays analyzed in this chapter, theatrical space mirrors the political and social realities of Argentina during the years of the dictatorship and the return to the democratic order in the 1980s and 1990s. Through innovative uses of the genre, Griselda Gambaro and Diana Raznovich reveal the centrality of theater in re-creating the way we perceive, conceive, and live space. Their plays unveil the fictions of a homogeneous social order; they uncover the possibilities for a critical examination of how space is a critical element in the building of new social awareness and change. Like Foucault's "other spaces," their plays explore the endless possibilities for remaking space from the perspective of a radical otherness. Their plays show the plastic quality of spatial formations by juxtaposing, "in a single real place several spaces, several sites that are in themselves incompatible" ("Of Other" 25). And although such juxtapositions may at times seem grotesque, as in Gambaro, or tragicomic in Raznovich, their heterotopias reflect the dissimilar realities of a society torn between the legacies of authoritarianism and the possibilities of a democratic order.

I will never forget the ringing of the bell that Thursday night. My father was then a public employee working for the Provincial Administration of Water in the province of Tucumán. It was during the height of Antonio Domingo Bussi's de facto governance. It must have been midnight, and my father was called into his office. In the morning, I learned that he had been commissioned to oversee the installation of water systems for four new small towns being built in the south of Tucumán, named after four members of the military who died during the Operativo Independencia, the military campaign that Bussi led in Tucumán: Soldado Maldonado, Teniente Berdina, Capitán Cáceres, and Sargento Moya.[24] A few months later, my father drove us to see the place. Built in a very symmetrical way, the towns stood out because of the impeccable condition of its facades. All the buildings were white, with the exception of the Argentine flags painted on top of the water tanks. In their intentionally utopian design, even as a child I could perceive the artificiality of their demeanor. In 1995, despite his record of human rights violations, Antonio Domingo Bussi was democratically elected as the governor of Tucumán. His campaign claimed order and cleanliness as one of the new government's slogans. What is the role of literature in the light of such historical distortions? I would like to think that it enables us to see a different view of our past—that as a critical tool, it sheds light on the dark corners of history. Theater more than any other literary genre allows for this form of historical revision. The plays by Gambaro and Raznovich are keen examples of the importance of the stage as a location that restores vitality to social practices and questions processes of authoritarianism and violence. As a powerful counterspace, theater opens up new perspectives on how our social identities and our collective memories are shaped by spatial processes. The stage's "other spaces" offer us a way of reflecting on our role as historical actors and also a means to build new places of memory, social awareness, and change.

CHAPTER 3

Global Patagonia: Rewriting the National Space

1. Global Imaginations of Place

Argentina and Brazil organized the Primera Bienal del Fin del Mundo [First Biennial of the End of the World] in 2007. Seeking to connect the Arctic and Antarctic regions through art, the biennial focused on some global concerns of the twenty-first century: time and its metaphors, ecology, urban topographies, and virtual or possible worlds. More than one hundred artists from 25 countries gathered in Patagonia and exhibited their works in different settings in Tierra del Fuego, the Beagle Channel, and Antarctica. One of the works, "Antarctic Village Project," exemplifies how the biennial addressed the spatial changes of globalization. Composed of fifty tent-like dwellings made of flags, clothes, or prints and set up in Antarctica by Argentine artist Jorge Orta and English artist Lucy Orta, this "ephemeral installation" drew attention to the problems of international borders. The project aspired to transform the Antarctic territory into a global nation for humankind, a promised land where millions of displaced people could escape from terror, racism, or economic injustice. In the artists' words: "Antarctic Village is a symbol of the plight of those struggling to traverse borders and to gain the freedom of movement necessary to escape political and social conflict. Dotted along the ice, the tents formed a settlement reminiscent of the images of refugee camps we see so often reported on our television screens and newspapers" (http://www.bienalfindelmundo.com/eng/index.html). As "Antarctic Village" demonstrates, the biennial melded the social and artistic implications of globalization in the areas of politics, ecology, and technology. Hence, the biennial explored what Néstor García Canclini defines as global imagery, an "imaginario global" [global imaginary] that links multiple territorial relationships and shapes social processes in global societies (*La globalización* 62). In García Canclini's view, material changes, such as the transformation of technology, the modernization of communication, the processes of the deterritorialization of capitalism, and the reshaping of national and international borders, are embedded in cultural imaginations of local and global identities. As such, territorial identities are shifting in a world where imaginations of place are being transformed by the cultures of globalization. In the case of Argentina, global transformations impact several aspects of postdictatorial society, such as the discussion on human rights and memory, political participation and citizenship, and in the cultural arena, the scope and goals of the literary and artistic cultures of the country.

As Francine Masiello describes in her work on neoliberal crises in Latin America, the notion of "transition" offers an appropriate means to frame the changes taking place in the postdictatorial societies of Argentina and Chile affected by globalization: "A transition in political strategy from dictatorship to neoliberal democracy; a transition in cultural practices from focus on social class alone to matters of sexuality and gender; a transition in styles of representation that waver between modernist yearnings and postmodern pastiche" (*Art* 3). The question of space is highly relevant to the transitions Masiello summarizes. The nation-state is the site where two antagonistic forces play out: on the one hand, the need for reconstructing a traumatic past that moves the country toward the past and the dwellings of memory; on the other, the urgency of neoliberal agendas that propel society toward the global economy and the modernization of technologies. Market deregulation and privatization were two key economic forces of the 1990s and 2000s that impacted several areas of the cultural field. For instance, Argentine literature during the neoliberal years suffered a number of changes, the reduction of its reading public due to the economic and social transformation of the middle classes, the weakening of a previously robust publishing market as demand for published materials decreased, and finally, the erosion of the importance of print culture in the new primacy of image-centered products (Hortiguera and Rocha 25).[1] Under the influence of global forces, the nation-state was transformed as its citizens lost confidence in governmental and political safety nets. In effect, global forces undermined the structure of the "planning state," which since the nineteenth century had labored to modernize the region by delivering better economic and social conditions for some areas of the population. Central themes emerge in the literature and culture of this period: the interlacing of global and local forces and the role that minorities or new citizens play in them, and the predominance of memory as "master narratives" collapsed after 1989 and a "more reflective type of narrative directly related to the examination of the past" came forward. (Rocha 39). If we take a quick look at the literature of the period, it becomes evident that global imaginations of place are central in fictions that, for instance, are located in foreign or oriental settings, such as *El Cangrejo* [*The Crab*] (1995) by Graciela Safranchik or *La perla del Emperador* [The Emperor's Pearl] (1990) by Daniel Guebel. Moreover, as I make clear in the next chapter, poetry in the 1990s and 2000s registers global and local exchanges through the "displaced" locations found in the works of Diana Bellessi, Luisa Futoransky, and Maria Negroni. Other writers, such as Washington Cucurto, focus instead on internal displacements and the role of immigrants and new waves of racism in the social scene of Argentina. Also evident are the importance of memory and the rewriting of national narratives, as in the examples of *Santo oficio de la memoria* [*Inquisition of Memory*] (1991) by Mempo Giardinelli, *La madriguera* [*The Warren*] (1996) by Tununa Mercado, and *Realidad nacional desde la cama* [*Bedside Manners*] (1990) by Luisa Valenzuela. In this regard, the national territory is a central metaphor for the complex set of negotiations that dominated the country in the 1990s and 2000s. Representations of space in the literature of the period are linked, therefore, to complex exchanges between the global and the national, as well as to the social and cultural transformations of globalization; cultural images of displacement and location are symbolic of a series of social exclusions taking place in Argentina over the past two decades.

In this chapter, I consider works by Sylvia Iparraguirre and Belén Gache and the transformation of national imaginations of place under global influences. The formation of a "global Patagonia" is evident in both authors, whereby the region transforms into a borderland space, an imaginary geography where global and national narratives intertwine. Although highly influenced by the imagery and rhetoric of a global society, Iparraguirre and Gache focus on national narratives and histories of gender and racial violence that shaped a spatial memory for Argentina. By addressing previous cultural images of Patagonia as the last frontier, they propose alternative readings to the cultural formation of the national space. In both cases, deterritorialized narratives question the identification of language and national territory by exploring the role of foreigners or historically displaced social subjects. In this way, their works focus on what Giles Deleuze and Félix Guattari define as a "minor literature," or a literature constructed by a minority within a major language ("What is" 16). Iparraguirre and Gache explore the meanings of "minor literature" within the Argentine context by addressing, for instance, the marginal positions women and indigenous populations have held in historical and literary imaginations of the national space. Through literary representations of geographical displacement, they propose alternative representations of the region of Patagonia, as their works invite reflection on the role of literary culture in the process of rewriting the national space and on the complex set of negotiations taking place between global and national forces in the past two decades.

2. The Formation of the Nation-State: Patagonia and the Writing of the National Borders

In the 1870s, Lucio V. Mansilla was commissioned to complete a topographical description of the southern Argentine frontier. A peculiar protagonist in Argentina's national life, Mansilla was both a member of the military and one of the most prominent literary figures of the nineteenth century. In 1861, he fought in the battle of Pavón, key in the internal civil war that eventually dissolved the Argentine Confederation and transformed Buenos Aires into the political center of the country, and in the bloody War of the Triple Alliance (1864–1870), in which he participated also as a journalist, publishing a series of articles in *La Tribuna* [*The Tribune*]. He supported Domingo Faustino Sarmiento in his run for the presidency, and as the newly elected president, Sarmiento appointed him in 1868 as commander of the frontier areas near the province of Cordoba. Published in installments in *La Tribuna* throughout 1870, *Una excursión a los Indios Ranqueles* [*An Expedition to the Ranquel Indians*] paved the way for civilizing missions to come, with a precise geographical characterization that ultimately awarded him a prize in the 1875 International Geographical Congress in Paris. A decade later, the Argentine government, through a series of exploratory and military expeditions, completed the extermination of the indigenous population of Argentina under the tenet of "Gobernar es poblar" [to govern is to populate], as declared by Juan Bautista Alberdi, the political theorist and a writer-member of the 1837 generation whose essay "Bases and Starting Points for the Political Organization of the Argentine Republic" influenced the drafting of the Argentine Constitution of 1853.

As David Rock states, the Argentine nation-state formed between 1852 and 1890. When interregional conflicts gradually ceased, economic expansion occurred on an unprecedented scale; the frontiers advanced rapidly as the Indians were exterminated or driven away, and a massive network of railroads and steamships revolutionized production and commerce and transformed Argentina into a leading exporter of wool, cattle, and temperate cereals—wheat, corn, oats, and barley—(131–36). A new relationship with

Britain also guaranteed the internal unification of the country amid a succession of export and foreign investment booms (119). Buenos Aires led the way in consolidating the new nation-state, which by 1880, had achieved complete supremacy. The establishment of the national territory between 1879 and 1884 followed this complex process of internal unification. Previously, writers such as Mansilla and Sarmiento, along with other members of the literary generations of 1837 and 1880, carried out the ideological and aesthetic project of defining a national space during almost forty years of writing about the connections between the nation-state and its territoriality. Echeverría's epic poem *La cautiva* [*The Captive*] (1837) and Sarmiento's biographical *Facundo: civilización y barbarie* [*Facundo: Civilization and Barbarism*] (1845) established a predominant perception among Argentine intellectuals and politicians of vast areas of the national territory as desert lands. In the 1880s, this image was exploited for the purposes of delimiting the national borders. As Perla Zusman and Sandra Minvielle state, the formation of the nation-state in Argentina was a planned process that required the "invention of a territory" involving the occupation—in a majority of cases by the use of military force—of the perceived "empty" internal territories which, in fact, were populated by indigenous peoples, the definition of international limits that lead to conflicts with neighboring Brazil and Chile at the end of the nineteenth century, economic investment in the areas recently added to the country, and in the ideological field, the formation of representations of a modern nationality. As Jens Andermann states in his study about "power maps" in nineteenth-century Argentine literature, literature had a key role in imagining this national space through three moments: first, writers from the 1937 generation "perceived and prepared" it by claiming a sense of displacement and disidentification with it; second, they "appreciated" it by exploring it and creating a "great topographic design" through realist descriptions that proposed reform and provided the necessary data for the technological and military expansion that followed, as revealed by Mansilla's text; and third, they reconfigured a national topology as in the Gauchesca writers of the literary generation of the 1880s, who appropriated the space previously perceived as marginal and empty—the space of the desert—and coded it as national by transforming it into a "place of memory" through a debate on the formation of a national patrimony (*Mapas* 21).

Beginning in 1872, the military occupation of areas of the Pampas, Patagonia, and Chaco was followed by a series of national laws that created the administrative units, and later, the provinces of Chaco, Chubut, Formosa, Misiones, Neuquén, La Pampa, Río Negro, Santa Cruz, and Tierra del Fuego (Zusman and Minvielle). In addition, the country's economic development required the expansion of land, on an unprecedented scale, at the disposition of the state to favor private investments in agriculture and cattle and sheep raising. The military campaigns of 1879 (The Conquest of the Desert) and 1884 (The Conquest of the Chaco Region), and the Patagonian and Andean campaigns of 1881 through 1885 were part of this national endeavor to aggressively incorporate new territories. This period also witnessed the annihilation of the majority of the aboriginal people in the country. In 1875, Valentín Alsina, the war minister under president Nicolás Avellaneda (1874–1880), sought to stop the *malones*, indigenous incursions into colonized lands in search of cattle, by building a 610-kilometer-long ditch running from the Atlantic Ocean to the Andes (Blengino 34–35). Known as the "Zanja de Alsina" [Alsina's Ditch], this was the first major attempt to consolidate the southern frontier along the Río Colorado, with the hopes that it would gradually advance farther south toward the Río Negro. It was never fully completed, only 370 kilometers were built; in addition to being harshly criticized by Alsina's contemporaries, the enterprise proved to be inefficient.[2] After Alsina's death in 1877, Julio A. Roca succeeded him as the next war minister and, in 1879, commanded a major military operation, "La Campaña del Desierto" [The Desert Campaign], which included continuous and systematic attacks to aboriginal settlements. To the north of the country, similar military operations took place, such as Benjamín Victorica's Chaco campaign. In 1884, as the war minister of President Julio A. Roca, he settled the first "civilizatory" colonies in this area where, under strong military control, both foreigners and indigenous people lived and were allowed to work exclusively for colonial establishments, the *obrajes*, the main economical activity in the Chaco region at that time (Lois). As Andermann explains, indigenous peoples living in the conquered areas were decimated through massive killings, the exhaustion and malnutrition that contributed to smallpox and measles epidemics, and deportation to sugar plantations in Tucumán and Entre Ríos (*Optic* 160–61). In Tierra del Fuego, local sheep barons destroyed the population of Selk'nam, Haush, Alacaluf, and Yahgan in about two decades by the end of the century (161).

The formation of the national territory concluded the project that writers such as Echeverría, Sarmiento, and Mansilla had outlined decades earlier. A number of cultural representations that included literature, photography, cartography, and the first scientific reports of the Argentine Geographical Institute, founded in 1879, established what Andermann calls the "spatial iconographies," which transformed the state into a visual form "where representations of nature and of history turned into figurations of the nation and thus attained a hegemonic function" (*Optic* 7). This is the moment of the formation of an imagined territoriality that had a central function in the creation of the national identity for the country. As Jean Gottmann explains, the notion of a territory implies a central authority that exercises sovereignty "over the people occupying or using that place and the space around it" (5). Although its legal uses imply the distinction of a portion of geographical space under the jurisdiction of certain people and separate from adjacent territories, Gottmann states that the term also means a "geographical expression both of a social function and of an institution rooted in the psychology of peoples" (7). Andrew Gray, referring to how indigenous peoples understand this notion, explains that it works alongside the concepts of land, earth, and landscape as aspects of a "polythetic" definition. Territory refers to political control over a geographical area; land, to the resources contained in it; earth, to a religious or spiritual relationship; and landscape, to the historical and semantic connection certain peoples maintain with their territory (27). Accordingly, the notion of a national territory, as evidenced in the complex process of nation-building during nineteenth-century Argentina, implies a series of material and symbolic strategies that include the reinscription, enclosure, and hierarchical structuring of space through a series of political, economic, and cultural processes. Literature and the incipient geographical discourse of the late nineteenth century had a leading role in linking the symbolic functions of the nation-state and its material powers over the territoriality it controlled. Pedro Navarro Floria calls this process the social construction of the national space, where the "territorial consciousness" of a country with preexisting effective territorial occupation, is transformed by the ideological construction of the national territory in which the new geographical institutions and publications—such as the *Annals of the Argentine Geographical Society* (since 1876), the *Bulletin of the Argentine Geographical Institute* (since 1879), the *Argentine Scientific Annals* (1874–1876), and the *Argentine Geographical Review* (1881–1883)— had a central role.

Since the sixteenth century, European travelers described Patagonia as a mythical land, the land of the City of the Caesars, also known as City of the Patagonia or Trapalanda, El Dorado, and the place where giants and fantastic beings lived, as described by Antonio Pigafetta, a sailor on Magellan's expedition, in his travel journal, *First Voyage around the Globe* (1524). As a place for the global imagination, Patagonia has been the inspiration of many fictional and nonfictional accounts, such as Darwin's *The Voyage of the Beagle* (1839), Herman Melville's images of Cape Horn in works such as "Benito Cereno" and *Moby-Dick* (1851), W. H. Hudson's *Idle Days in Patagonia* (1917), and Bruce Chatwin's *In Patagonia* (1975). As Andermann explains, the Argentine state in its expansion had to reclaim Patagonia from the imperial discourses that had produced "images of an archetypal space of liminality and passage, of beginning and end of the world, revisited in the nineteenth century by Fitz Roy, Darwin, and others" (*Optic* 131). The perception of Patagonia as the outer limit of a global order challenged the "spatial production of the State as a territorial entity" (Nouzeilles, "Patagonia" 36). The national government sought to "re-invent" Patagonia with two central images: an untapped resource yet to be fully exploited and an unbridled terrain well-suited to the embodiment of an incipient nationalism (37). In the nineteenth century, the image of Patagonia as the source of paleontological and natural resources transformed the area into a rich territory for scientific investigation (Blengino 89), evident in a vast number of scientific works, such as those of Estanislao Zeballos and Francisco Moreno.[3] The Patagonian space was made to represent both a past and a future, "the mythological origins of nationality and, as a source of wealth yet to be exploited, the spatial image of a glorious future" (Andermann, *Optic* 130).

Beginning in the 1930s, the opening of the area to national and international tourism transformed the Patagonian landscape into an object of mass consumption (Nouzeilles, "Patagonia" 3); meanwhile, this space adopted different textual representations that moved from an attempt to consolidate the area as part of the national territory, as in the accounts of Moreno or Zeballos, to an ironic depiction of such civilizing efforts, as in the *Aguafuertes patagónicas* [*Patagonian Etchings*] (1933) by Roberto Arlt.[4] During the twentieth century and the beginning of the twenty-first century, multiple images of Patagonia held sway over the national consciousness. In *Final de novela en Patagonia* [*End of the Novel in Patagonia*] (2000), Mempo Giardinelli depicts Patagonia as a place that challenges the construction of literary cartographies, and Cristina Siscar in *La siberia* [*Siberia*] (2007) also engages in an ironical travel narrative about the influences of global tourism in the conflict-ridden Argentina of the 1990s. Patagonia as the Argentine Siberia is the space where the dreams of an unrestricted global mobility collapse when a group of international tourists are stuck in the middle of the Patagonian desert.[5] Cultural representations of Patagonia develop from complex sets of rhetorical images that, since the sixteenth century, have connected local and global imaginations of place. Ernesto Livon-Grosman calls those representations "bricolages," as they take the form of narrative collages (11). Intersections of writing and geographic space in Patagonia assemble territorial representations of national and international orders by depicting the region as a mythical land, a territorial frontier, a global borderland, or a natural refuge in the light of global collapse.

What is the role of Patagonia in the literary imagination of Argentina in the 1990s and 2000s? First, we need to consider that the notion of territoriality previously described has considerably weakened because the idea of a national sovereignty is no longer placed in the nation but instead in different supranational organizations, most of which are private or not related to specific governments (Sassen, *Los espectros* 125). As Saskia Sassen states, global processes and formations destabilize the scalar hierarchy centered in the nation-state and, although this is yet an issue of relevance in the midst of global processes, "specific structurations of the global inhabit what historically has been constructed and institutionalized as national territory," causing a "partial denationalization of specific components of national states" (*Sociology* 22). As Renato Ortiz postulates, as a consequence of such denationalization, other agents have taken over the role of the nation-state as the producer of social and cultural meanings. Globalization breaks up the relationship between culture and place; thus, "deterritorialization" is a term that helps in the understanding of changes in the fields of economy and production (e.g., the global factory), technology (e.g., the mass media and other electronic means of communication), and culture (e.g., the production of global image reservoirs) (Ortiz 107–08). The works of Iparraguirre and Gache critically examine the effects of these global processes in the denationalization of the Argentine state through a rewriting of central historical narratives about the area. Centered in Patagonia and Tierra del Fuego and in the creation of a southern frontier during the nineteenth century, both authors consider the invention of a national space from a postcolonial perspective (Iparraguirre) and from the impact of media and technology on notions of space and territoriality (Gache). Written in a period when globalization is profoundly challenging the foundations of Argentina's national identity, *La tierra del fuego* and *Diario de la luna caníbal* [*Diary of the Cannibal Moon*] examine the historic role of Patagonia as a literary and aesthetic borderland and its influence in the configuration of narratives of spatial identity in the country. As a site that produces military and social repression (Viñas), establishes limits in territorial narratives (Andermann), and questions the shape and scope of the nation-state (Fernández Bravo), the frontier has been central to the writing of the national space, as represented in the literature of Argentina. By focusing on Patagonia as a frontier producing "symbolic meanings," Iparraguirre's and Gache's works redefine how the discourse on territoriality of the nineteenth century constructed an imagined community linked to the production of certain discourses on identity and to systemic forms of violence against and alienation of certain groups in the country. Further, the global influences of the period allow both authors to engage in a critical revision of the role of minorities such as women and indigenous peoples as key protagonists in the process of rewriting national ideals on space and territoriality. As Amy Kaminsky reminds us, the national acts as a "refracting lens between the global and the local that allows us to see the complex relations among all three scales. Moreover, the nation is itself constructed and held in place by the global and local forces upon it" (*Argentina*, 11). I will argue, then, that the global opens up new possibilities for rewriting a national identity; through the complex set of interactions described by Kaminsky, both authors engage in a redefinition of the national space while they also contest the role of literary production in the creation of a spatial identity for the country.

Globalization is neither a uniform nor a neutral process, and its complex effects on the nation-state are better perceived on what Sassen calls the "subnational scales," such as the region (*Sociology* 30). The notion of a "global Patagonia" as a "cross-border region" enables us to examine the role of supranational entities such as global electronic markets in national imaginations. In this context, Iparraguirre's and Gache's works make visible how the territorial identity of Argentina was transformed in the 1990s and 2000s. Both writers establish a dialogue between the local and the global that redefines the symbolic meanings the Argentine frontiers adopted in the nineteenth and twentieth centuries; furthermore, they rewrite the social and historical repressions that materialized in those territorial limits. They question the processes of identity production as they establish frontiers as liminal and porous sites for artistic and literary exchanges. Their works function as "archeological investigations" in that they delve into images of foundational representations of space in the country and explore their connotations of social exclusion. They move toward deterritorialization because they embed local narratives in global exchanges; they stress the importance of a global imagery—technological networks in the case of Gache, or travel literature in Iparraguirre—and last, they denationalize space by questioning the identity constructs at the foundation of the Argentine nation-state of the nineteenth century. By redefining the national space from a global perspective, they also question the role of authoritarianism, violence, and memory and the importance of literature in forming an idea of place. In addition, they examine the intricate connections between territoriality and the idea of a national literature as they examine notions of authorship and readership, as well as redefine the role of writing in global societies.

Iparraguirre's fiction reflects the analogies between territory and writing through a postcolonial perspective that is particularly evident in *La tierra del fuego* (1998). Though her later works do not deal with Patagonia—her latest novel, *El muchacho de los senos de goma* [*The Boy with Rubber Breasts*] (2007) is, as the author confirms, a testimony of the Menem years—her overall literary project builds on a cultural memory that revises the territorial implications of the country's national projects.[6] In *La tierra del fuego*, she focuses on Patagonia and Tierra del Fuego, the European expansion of the nineteenth century, and how it conflicted with Argentina's demarcation of its national limits. In her later fiction, the city of Buenos Aires becomes the site of internal borders that delineate economic, social, and linguistic exclusions. Iparraguirre's works set the stage for those voices that have been historically marginalized and, as Jorge Monteleone states, experiences of otherness are central in her narratives' cultural memory (26). In this chapter, I consider Iparraguirre's novel that fictionalizes the two survey expeditions of the Beagle to South America from 1826 to 1836. The central characters include Jemmy Button, one of the four Fuegians taken back to England in 1830; John William Guevara, the fictionalized, illegitimate son of an English officer who fought in the English invasions of 1806; and two Creole women, Lucía de Guevara, John's mother, who dies when her son is still young, and Graciana, a servant who, while having only a minor role throughout the novel, gains importance at the end when we learn that she is the heiress of Guevara's project and the person in charge of disseminating his work. This novel has been interpreted as a rewriting of history. Magdalena Perkowska contends that *La tierra del fuego* revises foundational fictions that sustained the formation of the nation-state throughout the nineteenth century, and for Juan Pablo Neyret, the novel is a metatextual reflection on the writing of Argentine history and, on the whole, on the exercise of literary writing as well.[7] I focus here on how such a reworking of history is bound to a territorial project that rewrites the national space through postcolonial literary topographies that cast women and indigenous peoples as the protagonists of powerful spatial counternarratives. Memory plays a central role in this process because the novel explores the connections between territories and images and suggests how a national project is built upon spatial constructions. The frontier is a key element insofar as it historically has been the central focus of the territorial expansion of the nation, as in the case of Argentina during the nineteenth century. Iparraguirre rewrites the southern Argentine limits as well as the interoceanic space between Argentina and Europe, an in-between space that also, throughout history, has been a cultural border, shaping the literary and cultural imagination of the country. As a metatextual exercise, this project configures a "minor literature," or an alternative literary project, within the Argentine tradition. Written from the marginal perspectives of Button and Guevara and centered on the Creole woman, Graciana, as the virtual author of new spatial narratives, the novel defines the literary spaces of the nation as borderlands yet to be fully defined, where linguistic and cultural exchanges acquire key relevance.

Gache is a writer and visual artist whose works connect writing and electronic media. She is the codirector of the Web site *Fin del mundo* (www.findelmundo.com.ar) and, in addition to her fiction and essays, has explored writing digital and video poetry. On her Web site, one finds *El diario de la luna caníbal* (2007), an installation she realized for the Primera Bienal del Fin del Mundo. This work is set in the penitentiary of Tierra del Fuego and, in the context of this biennial and its goals of connecting art, politics, and literature, proposes new ways to read the history of Argentina at the turn of the twenty-first century. Along with *Escrituras nómadas* [*Nomadic Writings*] (2006), the second book considered here, *El libro del fin del mundo* [*The Book of the End of the World*] (2002) bridges the gap between literary writing and electronic media. By following the format of an "object book," because it is highly interactive and explores the "materiality" of the print work, this book comes with a CD that encourages alternative readings by its users.[8] Likewise, two novels by Gache, *Luna india* [*Indian Moon*] (1994) and *Lunas eléctricas para una noche sin luna* [*Electric Moons for a Moonless Night*] (2004) are also of interest because the author's avant-garde notions of narration and readership echo the futuristic imagery of her mixed format works. I believe deterritorialization is a concept central to an understanding of Gache's works. Her notions of nomadic writing and her use of fiction and poetry based on hypertexts contribute to the fragmenting of the connections between language, territory, art, and literature. Most important, the uses of memory in *Diario de una luna caníbal* further open the discussion on how memory can be a key interpretative tool for understanding historic omissions in the collective building of Argentine territoriality. Finally, by displacing the locus of enunciation to territorial and artistic borderlands, Gache addresses the role of "cyber-identities" in literature, such as the ones Carlos Jáuregui describes for "writing communities on the Internet"; that is, identities that contribute to geopolitical simulacra and redefine the cultural geography of Latin America (293), a task that Gache undertakes in the virtual worlds of her Web-based fiction and poetry.

3. Postcolonial Geographies: La tierra del fuego by Sylvia Iparraguirre

In *Tierra del Fuego: Una biografía del fin del mundo* [*Tierra del Fuego: A Biography of the End of the World*] (2000), Sylvia Iparraguirre writes a "visual biography" of Tierra del Fuego, a history of the brutal colonization of the area and the disappearance of its original inhabitants, the Selk'nam, Haush, Alacaluf, and Yahgan. The book alternates between interviews with descendants of the aboriginal inhabitants and a history of the "legendary sailors" who, beginning with Magellan, established a transoceanic route through the Beagle Channel. An interview with Carlos Vairo, director of the Maritime Museum of Tierra del Fuego and a maritime ethnographer, unveils details of the maritime history, which includes the atrocious shipwrecks that took place in the Magellan Strait, Cape Horn, Le Maire Strait, and Staten Island. This biography of Tierra del Fuego intends to overcome the absence and lack of information that characterizes its history. *Tierra del Fuego: Una biografía del fin del mundo* plays with a double image of Tierra del Fuego that is both spectacular, a pictorial landscape assembled for the eyes of a global audience, as evidenced in breathtaking photographs by Florian Von Der Fecht accompanying the historical narration and interviews, and spectral, revealing the hidden histories of abuse, genocide, and stormy deaths that took place in the area and that give the text the resemblance of a memorial.[9] The title's reference to Tierra del Fuego as the "end of the world" further develops its image as a "cultural border" where history and myth intersect, according to Iparraguirre. The lasting nature of some of those myths can be explained by the history of mass killings and cruel repression that began with the "Conquista del Desierto," led by President Roca, which started in 1879 (personal interview, June 26, 2008). Thus, the role of memory and testimony is crucial in *Tierra del Fuego: Una biografía del fin del mundo,* for it reworks, in the words of Nouzeilles, the "desert dreams" of nomadic tourists that, since the turn of the twentieth century, transformed Patagonia and Tierra del Fuego into mercantile experiences of the natural world ("Desert Dreams" 258). The text by Iparraguirre and Von Der Fecht introduces mourning and memory as cultural counterforces to the touristic gaze. As in her novel, *La tierra del fuego,* the interruptions of memory challenge the uses of the Patagonian space for utopian dreams of modernization that include the capitalist expansion and subsequent annihilation of indigenous inhabitants, as well as the later touristic exploitation of the area. And in the context of the Argentine transition of the late 1990s, with its predominance of a visual culture and politics characterized by what Masiello describes as the "official insistence on forgetfulness and constant erasures of justice" ("Este pobre" 243), this book is a timely reflection on the complex dynamics between visuality, space, power, and the role of historical memory in unveiling the social legacies of historical spatialization processes in Argentina.

By following the format of many travel narratives, *La tierra del fuego* establishes textual dialogues with previous accounts of Patagonia. As Adolfo Prieto states, British travelers were influential to many Argentine foundational texts of the nineteenth century. In his study *Los viajeros ingleses y la emergencia de la literatura argentina, 1820–1850* [*English Travelers and the Emergence of Argentine Literature, 1820–1850*], Prieto states that English travelers developed a spatial rhetoric that complemented the cultural representation of landscape as a site of civilization or barbarism, as represented in many of their contemporary Argentine writers. Authors such as Francis Bond Head, Joseph Andrews, and Edmond Temple, who in the 1820s traveled to Argentina in search of mining resources, influenced Argentines such as Juan Bautista Alberdi, Esteban Echeverría, and Domingo Faustino Sarmiento, three pivotal writers who in the nineteenth century,coined the image of the internal areas of the country as a desert that needed to be modernized through the construction of railroads and cities. In this period, Robert Fitz Roy's *Narrative of the Surveying Voyages of His Majesty's Ships Adventure and* Beagle (1839) and Charles Darwin's *Journal and Remarks* (1839) were also influential, as references in articles by Sarmiento in the Chilean newspaper *El progreso* [*The Progress*] demonstrate. Head and Darwin were the first to adopt a number of images created by Alexander Von Humboldt in his *Personal Narrative* (1807), and were later followed by Sarmiento and Echeverría. The most relevant of those images is that of the desert land, the plain topography of which could be compared to the ocean; the Pampas as a sea will later become the image of America as a wasteland that legitimated territorial expansionism in Europe and aggressive modernization and internal colonization in Argentina (Prieto, *Los viajeros* 22–23). Fitz Roy's and Darwin's accounts of the expedition of the Beagle are central in Iparraguirre's *La tierra del fuego*, not only in its references to Jemmy Button, but also because they shed light on how English explorers shaped a territorial image of the most southern areas of Patagonia which, in turn, influenced the construction of a spatial image of the region. As Prieto states, Darwin expanded the image of the Argentine territory by adding Patagonia, Tierra del Fuego, and the Falkland Islands to the national imagination. Previously, when Domingo F. Sarmiento had depicted the landscape of Argentina in *Facundo: Civilización y barbarie* (1845), those territories were completely absent (Prieto 207). Thus, *The Voyage of the Beagle* and its references to southern Patagonia and Tierra del Fuego are fundamental pretexts of *La tierra del fuego*.[10] Moreover, Darwin's descriptions of the indigenous people as inferior and demonic set the foundation for the colonial enterprise of the Beagle that Iparraguirre deconstructs.

The novel opens with two epigraphs by Sarmiento and Melville, references to maritime and territorial projects that since the sixteenth century had established territorial limits in Patagonia. *Facundo* and *Moby-Dick* are two central allusions to the "civilization and barbarism" binary, the ideological subtext contemporary to the novel's narrative time. The narrator is John William Guevara, a mestizo who embodies ideas of both British and Argentine imaginations—Magdalena Perkowska calls him a "gaucho-sailor" (188). He introduces himself as the heir of a double genealogy while describing the two languages and two cultures influencing his identity: his mother tongue, rooted in the identification with the land; his father's, the language of an exile and maritime wanderer: "Por la corriente de las lenguas le fueron dadas involuntarias inclinaciones: a lo elemental y a lo firme, por parte de su madre; al desarraigo y a la melancolía, por parte de su padre" (44) ["The melding of languages gave him certain involuntary tendencies: toward the elemental and steadfast on his mother's side; toward uprootedness and melancholy on his father"] (St. Martin 24). The novel explores the potential of this hybrid identity as a source of literary creativity. There are autobiographical elements, but this is not an autobiography as such; it resists the autobiographical identification that characterizes the genre. Instead, I propose that there is a distanced representation of the subjective consciousness of the narrator evidenced in the proliferation of doubles, a common trait in Iparraguirre's overall narrative project, as many of her protagonists come from mixed cultural origins.[11] In *La tierra del fuego*, Guevara's doubles are Jemmy Button, who depicts his indigenous ties to America, and his father, the wanderer who relinquishes his British origins. As Amy Kaminsky states, Jemmy Button acts also as the British wanderer's double; in general, the doubles refer to the complex process of "othering" that signals the internal conflicts of territory and nationality (*Argentina* 59). Further, doubles expose "the disastrous consequences of othering for the colonized in the context of the relations of domination of imperialism and colonialism" (60), and such multiple representations of the self allude to the paradoxical formation of territorial identities that are marginal to the civilizing projects of England and Argentina. The mestizo, the epitome of the hybrid cultural identity of Latin America, gains his own voice in the history of Guevara. Many of the novel's characters live, like Guevara, between cultural and political borderlands. For instance, his father, after having arrived in 1806 as a member of the British navy, fought in England's invasions of Buenos Aires and ended up as a soldier in the Argentine army combating the Ranquel Indians in 1823. Moreover, the novel can be read as a parody of the main motives of foundational discourses of Argentine territoriality of the nineteenth century, namely the European journey, the city, and the ideals of European rationality (Perkowska 216).

However, this work is also a tribute to the hybrid identity of the Latin American intellectual of the nineteenth century. Though the tension between civilization and barbarism predominant in Sarmiento's *Facundo* is a key intertext of Guevara's narration, which the novel challenges through a postcolonial perspective, Iparraguirre's text also pays homage to the figure of Sarmiento as an intellectual who both affirms and questions European modernization. Guevara as Sarmiento is an autodidact whose father teaches him to read with the help of *Robinson Crusoe*. His fascination with books and the lettered culture is evident in the scenes in which he recounts his reading of *Moby-Dick*. Carlos Altamirano and Beatriz Sarlo have stated the importance of autodidactic knowledge in Sarmiento's own autobiographical figuration in *Mi Defensa* [*My Defense*] (1843) and *Recuerdos de Provincia* [*Recollections of a Provincial Past*] (1850). Produced through a chain of intertextual references, Sarmiento's "learning machine" interweaves texts, and employs a mixed Spanish "contaminated" by the use of European languages, a goal of Sarmiento's autodidactic literary model (Altamirano and Sarlo 160–61). Guevara embodies quite well the description of what Ricardo Piglia calls Sarmiento's mestizo intellectuality (127). Sarmiento, like many traveling intellectuals of the nineteenth century, was fascinated by the interlacing of dissimilar traditions; and his works, especially *Viajes por Europa, África, América* [*Travels through Europe, Africa, and America*] (1949), refer to the cultural heterogeneity of travel narratives of the period that are formulated as "narrations of self affirmation, emancipation, and decolonization" (Piglia, "Sarmiento" 128). Sarmiento is a good example of the intellectual traveler of the nineteenth century who, as a subject from a peripheral culture, seeks to rewrite the dominant ideological models of the central cultures of the century, such as Europe or the United States (Colombi, *Viaje* 15). Therefore, even when Iparraguirre's novel parodies European ideas of civilization and urbanization, it also connects Guevara to the hybrid cultural and literary identities of the intellectual lineage of figures like Sarmiento. Moreover, as a meta-reflection on writing, it reveals the other side, the American reception of travel narratives of European expansionism.

La tierra del fuego can be read against *The Voyage of the Beagle* as a postcolonial critique of British expansionism and its construction of a romantic imperialist subjectivity. The foundation of the myth of Patagonia that Antonio Pigafetta, Thomas Faulkner, and Charles Darwin created through their accounts (Livon-Grosman 39) is based on the articulation of forms of racial and sexual differences. Stereotyping is a key rhetorical strategy of colonialism because the body is the site where such differentiation takes place. The mythical construction of Patagonia embodies the ambivalence of colonial stereotypes, as bodies are constructed as both objects of desire and domination and power. Thus, colonialist discourses are based on "scenes of fear and desire," as "this function of the stereotype as phobia and fetish...threatens the closure of the racial/epidermal schema for the colonial subject and opens the royal road to colonial fantasy" (Bhabha 72–73). By expanding the complex desire/rejection binary of colonialist discourses in the image of doubles, Iparraguirre resorts to mimicry, another rhetorical device by which natives are depicted as cultural others, and reworks this image by introducing the complexities of colonial encounters. In key scenes, this novel depicts mimicry as a method of contesting imperial domination, as in when Guevara acts as a postcolonial ethnographer, describing the complex exchanges taking place between the Yahgans and Europeans. As a borderland subject, the novel presents him as someone with the capacity to ironically distance himself from an identification with colonialist discourses.

When we consider some examples of Darwin's descriptions of Patagonia, the novel's parody of the imperialist history of Patagonia becomes evident. Darwin's account describes the Yahgans as demonic beings, the possessors of an inferior language: "The language of these people, according to our notions, scarcely deserves to be called articulate. Captain Cook has compared it to a man clearing his throat, but certainly no European ever cleared his throat with so many hoarse, guttural, and clicking sounds." Further, they need to mimic in order to make themselves understood. Darwin states: "They are excellent mimics: as often as we coughed or yawned, or made any odd motion, they immediately imitated us. Some of our party began to squint and look awry; but one of the young Fuegians (whose whole face was painted black, excepting a white band across his eyes) succeeded in making far more hideous grimaces" (221). Iparraguirre alters this imperialist description; in a central scene, her protagonist Guevara compares the need for mimicking in Jemmy Button and the Yagans to the capacity for learning a foreign language:

> Aprendían el inglés a una velocidad pasmosa. Su capacidad era mimética, copiaban un idioma como se copian los gestos, las actitudes o las capacidades necesarias para sobrevivir. Lo primero que el Capitán enseñó a Button fue: *Pueden llamarme Jemmy Button*, y él lo repetía sonriente caminando por cubierta. Se paró frente a mí y repitió por centésima vez: *Pueden llamarme Jemmy Button*. (Emphasis in the original, 94)
> [They learned English at a staggering pace. They possessed a mimetic gift; they copied language the way one copies gestures, attitudes, or skills needed to survive. The first thing the Captain taught Button was *You may call me Jemmy Button*, and he repeated it, cheerfully pacing the deck. He stopped in front of me and repeated for the hundredth time: *You may call me Jemmy Button*.] (emphasis in the original, St. Martin 60)

Later on, Jemmy's mimicry is a symbol of his rejection of European capitalism; he imitates Guevara and Captain Fitz Roy when they exchange objects for coins, although for him, "otra cosa era el poder abstracto del dinero; la idea de su posesión por sí misma pertenecía a un universo de valores inmateriales, de influencia misteriosa, que Button jamás pudo asimilar" (118) ["the abstract value of money was something else. The idea of possessing it for its own sake pertained to a world of immaterial values, of mysterious influence that Button was never able to assimilate"] (St. Martin 79). In a London scene, Button "wastes" all the coins the Captain had given him while playing games, throwing them onto the streets of London so that they could be picked up by poor children. After the scene, Guevara concludes:

> Así perdió Button el único dinero que poseyó nunca, pero ganó una experiencia extraordinaria: alcanzó a concebir la idea abstracta del poder que otorga la riqueza. De allí en adelante, para lo único que pedía monedas era para tirarlas en la calle. Para un yámana, la idea de comprar un objeto o alimento era inconcebible; en el Cabo de Hornos cada uno obtiene lo que necesita y lo demás es de todos, pero esto, como muchas otras cosas, nadie se había preocupado por averiguarlo. (119)
> [That's how Button lost the only money he ever had but gained an extraordinary experience: he was able to conceive the abstract idea of the power money confers. From then on he only asked for coins in order to throw them into the street. For a Yámana the idea of buying any object or food was inconceivable; in Cape Horn each individual obtains what he needs, and the rest belongs to everyone, but this, among many other things, no one had ever bothered to find out.] (St. Martin 80)

The last sentence reveals the transition from mimicry to mockery in Button's actions as the novel displaces the British empire's "disciplinary gaze"; Button learns of the value of money only to transgress its capitalist ideals. As Bhabha states, mimicry is "one of the most elusive and effective strategies of colonial power and knowledge" as it describes the tension between the synchronic panoptical vision of domination...and the counter-pressure of the diachrony in history—change, difference—..." (85–86). In Guevara's borderland narrative, Jemmy Button, contrary to *The Voyage of the Beagle*, now in the role of the protagonist, embodies the complex visual dynamics of identification and rejection embedded in relationships of mimicry and mockery between the colonizer and the colonized.

The representation of Tierra del Fuego as the border of imperialist fantasies is evident in the novel's last chapters, which narrate the killing of a group of people living in a mission that Reverend Despard established on one of the Falkland Islands. Guevara reconstructs the trial, which took place in 1860 following the events and in which the Yahgans are judged for committing the crimes.[12] Two witnesses are brought in: Alfred Coles, the only survivor of the killings, and Jemmy Button, who is found at the crime scene and who volunteers to give his testimony. The trial is key in deconstructing England's expansionist project and its interests in capitalism, science, and religious conversion. Previous authorities had opposed the mission because of the obstacles it would have imposed to a smooth administration of the islands' affairs. Published in a newspaper four years earlier, a letter by ex-governor Mr. Rennie explains these difficulties. During the trial, the appalling testimony of the only survivor, Alfred Coles, is set against that of the angry Parker Snow, who had been fired by Despard because of his own disagreements with the way the mission was being run. While the trial is taking place, Snow also carries on a labor dispute in England against Despard; in his testimony, he explains that the mission exploited the Yahgans in the same way he had been financially exploited by Reverend Despard. Jemmy Button's testimony serves its only purpose—to scare away future expedition trips; he explains that different tribes live in the area of Tierra del Fuego and that it is one of them, probably the Selk'nams, that is responsible for the murders. Although he later confesses privately to Guevara that he had been involved in the massacre, he uses the trial as an opportunity to deepen the fears of the Europeans by presenting some inhabitants of Tierra del Fuego as cannibals and fierce contenders. As Guevara's states, Button attended the trial only to find out more about the Europeans' intentions and to protect his own people from further threats. Contrary to the stereotyping present in colonialist discourses, Button's testimony depicts his complex subjectivity, forced to lie in order to protect his people's lives and traditions. In addition, the trial makes evident the contradictions of British imperialism and the futility of laws and regulations that attempt to rule the area. As Guevara states, no one is charged in the trial; Button is allowed to leave while many outside the courtroom are still discussing the complicated developments uncovered by the testimonies. The narrative purposes of the trial scenes are tied to the novel's testimonial intentions. Guevara is described as a skilled translator of the complex set of events unfolding during the trial. An editor, a narrative figure who appears only during these scenes, explains to the readers that a set of documents, some testimonies in their original language, English, are stapled to Guevara's journal. This insert not only demonstrates the extensive archival work done by Iparraguirre during the novel's composition, but also makes evident the relationship between historical facts and fiction and the denunciatory goal of Guevara's narrative.[13] Guevara acts as a modern ethnographer unveiling the binaries that sustain the composition of the colonial subject.

The novel's format combines testimony, fiction, and history and brings forward a series of important issues regarding readership and authorship. *La tierra del fuego* follows the model of the epistolary novel, its seven folios referring to the epistolary communications that many explorers maintained when reporting to the colonial authorities that had financed their trip. The narration begins with the arrival of a letter by an unknown Mr. MacDowell or MacDowness, an officer of the British navy, who writes to Guevara requiring a detailed report of the trip taken by the Beagle 35 years before. The letter reports that on April 30, 1865, Jemmy Button, the Yahgan abducted by Fitz Roy and brought to England as an experiment in civilization, had committed suicide. The identity of the writer is hard to establish because of the poor quality of the paper; the letter arrived following a long itinerary until it reached Lobos, the solitary town in the Pampas where Guevara lives. The arrival of the letter prompts Guevara to begin writing a response that, following the format of the maritime report, is structured in a series of manuscripts—the folios—that Graciana, Guevara's only companion and caretaker, sews with devotion after its completion. The circuit of communication between Guevara and the British Empire represents a weak connection very well described by the random itinerary the letter followed until it reached Lobos: "Liverpool o Plymouth, el Cabo Verde, posiblemente las Azores, el Brasil, el Puerto de Montevideo, Buenos Aires. En algún punto de la previsible ruta había intervenido el azar. El azar y la monotonía son las dos constantes del océano" (19) ["Having discarded this possibility, I visualized the letter's itinerary: Liverpool or Plymouth, the Cape Verde Islands, possibly the Azores, Brazil, the port of Montevideo, Buenos Aires. At some point on the foreseeable route, blind chance had stepped in. Chance and monotony are the ocean's two constants"] (St. Martin 6). Such fragile communication is a metaphor for the distanced position the protagonist has as a member of both the British Empire and the incipient Argentine state. He thus chooses a response that, from a rather subjective perspective with autobiographical tones, contests the objective order evidenced in the genre of the official report. As a self-searching experiment, a testimony of the cruel history of the nineteenth century, and a meta-reflection on writing, Guevara's text establishes a postcolonial critique of the intricate relationships between Europe and America. The narrative characters of Guevara and Graciana, both marginalized subjects who experience their own fragility on the borders of the colonial order, reconstruct a symbolic domain of a world from which they had been displaced.[14]

The novel is also a testimony and has the intention of denouncing the atrocities that took place during the colonization of Tierra del Fuego. Over and over, Guevara questions himself about who is his writings' addressee; evidently, the confusion of the British officer's name, MacDowell or MacDowness, makes clear he is not interested in directly responding to the empire's request. At a certain point in the novel, Guevara also confesses that he is writing for his own purposes: to gain a deeper understanding of his identity and the history he lived three decades ago. However, at the end, it becomes evident that Graciana is the implied addressee, and this gesture recognizes her presence while giving her the power to interpret the legacy of colonialism in Latin America. As Perkowska states, Graciana is Jemmy's "alter ego" in the official story (196); she represents the dispossessed genealogies of America. In the final scene, Guevara teaches Graciana how to read:

> Mañana, o tal vez esta noche si encuentro voluntad, voy a despejar la mesa, voy a plantar en el medio el candil y le voy a enseñar a sostener la pluma, a entintarla, a trazar y a comprender los signos enigmáticos con los que, pacientemente, me ha visto convivir tantos meses. Si éste es un relato para nadie, quizá yo mismo deba crearle un lector, y tal vez sea ella, míster MacDowell o MacDowness, la que algún día pueda alcanzar el sentido de estos papeles sin destino. (285)
> [Tomorrow, or perhaps this evening if I can find the will to do it, I am going to clear the table, set the oil lamp in the centre, and show her how to hold the pen, dip it into ink, and trace and learn the enigmatic symbols she has patiently watched me living with for so many months. If this is a story for no one, perhaps I should create a reader for it, and perhaps it is she, Mr. MacDowell or MacDowness, who will some day be able to make sense of these papers addressed to no one.] (St. Martin 199)

As Guevara's ultimate addressee, Graciana embodies the complex intersections of race and gender addressed by the novel and their impact on literary culture. The final image of the book, as composed by a mestizo and an illiterate woman, proposes alternative views of the intended role of literature in society, which is particularly relevant in the 1990s and 2000s, when globalization impacted the foundations of Argentina's literary culture. This fragmentary composition can be interpreted as an example of the scattered, deterritorialized, or "minor literature" that Deleuze and Guattari describe, the literature that underrepresented subjects write within a major literary tradition ("What is a minor literature?" 18). In Iparraguirre's novel, the notion of a "minor literature" has multiple connotations. First, the novel's composition makes tangible the process of writing as a craft that cannot be massively reproduced, a tribute to writing in the media-ridden Argentine society of the 1990s and 2000s. Second, it is also a tribute to those books yet to be written, the powerful historical counternarratives of those subjects silenced by the cruel histories embedded in the spatial and political formations of the nation-state, particularly women and indigenous peoples. The final gesture of Guevara teaching Graciana to write refers to the tensions of orality and writing and the "minor" place oral traditions have held in the country's literary genealogies where, since the nineteenth century, intellectuals have maintained a role of interpreters and leaders of the illiterate masses in Latin America. This ending also highlights the importance of women in rewriting national narratives in the context of the globalization and redemocratization of the 1990s and 2000s, as well as the emergence of new social actors and their struggles in gaining new levels of political and social representation. Although the novel does not have open feminist claims, its focus on the decentering of cartographies of knowledge and power by questioning, for instance, the construction of women as peripheral subjects in both local and global traditions, is highly relevant. This, I believe, is an implied critique of how symbolic and material struggles over a definition of territoriality impact the location of women in both imperialist and nationalist discourses. Thus, *La tierra del fuego* engages in a revision of the historical importance of colonial others as subjects bound by hegemonic discourses on both race and gender. Iparraguirre astutely locates these reflections at the cross-border region of Patagonia and Tierra del Fuego, an area that historically has shown intricate spatial dynamics and has served as a place for the definition of global and national identities.

Sarmiento's project on literacy and education as key in the modernization process of Argentina is central in understanding Guevara as a recipient of such a tradition. However, Guevara's project is carried on not only in the margins of British imperialism, but also in the outer limits of the national space that Sarmiento, as well as the writers of the generations of 1837 and 1880, sought to establish as a symbol of a national identity. As a frontier narrative, *La tierra del fuego* represents those virtual geographies built upon alliances of marginalized historic subjects. The fact that a woman is the heiress of this literary genealogy is also significant, for Argentina's main literary traditions have since the nineteenth century turned both European and indigenous women into "objects of repression" (Masiello, *Between* 5). As a counternarrative, Iparraguirre's novel echoes the project by which Argentine women carried out a critique of the incipient nation-state of the nineteenth century.[15] Thus, *La tierra del fuego* also offers a disillusioned narrative of the complicities between literary culture and authoritarianism, territorialism, and the building of a modern political and literary identity for Argentina based on cartographies of exclusion and internal colonization. A tribute to Sarmiento and his project of "uniting" civilization and barbarism, the novel also challenges, in both its aesthetic and thematic implications, the ways in which authors like Sarmiento sought to modernize Argentina by imposing a territorial national identity that repressed racial and cultural differences. As a defense of the interpretative power of social subjects historically displaced by race and gender and of the importance of new social movements in the twenty years that followed the return of democracy in 1983 in Argentina, *La tierra del fuego* addresses the creation of "alternative versions of history and social commitment" (Masiello, "Este pobre" 250). The "global" Patagonia to which Iparraguirre's novel indirectly refers is both a space of memory and historical reconstruction and the utopian land for new territorial formations at the turn of the twenty-first century.

The descriptions of landscapes are central in understanding the connection between territoriality and writing, since *La tierra del fuego* rewrites a long-standing tradition that, since Sarmiento, saw in the Argentine landscape a metaphor for literary or political dreams of modernization. The images of civilization as an urban culture of European traits and of barbarism as the emptiness of the geopolitical landscape of the Pampas or Patagonia are central here.[16] As W. J. T. Mitchell states, landscape is a cultural medium that works as ideology because while it "naturalizes a cultural and social construction, representing an artificial world as if it were simply given and inevitable," it also "makes that representation operational by interpolating its beholder in some more or less determinate relation to its givenness as sight and site." More important, landscape is a "dynamic medium," for it circulates as a medium of exchange in cultural relationships through visual appropriation and the formation of identity (2). It is a "vast network of cultural codes" and, as an international or global phenomenon, is "intimately bound up with the discourses of imperialism" (9). *La tierra del fuego* carefully articulates and disarticulates the differences between nature and convention as Iparraguirre shows the role Patagonia has played in the representation of imperialist and nationalist territorial projects. In so doing, she creates an "aesthetic alertness to the violence and evil written on the land, projected there by the gazing eye" (29). Guevara, as a mestizo and a modern ethnographer, seems to be highly qualified to unveil the cultural implications of Patagonia as a landscape of imperial and national domination. In the novel's descriptions of Patagonia, a number of conventional images surface, such as those of the area as an inferno, the ends of the world, and a silent plain evocative of the ocean. As Mallory explains to his son, Guevara, "—Así es el mar—dijo—, como esta tierra inacabable y monótona, pero de agua. La casa es como el barco" (57) ["The sea is like that, he said, like this endless, monotonous land, but it is all water. The house is like a ship"] (St. Martin 33), an image shared by English and Argentine writers (Prieto, *Los viajeros* 22–23). Allusions to visual constructions of Cape Horn in Melville's *Moby-Dick,* as well as the epigraph in Sarmiento's *Facundo,* point to the construction of a Patagonian landscape; Guevara is the heir of a tradition of literary landscape that he learns to master through a complex cultural apprenticeship. The storms taking place in Patagonia are compared to paintings by Joseph Mallord William Turner, the master of Romantic English landscapes, widely famous for his depictions of stormy seas. Complementary to the seascapes, Patagonia as a deserted land is evoked from the opening epigraphs. Immediately after his description of Cape Horn, Guevara describes the emptiness of the Patagonian desert:

> Tengo una gran cantidad de mapas en el baúl; siempre me fascinaron. Una enorme porción de tierra patagónica aparece en esos viejos mapas bajo la denominación res nullius, cosa de nadie. Es mi país. ¿Ha estado usted alguna vez en la Patagonia, míster MacDowell o MacDowness? ¿Puede siquiera imaginársela? ¿Puede imaginar un colosal corredor de vientos cuyo piso es una meseta que baja desde las montañas hacia el este, asomándose sobre el mar en acantilados gigantescos y cóncavos?. (89)
> [I have a large number of maps in my trunk; they've always fascinated me. An enormous portion of Patagonian territory appears on those old maps under the name *res nullius*, no-man's land. It's my country. Have you ever been in Patagonia, Mr. MacDowell or MacDowness? Can you even imagine it? Can you imagine a colossal corridor of winds whose floor is a plateau which descends from the mountains toward the east and leans out over the sea in gigantic concave cliffs?] (St. Martin 57)

In addition, numerous references to the city and its landscapes of civilization are transformed by the description of a corrupted London, thus contrasting with the image of the city in Sarmiento's project of modernization. The precarious settlement Fitz Roy establishes for the Yahgans when he brings them back to Tierra del Fuego on the Beagle's second trip is a metonymic reference to nineteenth-century dreams of populating the empty Patagonia by building urban settlements. As detailed through Guevara's observations, these dreams will not materialize in Patagonia, where nature resists any impulse for its domination. His is an ironic account of settlements for Fuegia, York, and Button:

> En pocos días quedó armada la casa de madera y delimitado un huerto con zócalos de piedras; un campamento donde, según lo planeado por el capitán, quedaría Button con todo lo traído de Inglaterra; allí también, según su bucólica imaginación, armarían su hogar y crecerían los hijos de Fuegia y York. Yo mismo me daba cuenta de lo disparatado de todo esto. A miles de millas de distancia, la idea era una cosa aceptable y hasta loable; cuando la idea se materializó en el lugar, se hizo absurda. La naturaleza no dejaba resquicio a la imaginación. (192)
> [In a few days, the wooden house was erected and the vegetable garden marked off with a stone wall. It was a camp where, following the Captain's plan, Button would be left with everything brought from England, and where also, in his bucolic imagination, Fuegia and York

and their children would make their home. I saw how senseless all this was. Thousands of miles away the idea had been acceptable and even praiseworthy, but when it materialized on the spot, it became absurd. Nature does not give imagination a chance.] (St. Martin 133)

The "absurdity" of the captain's project thus reinforces the ironic reconstruction of Argentina's formation of the nation-state in the nineteenth century. As evidenced in the use of literary landscapes, *La tierra del fuego* rearticulates cultural relationships between binaries that were crucial in the nineteenth-century Argentine and European imaginations: civilization and barbarism, the country and the sea, and the empire and its colonies. Landscapes emphasize how Guevara's identity is formed through the appropriation of literary and cultural traditions. As intricate representations, Guevara seeks to decode them, for instance, in describing London's architectural marvels. However, he describes the need to create new spatial images for Latin America, new landscapes that appropriate and rework previous cultural icons, as he states when he associates landscape and the writing of a new history for Latin America:

> De donde nosotros veníamos no había tiempo, no se sabía cómo había transcurrido porque la vida parecía volver siempre a la tierra sin dejar huella. Había que atar los hechos a la llanura para que no se volaran. La historia estaba por empezar, mientras que allí, en Londres, años, siglos, épocas pretéritas retrocedían vertiginosamente por el solo hecho de mirar. (124)
> [Time did not exist where we came from, no one knew how it had passed, because life always seemed to return to the earth without leaving a trace. Facts had to be tied down to the plain to keep them from flying off. History had yet to begin, while there in London the years, centuries, past ages receded at a dizzy pace simply through the act of looking.] (St. Martin 83)

La tierra del fuego describes the construction of alternative territorialities against those that sought to mold, during the nineteenth century, local identities according to transnational fantasies of modernization and order. The novel links this virtual territoriality to a literary model located at the margins of global designs, a postcolonial project that deconstructs both nationalist claims of the Argentine state and the imperialist forces of British expansionism. As evidenced in the description of Patagonia as a liminal space, the geography of the borderlands seems the most appropriate for carrying out the writing of new forms of territoriality that the novel proposes. *La tierra del fuego* describes those territories as virtual and ghostly because they are not yet fully realized in either the history or the literature of Argentina. Guevara describes his last encounter with the land of Jemmy Button, Tierra del Fuego, as follows:

> Finalmente bajé y comencé a remar. Estábamos cerca del estrecho Murray, en la desembocadura del fiordo Ponsoby, en el centro del país de Button. Era un lugar que yo recordaba muy bien. No obstante, la niebla lo volvía fantasmagórico, espectral y, para mi inquietud, desconocido. Habían desaparecido las montañas, las laderas, toda referencia se esfumaba en una claridad lechosa que envolvía en ráfagas y remolinos todo lo existente. (201)
> [I finally stepped down and started to row. We were near the Murray Strait, at the mouth of Ponsonby Fjord, in the middle of Button's country. It was a place I remembered very well. Nevertheless, the fog made it phantasmagoric, ghostly and disquietingly unfamiliar to me. The mountains and hillsides had disappeared; all points of reference were vanishing into a milky brightness which enveloped in flurries and eddies everything that existed there.] (St. Martin 141)

Tierra del Fuego represents the limit of existing territorial identities and a borderland of new possibilities, thus making evident the importance of space in the configuration of identities studied here. Whereas *La tierra del fuego* is a tribute to the importance of literary culture, it also questions literary topographies that have built national identities on exclusionary dreams of modernization and progress. The issue of language and translation is central here. Guevara is a skilled translator, navigating the multiple linguistic encounters of the borderland, who defines a new literary topography questioning the "traditional contiguity between nation and language" at the same time that he rewrites national space, as defined by predominant cultural traditions (Rosman 18). Guevara as the epitome of a dislocated, displaced writer who cannot fully inhabit a particular literary or national tradition deterritorializes the concept of the nation as capable of defining literature and culture. In *La tierra del fuego,* we can also find echoes of Diana Bellessi's ideas on translation as a complex cultural exchange. As discussed in the next chapter on poetry and location, Bellessi's poetic project is based on an implicit dialogue with the indigenous American peoples. In her collection *Sur,* she explores ways in which poetry enables a virtual communication with those voices that, as the poet reminds us in the opening epigraph, are "aún forzados en la escritura, violentados en la traducción" [still forced in writing and distorted in translation] (5). Poetry enables a virtual communication that, as Eliana Ortega reminds us, "grasps without possessing" the multiple voices embedded in histories of colonization and builds a "Southern resistance" against acculturation (Ortega). In fact, *La tierra del fuego* could be read as a parallel project to *Sur*. Contrary to the colonization of language that takes place in certain instances of translation, both texts build linguistic crossovers that establish liminal spaces for historical memory.

The last section of this chapter will review how electronic media, a pivotal force in remaking the literary culture of Argentina in the 1990s and 2000s, further complicates the intricate connection among territory, language, and literature. Argentine writer and artist Belén Gache destabilizes Patagonia's geographical imaginations that, since the nineteenth century, have been associated with ideals of cultural nationalism. Gache's notion of nomadic writing examines the position of minority discourses in global designs that were also explored in Iparraguirre's *La tierra del fuego*. Moreover, she analyzes how hypertexts question hierarchical notions about literature, such as the role of cultural producers in the creative process. Thus, her definitions of nomadic writing are examples of what Walter Mignolo calls "border thinking," a set of critical discourses by which minorities seek to decenter political and epistemological global designs.

4. Hypertextual Territories: Belén Gache's Nomadic Writings

Gache's works address the complex intersections between media and literature; in *Escrituras nómadas,* she explores the literary implications of a "nomadic writing" characterized by "rhizome-like" or hypertext-based structures. Influenced by both avant-garde traditions of collage and spatial simultaneity, as well as the ubiquitous presence of electronic media in global society, she experiments with artistic and literary formats that challenge the notion of linear writing and encourage different levels of interaction between reader and text, such as those present on a computer screen. An example of a "minor literature," her nomadic writings are, as in Luisa Futoransky, implicit references to the marginal role women occupy in society as cultural producers. In fact, Gache chooses nontraditional forms of approaching the creation and circulation of literary texts and challenges, for instance, traditional conceptions of authorship and the idea of the book as a cultural object by producing electronic texts that can be accessed through the Internet; both author and reader are combinations of textual influences and impersonal functions operating on the basis of patterns determined by a textual system. Her aesthetic exploration of literary and artistic forms of nomadism is also a reflection on the role of location, place, and dislocation, as well as the contemporary spatial displacements brought about by the technological transformations of globalization, on experiences of migration and transnational cultural encounters. As Mignolo states in "Linguistic Maps, Literary Geographies, and Cultural Landscapes," the changing linguistic and literary cartographies at the turn of the twenty-first century challenge the traditional identification of languages and territories (65). Along these lines, "nomadic writing" also refers to the dislodging of territoriality and writing and to the transformations of the literary culture under the influences of globalization and new technologies. In works such as *Diario de la luna caníbal,* Gache additionally applies notions of "nomadic writing" to issues of collective memory, such as the violent historical formation of territoriality and the obliteration and disappearance of nomad populations, namely the Selk'nam in Tierra del Fuego. Like Luisa Futoransky, Gache treats nomadism as a political and epistemological tool for questioning the complex relations among gender, race, and cultural production and the spatial histories of a country that systematically displaced and erased those considered to be minor or marginal social actors.

The notion of the hypertext is relevant here, a format that many believe is a direct consequence of the technological inventions of the twentieth century. Theodor Nelson coined the term to refer to nonsequential writing and the fusing of different semiotic systems that contain words, images, and sounds. His hypertext project, "Xanadu," includes a branching of texts and innovative organizations of materials that allow the reader to go through interactive screens. Hypertexts have been linked to critical theories on reading and writing, such as the decentering proposed by deconstructionism or Deleuze and Guattari's rhizomes. According to George Landow, "all hypertext systems permit the individual reader to choose his or her own center of investigation and experience [...] [which means] that the reader is not locked into any kind of particular organization or hierarchy" (58). In the history of hypertexts included in *Escrituras nómadas,* Gache establishes its antecedents in the phonic games of futuristic poetry, concrete poetry examples such as the "poesia letrista" [letterist poetry] by Isou in the 1940s, and the cultivation of "nonsense" by English writers such as Lewis Carroll in the nineteenth century. Her analysis focuses on how those aesthetic trends deconstruct logical supports of linguistic expression. An important section of *Escrituras nómadas* is devoted to space as a key component in nonlinear forms of writing. Such nomadic models were used more frequently after 1897 with Mallarmé's *Coup de dés* and the historic avant-gardes of the early twentieth century. Different spatial structures support the characteristics of interactivity, randomness, synchronization, and spatiality that are central to nomadic texts. In *Escrituras nómadas,* Gache analyzes different genres and textual examples of spatial nomadic representations: maps used in fictional accounts, travel narratives, encyclopedias, and collages are, for this author, examples of nomadic formats employed in literature or art.

Gache's interest in the intersections between literary writing and other media, in particular, the Internet, is evident in multiple examples of her work. She maintains a Web site, *Fin del mundo* [*The End of the World*] (www.findelmundo.com.ar), and besides her fiction and essays, has explored writing digital and video poetry. *Word Toys,* an interactive book that can be read only on the Internet, further exemplifies her interest in the ways in which digital media affect writing. In the chapter "Mariposas-libro" ["Butterfly-book"], Gache creates a digital book collection composed of "dissected words," or quotations that are visualized as butterflies pinned on an insect inventory. The reader has to click on each butterfly in order to access different literary quotations, thereby building a network of virtual connections in the text, this time aided by visual supports provided by the Internet. In *Word Toys,* Gache explores the notion of reading as an unpredictable and discontinuous operation led by the reader. The format of *Word Toys* resembles that of a book that can be read by clicking on different screens and moving through chapters in an order decided at each individual path of reading. In some instances, as in "Water Poems," we are invited to interact with areas of the screen that prompt a textual reference, for instance, poems dripping in the bathroom sink as we click on the image of a faucet.

In her preface to *Escrituras nómadas,* Gache states that electronic media transform literary culture by combining different semiotic systems, such as the linguistic, the visual, and the phonic, and by challenging the principles of linearity and spatial order that characterize writing. By subverting conventional writing formats, this nonlinear or "nomadic writing" also questions sacred notions, such as truth or authority, coined by certain dominant cultures (19). *El libro del fin del mundo,* a book that can be downloaded as a PDF and includes a CD and a direct link to a Web site, is intended to be an electronic encyclopedia; encyclopedias, examples of nomadic writing according to Gache, challenge linear reading models as the reader determines virtual itineraries tracing symbolic cartographies of knowledge (*Escrituras nómades* 99). Many of the texts in *El libro del fin del mundo* point to this "nomadic" understanding of the process of reading as an operation whereby the reader can challenge preestablished cultural conceptions. The repetition of the rhetorical questions in the sequence entitled "Is it true?," challenges the certainty of scientific knowledge and invites critical forms of cultural readership. Other examples point to the rupture of traditions, such as "Manual de caligrafía de la dinastía Sung" ["Manual of Sung Dynasty Calligraphy"], in which a poet, Wang-Hsi, is condemned for combining different calligraphic styles coming from a series of writing traditions:

> "Wang-Hsi, versado en poesía y música, solía adoptar en sus composiciones diferentes estilos caligráficos tales como el de finales de la dinastía Chin o el oficial de la dinastía Han y los combinaba con monocondilos persas, minúsculas carolingias, escrituras cuneiformes, letras griegas y runas vikingas."
>
> [Wang-Hsi, well versed in poetry and music, used to adopt different calligraphic styles in his compositions, such as that of the late Chin dynasty or the official style of the Han dynasty, and he would combine them with Persian monocondylia, Carolingian lowercases, cuneiform writing, Greek letters, and Viking runes.] (17)[17]

In its experimentation with different writing formats, "Manual de caligrafía de la dinastía Sung" can be read as a tribute to the historical avant-gardes of the early twentieth century, such as the graphic poetry in Apollinaire's calligraphic games or Isou's "letterist poetry."

Whereas *El libro del fin del mundo* challenges traditional literary notions through the use of writing formats based on electronic media, this collection is also a tribute to the culture of books, as in the direct reference to illustrations and encyclopedias, textbooks, and medieval catalogs. The short story "El elefante del Papa" ["The Pope's Elephant"] refers to a rhinoceros's image made by Dürer in 1515. Based on true events that took place in late 1515 when the King of Portugal, Manuel I, brought a rhino to Europe as a gift for Pope Leo X, Gache's story describes how the animal died in a shipwreck off the coast of Italy and how Dürer, who had never seen a rhino, created the woodcut aided by a shipwreck survivor's testimony. "El elefante del Papa" describes the rhino's icon as a result of a complex series of cultural intersections that gave this representation different characteristics, from Ctesias's unicorns in his history of India, to the armored and dangerous animal in Dürer, and the capricious and carefree rhinoceros in Georges Louis De Buffon *Histoire naturelle, générale et particulière* [Natural History, General and Particular] (1749–1788) (*El libro* 35). By playfully rewriting the format of medieval bestiaries, Gache demonstrates how beasts are arbitrary creations foregrounding anxieties of cultural contact. The story also refers, as other pieces in *El libro del fin del mundo,* to the endless labyrinth of cultural references readers may navigate as co-creators of cultural perceptions and interpretations, which are, without exception, influenced by global images circulating through complex networks of citations. As "nomadic writings," encyclopedic and the Web-based texts have similar characteristics:

La concepción del texto tal como la conocemos hoy, con sus convenciones de formato y paratexto, corresponde a la modernidad. Este libro es portable, mercantilizable y coleccionable. Sus tapas lo cierran al mundo, lo separan como una entidad aislada. En los textos digitales, por el contrario, es imposible hablar de una estricta separación entre los mismos. La capacidad de crear hipervínculos hace pensar incluso en la posibilidad de una biblioteca universal cuyos fragmentos estuvieran todos interconectados. El orden de los textos, por otra parte, estará determinado en cada caso por una particular lectura.

[The conception of a text as we understand it today, with its conventions of format and paratext, corresponds to modernity. This book is portable, marketable, and collectable. Its covers close [the book] to the world; they set it apart as an isolated entity. In the case of digital texts, however, it is impossible to establish such a strict separation between the two. The ability to create hyperlinks even makes us think of the possibility of a universal library with interconnected fragments. The order of the texts, on the other hand, will be determined by each individual reading.] (*Escrituras* 151)

Nomadic writings enable a certain type of spatiality that Gache describes as

[…] libre y pululante de posibilidades, traspasado por desviaciones e interacciones. Las formaciones espaciales funcionan como modelos estructurales a partir de los cuales la narración se va armando. Los mapas (de una ciudad, de una casa, del trazado ferroviario, etc.) dan pie a constelaciones textuales y permiten una lectura topográfica de los textos.

[[…] free and teeming with possibilities, traversed by deviations and interactions. Spatial formations function as structural models from which the narration is constructed. Maps (of a city, a house, a railway system, etc.) give rise to textual constellations and make possible a topographic reading of the texts.] (78)

El libro del fin del mundo points to the spatial volatility of hypertextual spaces, which contest the hierarchical disposition of spatial constructs such as the territory. The story that gives the title to the collection, "El libro del fin del mundo" narrates the creation of such virtual spaces. It tells the story of an emperor, Roberto "the Inopportune," who establishes a new language and imposes it on his entire empire composed of "hundreds of provinces, principalities, and kingdoms" where two hundred languages are spoken and one hundred different alphabets exist (11). Along with the new linguistic identity, Roberto creates territorial demarcations by building a wall that surrounds its empire and defines its limits. He burns all existing books and creates a unique book, the "book of the truth" containing the "true name of all things" (11). The story goes on to tell how later emperors, such as Ulrico "the Consistent," undo Roberto's changes and build a "book of the end of the world," which they compose by assembling the fragments of the books burned by Roberto. "El libro del fin del mundo" thus represents a hypertext and an unbounded territory, a postimperial geography where utopian worlds might exist. This story also probes how the interrogation of territoriality is embedded in a questioning of a culture of books. Gache deconstructs space in order to alter conceptions of literary authorship and readership as well as the role of writing within literary culture. Roberto and Ulrico are two examples of authorship; the despotic Roberto functions as the author who unsuccessfully seeks to condense all possible meanings into one, the "true," while Ulrico builds a book of infinite possibilities, a collage made of the little fragments of Roberto's authoritarian endeavors. Gache's story refers to the "ends of the world," or the world's farthest limits, as the place where alternative literary and artistic projects exist.

El libro del fin del mundo addresses the process of reading as a way of navigating complex spaces expressed by the rich structure of the hypertext. In The series promenades makes this connection between writing and space evident, as it presents different textual wanderings embodied in quotes by Charles Baudelaire, Edgar Allan Poe, Walter Benjamin, and Robert Walser, pasted on the streets of an imaginary city. "Southern Heavens" describes precartographic charts of thirteenth- and fifteenth-century navigators. As the reader hears the sounds of the sky played on the CD, the image of a constellation appears on the computer screen, and we are invited to travel through the "Southern Heavens" as we also listen to the voice of a flight attendant giving us "reading instructions" about what to do during the flight. As skilled sailors crossing over the sea, guided by the sole references to the sky, we traverse the virtual space in our computer, enacting a complex experience of reading.

In *Diario de la luna caníbal,* Gache goes one step further in exploring the complex intersections between literature, media, and spatiality. Located in the Old Prison of Tierra del Fuego, this work is a critical revision of the construction of the southern frontier of Argentina (fig. 3.1). Gache planned the installation so that the spectator could walk through different cells and corridors of the prison as she or he listened to a recording of a diary by a fictional inmate, a Spanish immigrant from Gibraltar stranded in Argentina and imprisoned for political reasons. Located at the "end of the world," at the last continental frontier, *Diario de la luna caníbal* questions the creation of national borders as well as the building of a territorial identity for

Argentina. In her works, Gache describes spaces and territories as textual and artistic constructions; she examines how they are crafted as arbitrary representations and how, as cultural constructions, they determine narratives of identity and literary patterns that are based on the identification of language, literature, and nation. Her overall artistic project is mainly an aesthetic examination of how literary and artistic systems build spatial relations. However, the installation in Tierra del Fuego deals with political implications of space, and in the context of the global changes analyzed by the biennial, *Diario de la luna caníbal* constitutes a critique of asymmetrical relations of power that are embedded in local and global spatialities.[18] It is relevant to read Gache's installation from the perspective of transnational feminist notions of how spatial relations build subjectivities, and how narratives, in this case those pertaining to both the formation of a national and global identity, are "meaning-making practices with their own logic and cultural specificity." Moreover, spatial relations bring to the fore the construction of stories that are "social practices... regulated by the institutions that produce, legitimate, and distribute knowledge" (Stone-Mediatore 132). Transnational feminisms investigate the ways in which transnational structures determine cultural exchanges and how gender, class, and race are determined by spatial networks that, in our contemporary world, are scattered, thus rendering the notions of center and periphery insufficient to explain how transnational power relationships are established. In Grewal and Caplan's words, "hegemonies are scattered" at a time when we can think of "multiple peripheries" built around transnational networks (20). In particular, transnational feminisms' analyses have been sensitive to the processes of nation-state building and how they reveal intersections of modernity and coloniality (22). Therefore, several issues brought up by transnational feminisms are relevant to the analysis conducted here: first, the determination of fluid relationships of power within transnational networks; second, the formation of the nation as a territorial process that brings to the fore the complexities of modernity; and finally, the construction of space as a narration of histories of national and global communities. I will focus here on the notion of "nomadic writing" as instrumental in understanding all of the above and, in particular, how the building of Patagonia as a symbolic space in the history of Argentina offers a productive example of spatial formations and spatiality as a territorial and textual identity.

The location of *Diario de la luna caníbal* in the Old Prison of Tierra del Fuego is highly relevant. The installation connects two spatial narratives of Patagonia. In the context of the biennial, it draws attention to the image of Patagonia as a media-produced geography exhibited for the consumption of an "imagined global community." As such, the installation

Figure 3.1 Usuhaia Prison (hallways), site of the installation *Diario de la luna caníbal*. Used with permission of Belén Gache.

foregrounds a questionable relationship with the twenty-first century global tourist that signals the determining influence of neoliberalism and globalization in Argentine national identity and, as Hortiguera and Rocha have studied, the impact those forces had on literary culture. In the context of the territorial history of Argentina, we could also state that *Diario de la luna caníbal* establishes a restructuring of what Roger Bartra calls the "cultural territory," depicting power relations among different cultural classes (116) as well as dialogues with the rich corpus of literature that used Patagonia as a source of inspiration. As Bartra demonstrates, territorial configurations are directly linked to cultural maps that regulate literary production (116). As evident in the example of Patagonia and its role in the national imagination of Argentina, territorial fluctuations and changes frequently overlap with reconfigurations of literary and artistic notions and the power that cultural elites have in shaping a national identity that is both spatial and linguistic.

Diario de la luna caníbal explores, however, a second narrative of how Patagonia has been key in configuring territorial identities. This second narrative contests the image of Patagonia as natural refuge or promised land and proposes a darker depiction that refers to state repression, such as ethnic cleansing campaigns, led by President Roca in the 1870s. The video that accompanies the installation makes clear this sharp contrast: the colossal beauty of Tierra del Fuego, its open bays and its coasts, and the clean presence of its blue skies, set against the oppressive interiors of the penitentiary. The video focuses mainly on the prison's installations; walls, corridors, and windows are transformed artistically by shots that place the spectator in the position of the protagonist's isolation and let us contemplate a sky and a promise of freedom that will never be reached figs. 3.2 and 3.3 The exterior and interior views are dissected by complex structures of grids and other geometric forms such as doors, windows, and columns, aesthetically representing the prisoner's confinement. Opposed to what critics of globalization have referred to as the "metaphor of unidirectional flux" (García Canclini 54) and the fantasies of an unrestricted mobility of first-class global citizens, the suffocation of the prison's interiors renders visible the hidden constraints of spatial practices in the age of globalization. Moreover, the prison functions as a metaphor for the national frontier as a repressive spatiality. As Ibis Hernandez, a curator of the biennial reminds us, installations such as Gache's that take place in the prison, "send us to experience the psychological time where the present exists only as a memory of the past or as a transit toward a future freedom. Some works staged there refer not so much to physical confinement, but to the temporal experience of being entrapped by invisible walls such as [the ones represented by] the obsession with fashion, the consumerist attitude, the hounding of the media, the restrictions imposed by false beliefs...." (www.finaldelmundo.org-BienalFindelMundo).

In *Diario de la luna caníbal,* Gache explores notions of temporal and physical confinement by depicting the prison's interior space as Patagonia's dark side. Thus, Gache's interior and exterior landscapes stress processes of cultural exchange and visual appropriation because they implicate previous representations of the area. As such, the landscapes depicted in *Diario de la luna caníbal* are a "dynamic medium" that interweaves a "vast network of cultural codes" (Mitchell 9). As spectators, we can appreciate the visual construction of Ushuaia as a site where different cultural codes clash as repressive perceptions of space supersede the exterior "openness" of the natural world. This interpretation is further sustained by the journal that accompanies the video, which tells a compelling narrative of the ways in which Patagonia, as the last frontier, has been a violent site of repression. In Gache's previous works, the moon is an icon of futurist imagery (e.g., *Lunas Eléctricas para una noche sin luna*) or a reference of textual and visual compositions that follow a collage-like structure (e.g.,

148 • Gendered Spaces in Argentine Women's Literature

Figure 3.2 *Diario de la luna caníbal* (video still). Photograph taken from inside a prison cell. Used with permission of Belén Gache.

Luna India [*Indian Moon*]). Here, the moon is a narrative agent and a cultural reference, which points to social and cultural constraints embedded in spatial structures.

The title of the installation comes from a Selk'nam myth that describes a lunar eclipse when the cannibal moon will turn red with the blood of men doomed to die in a coming battle. The text for the installation, organized around 21 journal entries that correspond to different moon cycles, reflects the protagonist's progressive psychological deterioration. The reference to the myth comes from a text by Anne Chapman that describes the importance of matriarchy in the mythical ceremony of initiation, the Hain, in Selk'nam society. According to the myth, women, led by Moon [Kreeh], held the Hain ceremony that guaranteed women's ruling or matriarchal system for centuries. Men were forced into all sorts of servile tasks and feared women because of the supernatural powers they supposedly displayed while the Hain was taking place. According to different accounts by Anne Chapman and Martin Gusinde, men eventually found out women's lies and murdered the moon and the rest of the women. A patriarchal system where men conducted the Hain was established, and women were forbidden from participating in the ceremony (Chapman 66–77).

The journal reenacts this myth and its references to women as cannibals. Gache employs a series of aesthetic images to represent the matriarchal order of the moon as a phantasmal or empty space where the inmate sees his delusional fantasies reflected. White imagery predominates in the descriptions of the moon as a shining mirror, a snowy presence, or a blinding light that confuses the sense of space and time and that progressively reflects the protagonist losing his mind. Contrasted with the history of Patagonia and the recurrent efforts to delimit and mark the national space, the representation of an ambiguous or empty spatiality described in the journal as feminine is quite pertinent. Feminist readings about the construction of women as an empty spatiality are relevant here. The image of the mirror has been analyzed, for instance, from a psychoanalytical perspective by Kaja Silverman, who studies the impact of the mirror-stage on male and female formations of subjectivity. In her study on psychoanalysis and cinema, Silverman explores how women have been characterized as men's reflections and how "woman

Figure 3.3 *Diario de la luna caníbal* (video still). Usuhaia Prison (exterior). Behind, the Cinco Hermanos Mountains. Used with permission of Belén Gache.

Figure 3.4 *Diario de la luna caníbal.* Promotional image for the installation. Used with permission of Belén Gache.

has been made the repository not only of lack but specularity" (26). Along these lines, Gillian Rose has made evident how geography represents women as an empty space where a holistic sense of self can be re-created—a "topophilia," an original place that can be equated with the idea of the mother (85). In other instances, women have been depicted as the empty nature in landscapes, a passive subject that can be observed, possessed, and represented by men (95). Gache employs similar visual constructs when she describes the moon as a phantasmagoric presence that eventually takes over the prison and the consciousness of the inmate. The moon is a mirror that creates fantastic duplications of the prison cell:

> En otras épocas, pensaban que la luna era un espejo. Si esto fuera así, supongo que en la luna habría otra prisión y, en ella, otro penado como yo. A veces pienso, en cambio, que soy yo el que está en la luna y, allá en la Tierra, hay un penado que se me asemeja.
>
> [In other eras, people thought the moon was a mirror. If that were true, I imagine that there would be another prison on the moon, and inside it

would be another prisoner like me. Sometimes, I think that it's the other way around, that I'm the one who is on the moon and that out there on Earth is a prisoner who resembles me.] (*Diario de la luna caníbal*, n. pag.)

The moon dematerializes space; its shiny light invades the cell to the point that the constraining interior becomes a site of delusion and madness. The presence of the moon is also compared to the empty space of the page that the inmate seeks to cover with "black ink": "En mis noches de insomnio, escribo a escondidas de la luna. Ella no debe enterarse. Ella quiere los papeles siempre blancos, plateados, brillantes. La luna siempre escribe con tinta blanca. Yo tapo el papel con la sombra de mis letras negras." [On nights when I can't sleep, I write in secret, hiding from the moon. The moon mustn't find out. She wants the papers to be forever white, silver and shiny. The moon always writes with white ink. I cover the paper with the shadow of my black letters] (n. pag.). At the end, his precarious writing is interrupted by intense migraines and the demonic presence of the moon: "Por las noches, cuando todos duermen, yo escribo a oscuras sobre las paredes de mi celda. Allí escribo verdades y denuncio injusticias; acuso traidores y develo secretos. Por las mañanas, cuando intento leer mis textos, sólo encuentro la pared cruzada por rayas sin sentido." [At night, when everyone is asleep, I write on the walls of my cell in the dark. There I write truths and I denounce injustices; I accuse traitors and reveal secrets. In the morning, when I try to read my texts, all I find is a wall covered with meaningless scratches] (n. pag.). (Fig. 4.4)

The fragility of the prisoner's writing as described here invites several reflections. Gache establishes a dialogue with the Patagonian imagery of travel journals and navigation diaries that proposes that writing in the borders of empires or national frontiers is a transitional passage of self-definition, although the diary represents a progressive dissolution of the exile's subjectivity, as the fantastic ending makes evident. Located at the "end of the world," this fantastic drive can be interpreted as a consequence of the cultural contrasts and perceptions the protagonist experiences, but read from the feminist frame proposed by Silverman and Rose, the "failing" to write and the progressive loss of reason can be directly linked to the impossibility of symbolization. In other words, the moon is the empty space that needs to be demarcated and symbolized in the process of identity creation; however, the attempt fails with the protagonist's disappearance. The maddening effects of the moon are, therefore, consequences of life on the border and, in this way, *Diario de la luna caníbal* establishes a dialogue with previous narrative accounts that have shaped the imagery of Tierra del Fuego as a site that disrupts cultural and epistemological codes, as previously discussed in Iparraguirre's novel, *La tierra del fuego*. Thus, Gache's installation plays with a double image of Patagonia that is both spectacular, a touristic construction for the global eyes, and spectral, for it brings forward the failed narratives of identity and space that historically have tried to accomplish the writing, for instance, of the national borders. On another level, the reference to the Selk'nam myth foregrounds the histories of repression and genocide and makes evident the role of memory in the territorial identity of Argentina, for it reworks many of the imperial fantasies that, through the discourses of nation-building and tourism, sought to "mercantilize" the experiences of a natural world ("Desert Dreams," Nouzeilles 258). *Diario de la luna caníbal* is a counternarrative that interrupts the historical association between Patagonia and utopian dreams of modernization, for it is memory that allows for the redefinition of these foundational discourses that, like the writers of the generations of 1837 and 1880, sought to define a territorial identity for Argentina. Thus, *Diario de la luna caníbal* is an example of a process of deterritorialization that questions the building of territories both as spatial and symbolic practices that create narratives of identity used in processes of nation-building and modernization. Read against other literary projects embodied by writers such as Diana Bellessi and Eduardo Belgrano Rawson in Argentina, or Juan Pablo Riveros and Clemente Riedemann in Chile, who also located their projects in Patagonia and Tierra del Fuego, Gache's *Diario de la luna caníbal* establishes a dialogue with these writers who also questioned the violent history of territorialization of the southern areas of Argentina and Chile.[19] The reference to the original inhabitants, such as the Selk'nams, Yahgans, or Mapuches, in all of these accounts is not accidental, for it makes evident how territories are the result of historic power struggles in the borders of national and global orders. Moreover, by stressing the importance of displaced voices in the historical building of the nation-state, a text such as Gache's establishes the need to question the construction of an imagined community and deconstructs the notion of territoriality as a discourse that enables dramatic narratives of place Andermann, The Optic.

I would like to emphasize two central implications of Gache's nomadic, deterritorialized writing. The first aspect has to do with how nomadic writing connects to feminist claims about transcending the negative restrictions of territoriality and literary authorship. In Latin America, Ana Forcinito has studied the political ramifications of nomadism as a feminist interpretative tool, and Rossi Braidotti claims in *Nomadic Subjects* that nomadism is a political and epistemological tool that can enable a feminist decentering (Braidotti 22). Forcinito analyzes, for instance, how during the 1990s, women writers' practice of nomadic memory deconstructs territorial forms of patriarchy and authoritarianism (20). As in the work of Iparraguirre, Gache's *Diario de la luna caníbal* resorts to memory as an instrument of denunciation that, in the context of twenty-first century Argentina, clearly connects with the issue of memory predominant in the cultural politics of the period. *Diario de la luna caníbal* represents memorializing as an act deeply impacted by globalization. The prisoner's "senseless scratching" that each night mysteriously disappears from the prison's walls serves as a metaphor for how electronic media threatens the culture of writing. Furthermore, the testimonial aspects of *Diario de la luna caníbal* cannot be overlooked. Like *La tierra del fuego,* this installation locates testimonial claims about authoritarianism and repression in the southern confines of Argentine territory and brings attention to the violence and power embedded in spatial constructions. Thus, by conflating space and memory, both Gache and Iparraguirre show that imaginations of place are bound to cartographies of power and knowledge that at both the global and national levels have produced different forms of social exclusion. Gache's tribute to encyclopedic knowledge and Iparraguirre's devotion to the intricate connections of the literary traditions of the nineteenth century are excellent examples of how both authors, even when acknowledging the overarching presence of media at the turn of the twenty-first century, emphasize the transcendence of books as solid artifacts that challenge the volatility of the cultures of globalization. They both propose a complex association between literary culture and memory, thus providing new meanings for a devaluated culture of books in the Argentina of the turn of the twenty-first century.

Additionally, Gache's nomadic writing decenters notions relevant to the literary culture of Argentina. By combining writing and electronic media, she delves into the tradition of interactivity, spatiality, and the exploration of new linguistic and visual formats that began with the avant-gardes of the twentieth century. Her works give the tradition of fantastic literature, cultivated by authors such as Julio Cortázar, new dimensions as she explores the transformations produced by electronic media. The composition of her works, namely the way in which notions of authorship and readership are reworked by the influence of electronic formats, follows a trend increasingly important in Latin American literature (Castillo 233). However, intersections of media and literature render visible the ways in which Gache also moves toward reterritorialization, or what Carlos Jáuregui calls "virtual territorialization," for writing communities on the Internet are characterized by the "*search for textual authority* and *virtual territorialization*; in other words, the mimicking of certain practices of the printed world as a response to the loss of cyberliterature's aura, to its deterritorialization and fleetingness" (emphasis in the original, 290). In this "virtual territorialization," Gache proposes alternative conformations of territoriality that contest previous literary and spatial models. By resorting to the notion of nomadism and spatial decentering, the Gache's works describe territories as textual and spatial networks of multiple localities, thus adopting the notion of territory defined by global digital culture (Sassen, *Territory* 338). Gache's virtual territories show how digital media can be a powerful tool for contesting social exclusions, thus emphasizing how digital global culture is embedded into "larger societal, cultural, subjective, economic, and imaginary structurations of lived experience" (Sassen 344). At the turn of the twenty-first century, when space seems to become volatile under the overpowering influences of media and transnational forces, Gache proposes that nomadism is a countercultural practice, a way to construct virtual textual and spatial networks that can lead to a transnational solidarity that challenges the limitations of territoriality and power (Mohanty 3).

To conclude, global imaginations of place play a central role in the works by Iparraguirre and Gache as they reshape nationalist topographies such as the frontier and the national territory. They focus on a global imagery of Patagonia and create virtual territorial configurations. Aided by a rich tradition of cultural references, Iparraguirre and Gache rework the Patagonian landscape as a place of national and global connections, a territory to be redefined as a liminal space or borderland that includes previously marginalized voices in the shaping of a spatial memory for the country. Their works address how national territory and national literature are associated and create a critical dialogism that can be compared to what Mignolo calls "border thinking," a strategy that generates an epistemological and political decentering of "global designs"("Many Faces" 180). The works by Iparraguirre and Gache challenge historical legacies in Argentina and propose critical interpretations of space; they move from a process of deterritorialization to one that seeks to build new territorial networks that propose alternative forms of authority while questioning the concept of territory as a historic legacy of authoritarianism and repression. Iparraguirre resorts to a colonialist imagery of the maritime culture of the nineteenth century, whereas Gache employs the rich culture of premodern Europe and links it to media and hypertexts of the twenty-first century. They use memory as an interpretative tool for questioning territorialism and essentialist claims that link identity and space. And finally, they place their works in a geography of borderlands that explores new locations for Argentina's literary culture. By constructing these borderland topographies, they foreground the relationships that space maintains with gender, class, race, and nation. As their new cartographies rewrite traditional supports of writing through the use of the travel and the hypertext, Iparraguirre and Gache develop strategies for decentering the national literary canon. They reflect on writing and territorialism, both understood as key strategies in the composition of cultural maps of struggle and domination.

La tierra del fuego and *Diario de la luna caníbal* can be read as two examples of key critical interventions women can make in national and global imaginations of place. The critical examination conducted here of the associations among territory, writing, and the political "imagining of place" raises the question of the role of women's writing in the destabilization of territorial models and global designs as conducted by Iparraguirre and Gache. Although this feminist writing of the national space is yet to be consolidated, the area of the Southern Cone, as Masiello contends, abounds in tentative examples of feminisms of this sort. The works analyzed here can be placed within a corpus of examples in which neoliberal Argentina and Chile have questioned how women and other minorities are placed within the syntax of global exchanges, such as the south-north paradigm (Masiello, *The Art* 109). Journals such as *Feminaria* in Argentina and *Revista de Crítica Cultural* [*Journal of Cultural Criticism*] in Chile have also proposed a political and aesthetic decentering as the root of a reflection on globalization and transnational flows (118). As liminal experiences of the border are being reproduced in literary and artistic productions of the Southern Cone, the task of constructing a critical discourse to dismantle the "territorialities of masculinism" (Rose 151) still remains to be done. In this vein, productions by women like Iparraguirre and Gache open a new frontier for these critical inquiries.

CHAPTER 4

Poetic Crossovers: The Paradoxical Spaces of Women's Poetry

¿Por qué estás triste?—pregunta una mujer de ojos claros y me enseña algo. Es un globo terráqueo que puede deplegarse. Lo levanto y lo miro. Lo hago girar. Abro el mundo que empieza a transcurrir, a fluir sobre la gran pantalla de lo inexplicable. A deshacerse en mis manos como un canto inspirado, un archipiélago de silencios.
(María Negroni, *El viaje de la noche* 36)

[Why are you sad?" asks a clear-eye woman, pointing to something. It is a globe that unfurls. I pick it up and examine it. Set it spinning. I open the world that begins to take place, to flow over the large screen of the inexplicable. To come apart in my hands like an inspired song, an archipelago of silences.][1] Unless otherwise noted, Cindy Schuster has been in charge of all translations.
María Negroni, "The Map of Time"
(*Night Journey,* Twitty 37)

The woman poet as a nomad, an exile, an outcast. Navigating in a fragile boat, exiled in a desolated island, sitting at the location of an imaginary South. The poetic voices of the works of Diana Bellessi, Luisa Futoransky, and María Negroni depict these virtual geographies; they invite the reader, as the opening quote makes evident, to envision a world of endless possibilities. As a series of reflections on place and location, this corpus of poetry reveals the creation of spatial margins and the "persistent presence of difference" in social spatialities (Blunt and Rose 16). Written both within and outside the boundaries of national traditions, the poetry collections analyzed here cross over different geographies, poetic styles, and aesthetic traditions to form poetic paradoxical spaces that, in tune with social and political developments in Argentina, entice reflection on memory and mourning, the intersections of local and global realities, and the postnational and postcolonial experiences by women writers. In Diana Bellessi's *Crucero ecuatorial* [*Ecuatorial Cruise*] (1980), *Tributo del mudo* [*The Tribute of the One Who Cannot Speak;* trans. Le Guin] (1982), *El jardín* [*The Garden*] (1992), *Sur* [*South*] (1998), and *Mate cocido* [*Mate Tea*] (2002), images of nature, landscape, and travel are at the root of a proposed spatial decolonization of women's and indigenous peoples' social imaginaries. Luisa Futoransky's *Babel, Babel* (1968), *Partir, digo* [*To Leave, I Say*] (1982), *Prender de gajo* [*Transplant*] (2006), *Inclinaciones* [*Inclinations*] (2006), and *Seqüana barrosa* [*Muddy Sequana*] (2007) employ nomadism as an aesthetic strategy to deterritorialize the politics of memory through a postmodern use of collage, humor, and artifice. In *Islandia* [*Iceland*] (1993) and *El viaje de la noche* [*Night Journey*] (1994), María Negroni rewrites national space through allegory; she compares the world of poetry to Iceland, a lost homeland for exiles seeking refuge in virtual memories taking place outside of the limits of national traditions. In all three cases, the politics of memory is central as these poets challenge identifications between memory and space—in particular, a national space, which is at the root of political practices that characterize Argentina's postdictatorial scene. In addition, by challenging how women and other underrepresented social groups, such as indigenous people or immigrants, are erased from representations of the national space, these poets rewrite imaginary national geographies from a decentered perspective that explores alternative symbolic topographies and new notions of identity and citizenship.

I am not proposing here that the construction of marginal spaces in poetry prevails only in poetry written by women authors. Rather, I analyze how this corpus of poetry offers a series of examples of the ways in which literature addresses the production of gendered social spaces. Gender works as one of the many ways in which the landscape of social relations is reinterpreted through spatial categories. The decision to focus on these particular women authors comes from the keen awareness that predominates in their works of the links between gender and space and the central role of poetic expression in unveiling the pervasive influence of spatial discrimination in Argentine society. In the social movements of postdictatorial Argentina, poetry has played a central role in producing a reflection on the main themes that dominate the literary imagination of the period: memory and the discussion on human rights, experiences of exile and internal and external displacement, the insurgence of new social actors, such as local activists from neighborhoods (the barrios), and young people, women, and union members (Jelin, 16–17). As Bellessi recalls, in 2001 and 2002, the years of the Argentine economic and political collapse, poets were present at numerous demonstrations or in picket lines against the shutting down of factories, and in certain instances, some poetry was printed on T-shirts that demonstrators wore during urban protests (personal interview, June 27, 2007). Although poetry has traditionally been considered a marginal genre in the editorial market and its readership has been perceived as limited, the collections examined here challenge this presumed marginality by proposing that the genre is a powerful discourse for investigating the role of literature in the social and political developments of a society in crisis. As Francine Masiello states, during the period of dictatorship and redemocratization in both Argentina and Chile, poetry unsettled the discourses of totalitarianism and neoliberalism, as well as the demands of the market; the impressive production of books and journals devoted to poetry, along with a number of activities that seek the cultivation of the genre, demonstrate the centrality of its role in the return to a democratic society in the 1980s and 1990s (*Art* 223–24). In Argentina, four seminal poetry journals published in the 1980s—*Diario de Poesía*, *Último Reino*, *XUL*, and *La Danza del Ratón*—as well as the appearance of independent publishing houses such as El Imaginero, Tierra Baldía, Libros de Tierra Firme, and Ediciones del Búho Encantado, allowed for a close communication between new and old poetic generations and a rapid circulation of new works (Fondebrider, 27–29). In a cultural scene increasingly dominated by global influences and themes, Argentine poetry in recent decades also challenges what Luis Cárcamo-Huechante and José Antonio Mazzotti describe as the "socio-cultural perception" that the genre enjoyed in the 1950s, 1960s, and early 1970s, which forged a close relation between poetic discourse and utopia and infused poetry with political undertones. Although poetry, such as that considered here, possesses traits of elegy, irony, parody, and allegory that challenge what Cárcamo-Huechante and Mazzotti consider the utopian force seemingly lost in contemporary poetry (12), I believe there also exists a lyrical vindication of poetry as an instrument of social awareness and political engagement, something particularly evident in the critique of social spatialities present in the works of Bellessi, Futoransky, and Negroni.

In the period from the 1970s to the 2000s, the region of the Southern Cone witnessed an unprecedented number of experiences of displacement, migration, travel, and exile, as evidenced in the poetry considered here. In the case of Argentina, this includes the generalized political repression and violence that forced thousands to flee the country in the 1970s and 1980s, the increase in immigration from neighboring countries like Bolivia and

Paraguay because of favorable economic conditions under the neoliberal policies of President Carlos Saúl Menem (1989–1999), and the growing possibilities for travel and international tourism due to the impact of globalization. Such displacements, as Caren Kaplan notes, are not all the same, even when modernist representations of movement, location, and homelessness in contemporary critical practices, "create ahistorical amalgams" that leave out the material histories behind them ("Becoming Nomad" 2). As Cárcamo-Huechante and Mazzotti explain, the advance of the free market and neoliberalism, as well as the effects of globalization in Latin America, has posed new challenges to the role of national and local cultural contexts. Poetry reveals these issues by depicting "abstract" or "deterritorialized" representations of signs and subjects (13). However, as evidenced by poetry considered in this chapter, women poets, who acquired a protagonist role within the poetic field of production of this period in Latin America, describe the specificity of languages and locations and the concrete, historic struggles of Latin America's politic and social bodies (15).

Experiences of travel, exile, and nomadism shape the poetry by Bellessi, Futoransky, and Negroni, wherein a rich and complex poetic language describes the difficulties of moving through local and global spaces experienced by women and other social subjects historically displaced in Argentine society, particularly migrants, indigenous peoples, political exiles. This poetry establishes what Gillian Rose describes as "paradoxical spaces," defying the construction of a fixed positionality and implying a politics of resistance and subjectivity: "This space is multidimensional, shifting and contingent. It is also paradoxical, by which I mean that spaces that would be mutually exclusive if charted on a two-dimensional map—centre and margin, inside and outside—are occupied simultaneously" (*Feminism* 140). Located both inside and outside of what Rose calls the "territoriality of masculinism," these women authors confront social locations determined by gender, sexuality, class, and race, as well as by a whole range of other relations that position women and other subjects in a situation of social disadvantage (151). Such "paradoxical spaces" challenge the ways in which we conceptualize space. Rose, a feminist geographer who disputes the idea that space is a transparent category, as certain geographic discourses want us to believe, states that "space itself—and landscape and place likewise—far from being firm foundations for disciplinary expertise and power, are insecure, precarious and fluctuating" (160).

What does poetry teach us about these paradoxical locations? In a global world where placelessness seems to be the rule, poetry invites us to reflect on how places still possess a symbolic role in defining identity and language. And although poetry critically examines the connections between place and identity through the production of paradoxical poetic spaces that are depicted as fragile and vulnerable constructions on the brink of collapse, the women authors studied here engage in a thorough reflection on places as social constructions very much in line with Doreen Massey's critical examinations on place from a geographical perspective. Massey conceptualizes places as processes where social interactions take place over time (therefore time is embedded in spatial categories); boundaries as porous connections with the global world ("boundaries may of course be necessary for the purposes of certain types of studies for instance, but they are not necessary for the conceptualization of a place itself"); and finally, as entities full of internal conflicts as they connect to identity not from the perspective of a "uniqueness" of a place: the specificity of a place is continually reproduced (155). Language and subjectivity play a central role in these poetic redefinitions of place. The collections studied here abound in examples of a paradoxical polyglossia that includes a number of poetic styles that, cultivated since the 1960s, acquire in the context of globalization a new and important role: conversational, neobaroque, indigenous poetry. Multiple languages characterize a poetic expression that, in the case of Bellessi, opens new places in the poem to invite myriad voices that had been erased from colonial and masculinist geographies. As a "poetic explorer," Bellessi rewrites the discourse of colonization in Latin America and stretches her poetic geographies in a dialogic space that is characterized by contradictory temporalities of eulogy and utopia.

1. At the Mercy of the Elements: Diana Bellessi's Earthworks

The aesthetic relationship with nature is a key force shaping Bellessi's poetic production. In her early collections *Crucero ecuatorial* (1980) and *Tributo del mudo* (1982), Bellessi examines the role of nature from what Eliana Ortega calls an "exploratory perspective," where the poet employs real and imaginary geographies of America as the soil for her poetry. Written during the dictatorships of the 1970s and 1980s, while Bellessi was living on the delta of the Río de la Plata, her works examine representations of nature as central in crafting a sense of poetic belonging and estrangement. *Crucero ecuatorial,* a set of vignettes about her trips throughout Latin America, focuses on foreign topographies and world wanderers, whereas *Tributo del mudo* uses references to Chinese poetry and oriental landscapes to build spatial defamiliarization through a series of contemplative images of death and memory. As poetic reflections about space and location and about nature and the role of poetry in transforming and building cultural landscapes, both collections address experiences of travel as ways of establishing connections between the individual and the universal, a topic that Bellessi addresses at length in the essays compiled in *Lo propio y lo ajeno* [*The Self and the Other*] (1996). For instance, referring to *Crucero ecuatorial*, Bellessi states in an interview with Alicia Genovese and María del Carmen Colombo that her travels throughout Latin America revealed the impression of both identification and distance with the places she visited, a sense of being at home in the world very much along the lines of Walt Whitman's poetry. As a Latin American explorer, Bellessi comments, she was able to experience firsthand the myth of the "Patria Grande," or Latin America as a continental homeland (Genovese and Colombo).

In *El jardín* [*The Garden*] (1993), aesthetic encounters with nature supersede the forces of authoritarianism that had dominated Argentine society during the majority of the twentieth century. In this collection, Bellessi elaborates on topics and poetic strategies also present in *Eróica* (1988), where she depicts an entrance to a primitive and sacred world by using metaphors of erotic and heroic encounters where love and hunting describe how the poetic speaker approaches a sacred connection with others. In *El jardín*, such an encounter is made possible by the aesthetic gaze that replaces vision as a tool of nature's possession and domination; the "garden" refers both to the geography of the Rio de la Plata's delta where Bellessi spent long periods of time, and to a depiction of "eden," the vegetable garden she cultivated as a child, the daughter of Italian immigrants working on farms in the province of Santa Fe. Poems like "Un día antes de la revolución ["The Day before the Revolution"] (trans. Le Guin) and "Manhattan Revisited" explore the culture-nature binary and the possibilities of decolonizing civilization by a return to a natural order. The latter juxtaposes a series of poetic images: a puma wandering the streets of New York, the works and images of primitive peoples, such as the cannibals in New Guinea, hanging on a museum's walls, and the spoken language of immigrants in the barrio. Through these poetic encounters of culture and nature, the poet explores the possibilities of a "counter revolution" in which the natural world reverses the powers of violence and authoritarianism. By building the poem as a carefully assembled sacred garden, the poet seeks in its natural space possibilities of reconciliation and internal dialogue:

> He construido un jardín como quien hace
> los gestos correctos en el lugar errado.
> Errado, no de error, sino de lugar otro,
> como hablar con el reflejo del espejo
> y no con quien se mira en él.

He construido un jardín para dialogar
allí, codo a codo con la belleza, con la siempre
muda pero activa muerte trabajando el corazón.
[I have built a garden like someone
who makes right moves in the wrong place.
Not the wrong of a mistake, but of another space,
like talking to the reflection in a mirror,
not the person looking into it.
I have constructed a garden as a place of dialogue,
shoulder to shoulder with beauty, with the always
silent but persistent death working the heart.] (*Tener* 469)[1]

Like Foucault's heterotopias, Bellessi's garden is both a real and unreal "other space" that mirrors society's own predicaments and failures to establish a more democratic and egalitarian order.[2]

In *Sur* (1998), the poet examines, through images of nature, the many places of colonization shaping the difficult dialogue between "lo propio y lo ajeno" and its legacies of linguistic and racial exclusions. From the onset, this reflection centers on experiences of displacement by the indigenous populations of America. Prefaced by the words of one of the last Selk'nam women of Tierra del Fuego, Angela Loij, "No tengo nada de tierra, ni cosa, no tengo" [I have no land, no belongings, I have nothing], this collection seeks to establish a cultural exchange among multiple histories of colonization of the continent:

A Lola Kiepja
Agustina Kilchamal
Ailton Krenax
Y a las voces anónimas que en los dichos y en los cantos de los Pueblos Americanos, aun forzados en la escritura, violentados en la traducción, han sido el manantial del que abrevan los poemas de este libro. Doy gracias a sus almas que se dejan oír, que sueñan y siembran en la oreja impropia de la hija perdida.
[Dedicated to Lola Kiepja
Agustina Kilchamal
Ailton Krenax,
and to the anonymous voices, which in the sayings and songs of the American Peoples, although stilted in writing and distorted by translation, have been the spring that feeds the poems in this book. I give thanks to their souls for allowing themselves to be heard, and for dreaming and sowing their seeds in the undeserving ear of their lost daughter.] (*Tener* 515)[3]

Sur is, above all, a reflection on how location impacts poetry. The first poem opens with an invocation to Lola Kiepja, another Selk'nam survivor: "Oh Kiepja no me dejes / sentar en hain equivocado" [Oh Kiepja don't let me / sit in the wrong *hain*] (emphasis in the original, *Tener* 520). The Hain, a mythical place in Selk'nam's matriarchal society where women performed secret ceremonies to perpetuate their power becomes in *Sur* a site for feminist resistance, a place to establish a collective memory of territorial, cultural, and linguistic exclusions on the continent.[4] Through this spatial image, Bellessi proposes a complex relationship between poetry and temporality in which the poem is both anachronic and utopic, as it recovers the lost wor(l)ds of those excluded from hegemonic historical narratives and establishes a space for virtual poetic exchanges, a tension that Bellessi later explores in *Mate cocido* (2002), *La edad dorada* [*The Golden Age*] (2003), and *La rebelión del instante* [*Rebellion of the Moment*] (2005).

Spatial constructions in *Sur* acquire both static and dynamic characteristics. Central to the collection is the idea of the local as a point of articulation or, a site for intersecting spatial networks (Massey 120) that connects different histories of colonization. Although the "South" adopts the form of a bounded place, a site of historical nostalgia, the "local," or a place of feminine identity and feminist resistance in references to the Hain, Bellessi describes this geopolitical location through another compelling spatial image, that of the "río de no retorno" [river of no return], a metaphor for the entire continent (122). Through the spatial dynamism of the river, the "South" represents a fluid medium, and the words of oral languages establish a conflicting relation with the lettered culture. In this oral quality of Bellessi's poetry, we can detect influences of the colloquial or conversational poetry popular in Argentina in the 1960s and 1970s. Authors such as Juan Gelman, Francisco Urondo, Juana Bignozzi, and César Fernández Moreno are among those who promoted the notion that poetry needed to be structured according to oral language. In "La experiencia de la poesía" ["The Poetic Experience"], Bellessi reiterates these ideas by contrasting poetic language, "un habla" [a kind of speech] that runs like a river, with formal discourses seeking to dominate and control. Poetry, in Bellessi's words, is

> un esclavo liberado, un gaucho detrás de la frontera, un compadrito en la cornisa del arrabal, una renegada que escapa de las células primarias construidas para fijar y repetir economías de opresión, como los roles sexuales y los modelos congelados y únicos de familia al servicio de productividades perversas.
>
> [a slave set free, a *gaucho* beyond the frontier, a *compadrito* at the margin of the slum, a (female) renegade who escapes from the foundational

cells constructed to prescribe and replicate economies of oppression, such as sex roles and rigid, singular models of the family that serve to perpetuate perverse productivities.] (15)

A river running through different oppressive spatialities, poetry has the power to transgress, rebuild, and transform historical locations. The poetic form of *Sur* reflects this mobility through space by re-creating the rhythms and metric structures of the spoken language, exemplified by breaks in the alignment of verse and syntax through enjambment; multiple internal and open-ended dialogues with different poetic subjects through the use of rhetorical questions; the inclusion of shorter verses, in many cases of less than nine syllables; and the creation of an emotional language through the use of diminutives. Bellessi's style, which she characterizes as "lyrical" in that it opposes other trends in Argentine poetry more centered on content than form, such as "objetivismo" [objectivism] ("La lírica vuelve a casa") ["Lyric Poetry Comes Home"], disrupts not only poetic ideals of contention within the form, but also highlights the complex connections between language, power, and location. Thus, the opening dedication to "the anonymous voices, which in the sayings and songs of the American Peoples, although stilted in writing and distorted by translation," (*Tener* 515) acquires new meanings. Poetry enables a virtual communication that, as Ortega reminds us, "grasps without possessing" the multiple voices embedded in histories of colonization and builds a "Southern resistance" against acculturation. Contrary to the colonized language and the violent linguistic encounters in translation, *Sur* builds poetic crossovers that challenge the spatial and linguistic dynamics of colonization while building new spaces for cultural memory within and outside the poem.

Images of nature as described in the history of American colonization are central in this investigation into connections between power, language, and space in *Sur*. In his study on rural scenery and society in English poetry from 1630 to 1660, James Turner examines the ways in which the European pictorial tradition formed an ideal of landscape that dominated European taste for centuries and influenced literary representations of nature. Organized theatrically according to principles of light and dark, wings and backdrop, landscape was conceived both in literature and art as an ideal and harmonious aesthetic structure through which the poet could obtain the "World's true image" (15–16). However, as W. J. T. Michell points out, landscapes bear ideological components as they represent exchanges, visual appropriations, and processes of identity formation (2). In *Sur,* the poet examines, through the building of a poetic landscape, the formation of social and subjective identities; landscapes therefore embody linguistic and cultural exchanges as they represent the geography of a "contact zone," a site of transculturation that describes the "spatial and temporal co-presence of subjects previously separated by geographic and historical disjunctures" (Pratt, *Imperial Eyes* 7). Bellessi's landscapes follow the poetic tradition of Juan L. Ortiz's "eco-poetry" in that the poems in *Sur* call attention to critical and vital connections between human and natural orders (Forns-Broggi 35). According to Francine Masiello, this ethical relation between the natural and the political shapes the "nature" of Bellessi's poetry. Collections like *Sur* establish novel geopolitical relations with the land in order to offer poetic and political possibilities for an imaginary community with strong bonds to the natural world ("La naturaleza" 69). The landscape is central in this geopolitical reformulation of space: it invites a dialogue with others that critically reexamines spatialization processes and their impact on identity formation in America. Keenly aware of the importance of nature as a critical element in denouncing the injustices on a global scale, Bellessi advocates through this dialogical use of landscapes the creation of a new poetic language that questions authoritarian discourses and the violence of territorial processes in the entire continent.

"Naturaleza encantada…" ["Enchanted Nature…"] re-creates, for instance, both spatially and linguistically, the tensions of colonial encounters. The title ironically refers to the image of an "enchanted nature" prevalent in depictions in early chronicles and travel diaries by Spaniards arriving to the continent. Contrary to European views of a colonized nature, the poet describes the American landscape as "sacred residence," a site to establish a cultural dialogue with painful memories of colonization. The title ironically refers to the transformation of nature into an "enchanted" product of colonization, a fetish built upon a series of European cultural codes and images. The implied tension between these two world views—nature as a product of capitalism, nature as a sacred resource—takes the form of an internal dialogue in which the poet questions the language of domination used by colonizers like Columbus to possess and domesticate nature. "Naturaleza encantada…" examines nature as a cultural and linguistic construction of language. The poem uses figures of speech like the synecdoche to name the aberrations of colonization, where words and swords have the same destructive effects on nature. Bellessi's poem reverses the meaning of "enchanted" and its implications on possessing nature through language by cultivating a sense of mystery around it. Nature is rather a space of uncertainties, a fragile residence, and a site to explore an "enchanted," original, and sacred relation with the natural world. By distorting and mimicking European aesthetic conventions on landscape, "Naturaleza encantada…" critically revises the links between the formation of cultural ideas on landscape and colonialism.

The poem's closing question—"¿Quién gime aquí?" [Who wails here]—highlights the dramatic transformation of the landscape into a memorial, a fertile soil for virtual encounters with the victims of colonization. As the "basis for a meditation on the advantage about dialogue and exchange" (Masiello, *Art* 163), the landscape in Bellessi's poetry describes a sense of poetic otherness and mystery through which the poet seeks to re-create new forms of cultural communication with the disappeared original inhabitants of America.

As "Naturaleza encantada..." prompts a reflection on language as a key element in cultural definitions of space, "Una moneda por el par de orejas..." [A Coin for a Pair of Ears] and "Ojo imperial" [Imperial Eye] describe the gaze as a way of constructing nature. Both poems refer to later stages in the colonization of America. "Una moneda por el par de orejas..." speaks directly about the 1886 gold expedition to Tierra del Fuego by Julius Popper and the violent extermination of the Selk'nams carried out by *estancieros* [ranchers] and gold miners like him at the end of the nineteenth century. Along with "Ojo Imperial," this poem recycles European travel archives by sailors such as James Cook who, since the eighteenth century, explored the most southern areas of the continent. "Una moneda por el par de orejas..." clashes two spatial perspectives, the land and the sea, as embodied by the figures of the mestizo in the Cordillera and the colonizer seeing from the ocean. The Fuegian landscape is the site where the poet establishes a dialogue between those perspectives; personifications of the wind, the mountain, the moon, and the native vegetation allow the voices of those murdered by the Europeans to surface. Such references to exploratory and colonizing travels of the nineteenth century can be read against experiences of neoliberalism and globalization that impacted Argentina in the 1990s when policies by then president Saul Menem sought to incorporate the country into a new global order. Written during this period, *Sur* examines the uneven effects of notions of global mobility in cultural encounters between Europe and America.[5] The "South" is a poetic geopolitical space that epitomizes these ideas. Anchored in sites such as Tierra del Fuego, this collection builds a virtual poetic space that crosses over different historical temporalities and spatial realities to invoke past voices coming back in a dreamlike enunciation. Open-ended questions, ellipses, and interrupted dialogues that form the majority of the poems in the collection shape this virtual geography of a South that refers both to South America and similar geographies of internal and external colonization, such as the southern areas of the United States. Poems such as "Arizona" or "Cazador de Sueños" ["Dream Catcher"] establish this hemispheric connection where the "bello joven de linaje návajo americano" [beautiful young man of Navajo-American descent] (*Tener* 576) dialogues with the indigenous peoples of South America. Like the Hain, the dream catcher is a tool to convey those violently silenced voices of America. The "South," a utopian land and an archeological site, represents the paradoxical geographies of an entire continent dreaming of a future but still struggling with the legacies of a painful past: "Oh río del no retorno, es sur/ el continente entero" [Oh river of no return, the whole / continent is the South] (*Tener* 646).

The "South" is thus a paradoxical space that mobilizes memories of a collective remembrance and the illusion of a return of an original place. As such, *Sur* adopts the poetic form of an elegy, a lamentation about the annihilation of the original peoples of America, which can be read against works such as those by Sylvia Iparraguirre and Belén Gache referred to in the previous chapter. The poems' open composition and the recurrent use of ellipsis, as in "Is South an illusion?...," invite the reader to adopt an active participation in crafting new interpretations for the meaning of certain locations, such as the collective "South." *Sur* proposes that poetry is an open place, a multilayered site for endless collective interactions between the reader and different poetic subjects. The paradoxical descriptions of space that abound in the collection make clear that poetry is a virtual geography that contests the fixity of spatial constructs of power and domination. For instance, "Sabe el pie si toca..." [The foot knows when it touches...] describes an invisible mountain chain that, as many of the imaginary places in Bellessi's poetry, interconnects different locations:

Virtualidad herida
De la palabra. Pequeño
Pago al que atraviesan

Los lugares, gente
Cuya mirada no alcanza
Pero siente, la invisible
Cordillera—oh Sur—
Que reposa al Este

[The word's wounded
Potential. Small
Locality crossed by

Places, people
Whose gaze cannot reach
Though it senses, the invisible
Mountain range—oh South—
That lies to the East.] (*Tener* 612)

In such unstable sites, the poetic subject chooses her residence along with many others who have experienced space as a site of displacement and violence. "Paisaje sin fijación/ capaz de sostener sólo / ligereza, fragilidad / que se renueva…" [Unfixed landscape, / able to sustain only / lightness, fragility / renewing itself…] (*Tener* 608), such are the fragile spatialities of poetry. Poetry is a virtual archipelago, and the poet a subject at the mercy of natural elements, Bellessi says in "Estas islas por ejemplo…" ["These islands for instance…"] where forms and volumes of spatial shapes are rapidly changing and decomposing. Although some places seem to expel us, even reject us, the poem says, it is only in this virtual "pago," in that Hain, or sacred and flimsy residency, where we can finally be at home by reconnecting to a global lineage of the dispossessed:

> Es allí donde sentamos
> Nuestra herencia, donde soy
> Tu hermana Ailton Krenax,
>
> De palabra, inasible
> Fluye como las aguas
> De los ríos. Soy viajera
> De las montañas y todo
> el Sur tras de mí habla…
>
> [That is where we locate
> Our heritage, where I am
> Your sister Ailton Krenax,
>
> Sister of the word, the intangible
> Flowing like the waters
> Of the rivers. I am a mountain
> traveler and the entire
> South behind me speaks…] (*Tener* 609)

Although the "South" is, as previous examples demonstrate, not a fixed residence but a virtual, ever-changing poetic geography, Bellessi engages in a defense of the local understood not as the "homeland" ("La patria"), but as a multilayered and paradoxical location, the "pago," a definition that very well fits into characterizations of feminist geographies outlined by authors such as Massey and Rose. As other poets before her, like Juan L. Ortiz and the fluvial geography of Entre Ríos, described by his poetic style, Bellessi creates such fluid places through a poetic language of fractures, instabilities, and internal mobility, her style sketching an "internal map" for virtual geographies that contrast with spatial constructs defined in official discourses that, since the nineteenth century, have sought to define a national identity through cultural representations of the Argentine landscape. Referring to the musical quality of poetry, she states in "La experiencia de la poesía":

> Y en este misterioso goce musical pleno de recursos dirigidos a la subjetividad del que lee, la sinalefas como arañitas uniendo a las palabras a través de sus vocales, las aliteraciones haciendo piruetas en pequeña escala, las rimas internas y externas abriendo o cerrando las cadencias, los hipérbaton desbaratando las valoraciones previas y cerradas de adjetivos y sustantivos, en este misterioso goce musical... surgen miríadas de imágenes que se encadenan, que se hacen y deshacen, portadoras de sentido, de lógica, de coherencia, de voluntad de decir.
>
> [And in this mysterious musical pleasure full of poetic devices that speak to the reader's subjectivity, synaloephas like tiny spiders linking words by eliding their vowels; alliterations doing small-scale pirouettes; internal and external rhymes opening and closing cadences; hyperbatons playing havoc with previous fixed valorizations of adjectives and nouns, in this mysterious musical pleasure... myriad connected images emerge, are created and destroyed, each bearing meaning, logic, coherence, and a will to speak.] (12)

Bellessi's poems give the impression of a voice or, better yet, multiple voices interacting in the sonority of a choral-like enunciation. This oral quality is particularly evident in the formation of a poetic subject who, anchored in the field of her own experiences and perceptions, brings to the poem an emotive memory and the changes and transformations of her subjectivity. For Alicia Genovese, who studies this construction of the poetic self as closely related to the poet's subjectivity in poetry by Juan Gelman, Olga Orozco, and Juan L. Ortiz, this identification and poetic style invites the reader to relive through reading ("Poesía" 17). In *Sur,* the poet is a chameleonic figure, a highly dynamic and fluctuating subjectivity adopting different textual identities and holding internal dialogues with herself and other poetic subjects. As in the poetry by Gelman, Orozco, and Ortiz, the poetic self's dynamic position inspects the poem as a space that builds hierarchies and positionalities, as well as the ethical role of the poem in conveying other voices and perspectives, including those of nature. This complex dynamic between the self and the other is central in the essays in *Lo propio y lo ajeno.* An important aspect of this reflection centers on translation and, in particular, the translation of poetry, an art that further exacerbates, according to Bellessi, the self-distancing and estrangement that dominates poetic writing:

> Translation—and I speak strictly of the translation of poetry—is, perhaps, closest to the writing of poetry; it is carried through a slow process of internalization and silence.... It also demands being receptive to—through one's own emotions—the thoughts and emotions of another voice. The poet recognizes in his or her own writing, when, on saying 'I,' she feels both a close and a more distant voice at the same time. It means translating into one's own voice something that comes from distant reaches of time. ("Gender" 26).[6]

Gender is a central aspect in this construction of a speaking subject in poetry:

> The speaking subject is seen as object and theme not only in her individual subjectivity but also in the singularity of gender. If we conceive language and its structuring of discourse as a primarily historical construction, this leads the producer of the original to explore in semantic and syntactic terms her place in it, with both approval and disapproval that imply a detailed process of remantization. The translator is also implicated in this process, as she watches her language broken apart violently by the original that she translates. ("Gender" 28)

In *Lo propio y lo ajeno,* Bellessi explores at length how the production of a poetic self is particularly difficult for women. Poetry by Alejandra Pizarnik exemplifies this internal struggle that the woman poet, like other "social captives" such as the poor, marginalized ethnic groups, those in prison, and members of sexual minorities, has to carry out in searching to overcome oppressive social positions that confine her to silence. In "Un recuerdo suntuoso" ["A Sumptuous Memory"], Bellessi states that Pizarnik's main character, the perverse countess of *La condesa sangrienta* [*The Bloody Countess,* trans. Graziano], Erzebet Báthroy, torturing and killing hundreds of young women in her dark castle, embodies Pizarnik's attempts to build a new poetic self "tensado en arco de oro cuya flecha rasga el silencio" [taut in a golden bow, whose arrow rends the silence] (49). Murder is the only resource left for the woman poet's liberation, and it is only by killing her other selves or those of her implied readers—women like her entrapped within the walls of society's rooms for them—when the poet can find "la liberación de un presente congelado donde no puede *sentir,* donde no puede articular un discurso de su sentir, y el único reparo es la cuna del silencio, o la mascarada de la muerte" [liberation from a frozen present where she cannot *feel*, where she cannot articulate her feelings in discourse, and her only solution is the cradle of silence, or the masquerade of death] (emphasis in the original, 48).

The essays in *Lo propio y lo ajeno* bring attention to the fact that women face the need for a double decolonization, that of the "pensamiento burgués Europeo" [bourgeois European thought] and of the "patriarcado autoritario" [authoritarian patriarchy] (50), and she calls for the liberation of women's imaginary "mortgaged" by experiences of patriarchy, *mestizaje,* European cultural domination, and educational systems that perpetuate class differences (97). Her poetry examines genealogies as a means of decolonizing women's imaginaries; poetry needs to be written, thus, "outside the culture," she says in "Los del infinito me han hablado" ["Those from Infinity Have Spoken to Me"], by sitting in "another Hain," assisted by voices such as those of Lola Kiepja, voices that, like the poet herself, have been erased and violated by their incorporation into dominant or official cultures. The woman poet finds her art in those quiet whisperings; in close contact with nature, she writes a poem that is eccentric and located outside the many orders that have historically confined women to a position of seclusion and silence. At the mercy of the elements, the woman poet learns from nature the greatest lesson of humility in acknowledging herself in others:

> Nuestra relación con la naturaleza es histórica, incluye un diálogo donde el ser humano se escinde, sintiéndose parte de ella y fuera de ella, lo que le permite hasta cierto punto *ordenarla,* no quedar sometido y expuesto a su poder omnipotente que le produce espanto sin darle lugar para experimentar la existencia y *la belleza de lo natural.* Es decir que lo coloca en un espacio fuera de la escritura. Un exceso de orden, con características utilitarias y autoritarias que produce efectos arrasadores como los que conocemos en la actualidad, incluye la desaparición de ese espacio de lo natural donde el diálogo se hace posible.
>
> [Our relationship with nature is historical, and it includes a dialogue in which human beings are split, feeling themselves to be both inside and outside of nature, and this allows them, up to a certain point, to *order nature,* so as not to be subjected and exposed to its terrifying, omnipotent power, which leaves no space to experience the existence and *beauty of the natural world.* In other words, human beings are positioned in a space outside writing. An excess of order, with utilitarian and authoritarian characteristics that produce devastating consequences like the ones we see today, involves the disappearance of the space of the natural world where dialogue is made possible.] (emphasis in the original, 101–02)

Shaped in those terms, poetry represents a dialogue, a place for a "double voice," and a refuge for those marginalized voices that have been whispering a discourse of resistance since ancient times, a site where multiple cultures can coexist in a poetic paradox:

> El tiempo es desafiado. Se mueve hacia atrás y hacia adelante quebrando la ilusión del binomio pasado-futuro. Las voces de Lola Kiepja, por ejemplo, la última Selknam de Tierra del Fuego, o la de Agustina Quilchamal, Tehuelche cuya etnia también ha sido borrada, no son tomadas desde un futuro interpretativo que las coloque en el pasado desde el presente del poema, sino que cohabitan en el tiempo, son parte del mismo proceso que produce el poema, aunque quien lo escribe haya sido entrenada en los recursos de la alta cultura, y no pertenezca al espacio social donde los códigos culturales de las primeras se organizaron. ¿A través de qué? De un gesto del corazón, el brujo del cuerpo. Y a través de un tratamiento del tiempo en el poema, que no es desplegado en la duración...En la palabra viva también, cuando no ha sido sometida y clasificada como objeto arqueológico, cuando se la deja rozar nuestro corazón.
>
> [Time is defied. It moves backwards and forwards, disrupting the illusion of the binomial past and future. The voices of Lola Kiepja, the last Selknam of Tierra del Fuego, or Agustina Quichamal, a Techuelche whose ethnicity has also been erased, are not interpreted from a future that locates them in the past of the poem's present. Rather, they coexist in time; they are part of the same process that produces the poem, even though the poet has been educated in the practices of high culture and does not belong to the social space in which their cultural traditions were established. How is this accomplished? Through an act of the heart, the body's sorcerer. And through the treatment of time in the poem, which does not unfold in the usual order....And in the living word, when it has not been subjugated to the status of an archeological object, when we allow it to touch our hearts.] (117)

"Lo propio y lo ajeno," what belongs to the self and what belongs to others, can come together only in the paradoxical space of the poem, a site of coexistence of otherwise irreconcilable realities. As in *Sur*, poetry becomes a "contact zone" where women and other "social captives" are invested as artistic and literary producers, those who in poetry reoccupy the scene from which they had been taken due to experiences of social exclusion (116).

Later collections such as *La edad dorada* y *Mate cocido*, from 2002 and 2003, extend this image of the contact zone to other socially displaced groups such as the "cabecitas negras," the migrants from the Argentine provinces and from Bolivia and Paraguay living in the neoliberal Argentina of the

1990s and 2000s. In *La edad dorada,* the "golden age" embodies moments of encounter and dialogue where "piqueteros" (picketers), their faces illuminated by street fires of protest, remind the poet of her family's faces evoked in kitchen fires warming the farm. As Jorge Monteleone states in the introduction to *La edad dorada,* these encounters have religious undertones in a cosmic sense of Christianity where the contemplation of this "other" is linked to a sense of divine alterity (4). Similarly, themes and imagery from socially excluded subjects occupy the center scene in *Mate cocido.* The title of this collection comes from a *cumbia* song by "Mona" Jiménez as well as from the name of a rural bandit, David Peralta, "alias mate cocido" (7). Poems like "El relato impossible" ["The Impossible Tale"] make direct reference to poetic language as a battleground where yet untold oral narratives clash with those written by official discourses. In *Sur* and *El Jardín,* this interrogation about language centers on place and location, images of nature embodying the poet's search for a poetry that incorporates the inflections and tones of discourses left out of the lettered culture. However, *La edad dorada* and *Mate cocido* are part of a new stage in this poetic project where languages from the street and the field are no longer references set in the background; they now occupy a central scene in Bellessi's poetry. As she states in an interview, her latest poetry "marries" lineages such as the indigenous and the European that for a long time had influenced her; she finally feels at home in a poetic style that she describes as deeply nourished by the popular (personal interview, June 27, 2007).

In *Mate cocido,* the poet employs the metaphor of the river once again to describe "universal circles of contact" connecting those voices with no place in the lettered culture, as heard in stories of immigration coming from ships arriving from Europe into Buenos Aires at the beginning of the twentieth century: "Bailando en el Titanic" ["Dancing on the Titanic"]; the songs of Bolivians dancing in the streets of the city—"Bolivia"; the candid conversation with a habitant of the delta's islands aboard a boat—"Río Abajo" ["Down River"], and the voices of "cabecitas negras," the immigrants from the provinces living in the Once neighborhood in Buenos Aires—"the drag queen." In the fluid geography of the river, the poet searches for a stream of collective memories of displacement and loss. *Mate cocido* represents a return to a popular soil in poetry where the poet re-creates a seemingly lost "golden time of childhood"; brushing on words that she has not heard in a long time, she captures, although only for a fleeting moment, a seemingly original relation to this lost, primitive language. Written in a period that witnessed the political transition from authoritarianism to the neoliberal state, Bellessi's poetic project, centered on how location and place determine language and social subjectivities, directly relates to the places women and other underrepresented social groups, such as ethnic and sexual minorities, occupy in the newly reestablished democratic society of Argentina. Her poetry "relocates social languages" as it questions the creation of subaltern languages and subjectivities through experiences of authoritarianism and political violence. Masiello states that this is a characteristic of women's poetry of the period that contests both the "territoriality" and the "authority" of state discourses (*Art* 229). Read against the essays in *Lo propio y lo ajeno*, collections like *El jardín, Sur, La edad dorada,* and *Mate cocido* establish a "counter-discourse" in poetry, carefully assembled with those broken speeches, the subtle whisperings of those subjects with no place in spatial formations of both militarized and neoliberal societies.

Common stories of dislocation take place in Luisa Futoransky's works as well. Like Bellessi, she is conscious of complex relations between poetic language and location, and her fictional and poetic personae adopt spatial and figurative mobility by using, for instance, humor and parody to destabilize cultural locations. Read from the lenses of what Ana Forcinito calls the "nomadic memory" of women's postdictatorial writing, Futoransky's works are located in the borders of traditional social spaces for women (14). As a postmodern nomad, Futoransky's poetic displacements question the role of place and location in the repressive state of the 1970s and 1980s in Argentina.

2. Nomadic Memories: Luisa Futoransky's Deterritorialized Quest

Experiences of exile, nomadism, and deterritorialization characterize Futoransky's poetry. Having left the country in the 1970s, she traveled and lived in multiple locations: Japan, China, and France. Written at the intersections between national and global geographies, her poetry has been compared to Juan Gelman's because of its representations of translation and polyglossia and its rich references to different cultural traditions (Masiello, *Art* 146). Mainly centered on women's experiences, her works reconstruct hidden stories of mobility and habitus in the postmodern metropolis.[7] Her poetic representations of placelessness and location describe ways in which, in Doreen Massey's words, "...mobility, and control over mobility, both reflects and reinforces power" (quoted in Kaplan, "Becoming Nomad" 153). Her collections *El corazón de los lugares* [*The Heart of Places*] (1964), *Babel, Babel* (1968), and *Partir, digo,* [*To Leave, I Say*] (1982), and her latest works, *Inclinaciones* [*Inclinations*] (2006) and *Prender de gajo* [*Transplanted*] (2007), examine memory's historical formations and the impact of gender, class, race, and nationality on mobility and the production of social locations. In her poetry, the voice of the woman nomad, the poetic subject, builds critical dialogues between multiple sites of enunciation.[8] In a style characterized by the postmodern use of collage, her works establish new geopolitical locations in poetry by reworking local and global enunciations and an estranged connection with language.[9]

In "Elogio del olvido" ["In Praise of Oblivion"], Futoransky examines the futile attempt to inscribe memory in a particular location, something she says that contemporary rituals and memorials try to do in commemorating society's historical milestones. On the contrary, memory is a dialogic, selective, and defiant mechanism, a cluster of multiple enunciations, a historical collage that also includes healthy and necessary moments of oblivion. Futoransky's novels *De Pe a Pa o de Pekín a París* [*From Pe to Pa or from Peking to Paris*] (1986) and *Son cuentos chinos* [*Tall Tales*] (1991) are, in fact, narrative collages critiquing the politics of memory, as represented in Latin American "exiled writing," and its nostalgic re-creation of a homeland. Opposed to the utopian nonplace of exile, Futoransky's fictional characters are bounded in specific spatial formations connecting global and local locations. Contrary to the idea that subjects can freely circulate through global networks, the novel's protagonist, Laura, painstakingly moves through places in China and Paris because of the tight network of cultural and literary discourses regulating both her spatial and social mobility. As Marcy Schwartz states, Futoransky reworks images of Paris, as depicted in exiled and travel narratives that since the nineteenth century have transformed the city in the most influential literary location for Latin American writers.[10] She rewrites the "Paris of exiles" in the sense given by writers such as Cortázar[11] by describing how women, immigrants, and refugees experience this imaginary space, following Schwartz's words, "under their skin." First in China and Japan and later in Paris, Laura addresses travel conventions about the cities where she resides. Both disenchanted tales about how the "orient" is the site of occidental fantasies, her novels critically examine the legacies of modernist "orientalisms."[12] As postmodern travelogues, Futoransky's fictions adopt the form of assemblages of thoughts, literary references, and the protagonist's daily experiences.[13]

The role of translation and a polyglot poetic space where "location" is traversed by multiple enunciations is also evident in Futoransky's poetry collection of 1968, *Babel, Babel*. This poetic travelogue engages in a dialogue with previous narratives of mobility and location in Latin American literature established, for instance, through the tradition of oceanic travel that since the nineteenth century shaped cosmopolitan exchanges between Argentina and Europe (Colombi *Viaje intelectual* 15). *Babel, Babel* explores representations of forced displacement and exile through literary and biblical references to shipwrecks from Noah to Jonah, as well rewrites literary representations of the city, often associated in Argentine literature to notions of cosmopolitism. However, Futoransky rewrites the tradition of cosmopolitan literary identities by describing instead her poetic subject as "Nuevo barco ebrio" ["New Drunken Boat"], a "wandering ship," crossing over stormy waters of personal and collective histories. Aware that a safe landing is no longer possible, this inexperienced sailor, this "new" ship is condemned to shipwreck:

> Bajel, cuando llegue la mañana
> serás alguien experto ya en la desolación de los naufragios
> y la tierra habrá bebido tu inocencia:
> la playa donde arribes te tiene reservado
> el más cruel de los desiertos
> y el más infernal de los silencios; no vuelvas tu cabeza
> porque es en vano que pretendas ayudar
> al que a tus espaldas ya emprendió la estéril travesía.
> [Vessel, by morning
> you will be practiced in the desolation of shipwrecks
> and dry land will have drunk your innocence:
> the beach where you pull into port has reserved for you
> the cruelest desert
> and the most infernal silence; do not turn your head
> for your efforts are in vain
> the one you mean to help has already embarked
> in secret on the futile crossing.]

Constantly attacked by exterior agents such as bad weather and dusty winds, this ship embodies a permeable subjectivity on the brink of collapse, a representation often associated with a female subjectivity in Futoransky's works. Other poems in this collection refer to the idea of the city as the space that a masculine desire seeks to conquer and civilize. "Llanos del Sur" ["Southern Plains"] addresses, following the tradition of Jorge Luis Borges's poem "Fundación mítica de Buenos Aires" ["Mythical Foundation of Buenos Aires"], the literary creation of the city as a way of producing the space of a nation, namely Argentina. However, as in other examples from this collection, the poet rewrites literary motifs of the intellectual map of Argentina from a different perspective. In this example, the poem refers to the literary image of the desert, a foundational icon in Argentine cultural landscape, and of the city as an imaginary geography that intellectuals sought to produce as the embodiment of the country's literary culture. In "Llanos del sur" the city becomes the space that is impossible to be named:

> Cuando los peces retiren sus ovas
> de los recovecos de tus construcciones
> otra vez un ingenuo, un loco, un guerrero
> un fanático, un ambicioso, o todos ellos juntos
> o alguien con todos y más de estos defectos y virtudes
> erigirá un fortín en el desierto
> y te llamará de alguna nueva o vieja manera
> Buenos Aires.
>
> [When the fish withdraw their roe
> from the niches in your constructions
> another innocent, madman, warrior
> fanatic, man of ambition, or all of them together,
> or someone who possesses all of these defects and virtues
> will erect a fortress in the desert
> and name you, in a new or old way
> Buenos Aires.]

Cities are fragments of a skin in disintegration in "Coração da Guanabara" ["Guanabara's Heart"]; the city wavers between the fluid geographies of the mountain and the sea. This poem describes experiences of spatial disorientation:

> la ciudad entonces se mece y aulla demente entre el sol, la montaña
> y el mar
> que no la dejan escapar
> [then the city then sways howling madly between the sun, the mountain
> and the sea
> that will not let her break free.]

Babel, Babel rewrites the virtual geographies of the sea and the city, two central tropes embodying notions of masculine mobility in urban and transatlantic narratives of space. Contrary to the harmonic cosmopolitanisms that founded Argentine literary culture, *Babel, Babel* raises dissonant voices embedded in a postmodern, postnational, and postcolonial space, as described by Schwartz, a deconstruction of the engendered cosmopolitanisms that characterize Latin American literature since *modernismo* ("Paris" 116).

In *Partir, digo* (1982) Futoransky prefaces the collection by describing it as a postmodern travelogue built upon fragments of experiences and memories of travels around the world. As reflections on displacement, many poems center on the imagined geographies of memory, whereas poetry is the futile attempt to assemble them in a coherent discourse, as in "Vitraux del exilio" ["Stained-Glass Windows of Exile"]. In the tradition of exile writing, this poem establishes an intimate dialogue with the unreal geography of a remembered country, parodied here through the poet's uses of humor and irony. Space cannot be truly shaped as a literary representation, the poem states, because places are assemblages formed through multiple layers of dialogical enunciations. *Partir, digo* describes places as collages shaped by an ironic memory, a "dynamic simultaneity"[14] connecting different localities. Through such ironic rewriting of places as futile constructions of memory, the poet contests hegemonic relations—economic, cultural, or political—embodied in the idea of location.[15] Against the tradition of travel writing that transforms places into exotic landscapes of a literary imagination, Futoransky's poetry addresses a conflictive and gendered spatiality that, in many instances, lacks the powerful seduction of picturesque images. Referring to Aimé Césaire's writing, the poet says:

> Porque ya no podré jamás escribir poemas a lo aimé césaire
> con tantísimas esdrújulas con soles radiantes y bucaneros
> que descubren tesoros con doblones sangrientos y escolopendras
> y hojas de plátanos como barcos y abrazos esplendorosos
> de jóvenes negros como el diamante que te abren
> el alma arco iris pompa de jabón con la mirada en las
> tierras fermentadas de germinaciones y podredumbres
> [Because I will never be able to write poems in the style of aimé
>   césaire
> profuse with proparoxytones with radiant suns and buccaneers
> who discover treasures with bloody doubloons and centipedes
> and plantain leaves like boats and the splendid embraces
> of young men black as diamond who open
> your soul rainbow bubbles with their gaze on
> lands fermented with germination and rot.]

Futoransky's poem is situated at the center of a blank page, an effective metaphor of how writing can also be an oppressive spatiality for women: "mis universos son mucho más reducidos entrarían en una / pequeña hoja de block cuadriculado de una sola línea" [my universes are much smaller, they would fit / on a small sheet of graph paper with a single line] (46).

In later collections such as *Prender de gajo* (2006), Futoransky further develops the connections between spatiality and writing. As a poetic manifesto for a new geopolitics in times of globalization, *Prender de gajo* reflects on memory as a powerful mechanism for the aesthetic production of space. The characteristics of an engendered spatiality previously outlined for Futoransky's works converge in *Prender de gajo:* a vanishing subject in a deterritorialized text, the use of collage and travel metaphors of intertextual quotations, the searching for a nomadic mobility outside of material constraints of gender and social locations, an estranged postmodern aesthetics and the use of humor as poetic artifice, and the questioning of memory in a contemporary "culture of amnesia." Futoransky's poetic language connects local and global utterances and shows subjects and words flowing into the cultural economy of pastiche that characterizes globalization. Feminist readings of these global itineraries are present in poems such as "Cartulina de Ljubljana" ["Card from Ljubljana"] or "La coleccionista" ["The (Female) Collector"], in which the wandering subject acts as collector of "spatial souvenirs." In "La coleccionista" she states, "Con la insensatez propia de los coleccionistas atesoro ciudades, qué digo, países enteros que no existen." [With a collector's foolishness, I amass cities, or should I say, entire inexistent countries] (62). However, her task is doomed to failure because memories of such places are unmarketable products:

> Yo también codicio el proyecto de poner en secreto toda la colección en venta y liquidarla de un solo tajo y de la misma vez. Rematarla en Sotheby's o Christie's no puedo; está prohibido. Pero andando con pies de plomo y mucho tino a lo mejor en el Mercado negro aún se puede.
> [I also covet the idea of secretly putting my collection up for sale so that I can liquidate the whole thing once and for all. I cannot auction it at Sotheby's or Christie's; that is prohibited. But if I proceed with great caution and prudence I might get lucky on the black market.] (63)

The quote ironically refers to the commercialization of space in experiences of global tourism, something that Futoransky addresses at length in her poetry. Through verbal games, irony, and humor, Futoransky traces an antitouristic version of the many places to which she traveled over the years. "Restaurante de Ekoda" ["A Restaurant in Ekoda"] narrates the experience of a lunch with uncooked fish at the Ekoda train station in Tokyo; the picturesque Japanese landscape of pagodas dissolves under the persistent rain, also slowly erasing the poetic subject-defined contours. "Palmares de San Remo" ["San Remo Palm Grove"] and the long poem in prose, "Con el escorpio puesto" ["Wearing Scorpio"], show the dark side of touristic destinations by exposing common places of abuse and corruption hidden in the construction of artificial touristic sites for the eyes of a global consumer. As the poet states in "Con el escorpio puesto," even the pigeons in Saint Mark's Basilica in Venice are trained to pose for the tourist (*Seqüana barrosa* 71). Described from this cynical perspective, these poetic experiences of place unveil a world of social injustices suffered by immigrants, women, and children, the main victims of an uneven global mobility denounced in poems such as "Arde París? Aquí vivimos" ["Is Paris Burning? We Live Here"], a title that, echoing the 1966 film by René Clement, parodies images of Paris as a global capital of freedom and social equality.

As in poetry by Bellessi, Futoransky's works articulate a paradoxical search for location, in this case through a postmodern aesthetics of artifice. In this "poetic economy," to use Kuhnheim's term referring to reorganizations of the poetic space that signals new forms of social spatiality,[16] locations in Futoransky's poetry are, in Caren Kaplan's words, "discontinuous, multiply constituted, and traversed by diverse social formations" ("Introduction" 182). The poet transforms locations into poetic memorials where different social actors bring new meanings to them through the incorporation of collective memories (Jelin and Langland, 3–4). She combines here the playfulness of a postmodern aesthetic with the search for memory through a complex set of spatiotemporal relations embodied in connections between memory, mourning, and place. Her poetry reflects on how individuals negotiate social relations through grief and remembrance, with places as central in giving voice to the effects of dislocation, disembodiment, and localization that constitute contemporary social orders. In her introduction to *Memory, Mourning, Landscape*, Kate McLoughlin states that this "affective terrain" of memorials includes different temporalities, those of "the displaced, the buried, the otherwise vanished." As loci where "memory is crystallized," certain locations are transformed, she states, by using Pierre Nora's term, into "places of memory" (ix). In "Tiananmen, 4 de Junio, 1989" ["Tiananmen, June 4, 1989"] the poet engages in the aesthetic re-creation of such spatial changes. Referring to the brutal repression that took place in Tiananmen, China, on June 4, 1989, this poem transforms the space of the page into a memorial, a landscape of collective and individual mourning. Its structure organizes space following avant-garde principles of experimentation with the visual form of the poem, two paradoxical directions of stillness and progression pulling the reader into a sense of being detained in a central image—"the moon lost centuries in Peking this morning,"—and moving through the network of poetic references to beauty and violence evoked in the enumeration. As a memorial site, the poem's form brings us into the present and the past, with the powerful images of experienced and remembered places:

la luna perdió siglos en Pekín esta mañana
esta mañana
la luna (el sol, las estrellas, las piedras todas de las estelas, las brújulas, el torno y el horno de cocer la terracotta, la cresta en llamas de los pájaros, los rayos y centellas de las bicicletas y la última mota de polvo que ocultó la uña)
en Pekín (laca brillante de la Ciudad Prohibida, un rumor de falanges, falanginas y falangetas, un cortejo de bubones y de ganglios estallaron en Pekín; Pekín, la sanguinaria)
perdió (los huérfanos granos de arroz abandonados entre los restos humeantes del Museo de la Larga Marcha y la luna que riela el caprichoso trazado de la Gran Muralla por la fidelidad al único monumento que desde su lejos y de nuestro tiempo le atestigua el sudor y lágrimas del hombre, de asco y de vergüenza olvidó en el fragor del dolor)
su madrugada
¿cuántos siglos perdió la luna en Pekín esta mañana?
[*the moon lost centuries in Peking this morning*
this morning
the moon (the sun, the stars, all the stones on the trails, compasses, the potter's wheel and the kiln that fires the terracotta, birds' crests in flames, bicycle spokes and sparks, and the last speck of dust hidden under the fingernail)
In Peking (brilliant lacquer of the Forbidden City, a rumor of phalanxes, small gatherings and multitudes, a procession of tumors and ganglia exploded in Peking; bloodthirsty Peking)
lost (orphans grains of rice abandoned among the smoky remains of the Museum of the Long March, and the moon shimmering the erratic route of the Great Wall faithful to the only monument that from its bygone and our time bears witness to man's sweat and tears, of revulsion and shame forgotten in the clamor of pain)
its dawn
how many centuries did the moon lose in Peking this morning?] (emphasis in the original, 42)

As McLoughlin states, memorials, like writing, may be durable but are not permanent; rather, they are protean and palimpsestic (xii). The poems in *Prender de gajo* demonstrate the sequential chains of common histories of memory and oblivion in the form of what Masiello names as Futoransky's "nomad's poetics," a "restless, multivocal, mobile" expression connecting fragments of histories of migration and their generic and social forms of oppression ("In Search of" 42). This collection echoes the debate on gender and location in Latin America, for Futoransky constantly refers to a material and bodily experience of space, something that Schwartz has studied at length in Futoransky's novels. In this process of remembrance, Futoransky engages in the engendered nomadic memory that Ana Forcinito describes as central in Latin American postdictatorial women's writing, where a rebellious corporality challenges authoritarianism; as military regimes have used bodies to destroy subjectivities or to construct terrorized subjectivities, Futoransky's poetry gives the female body a new legitimacy, as it denounces ways in which bodies are domesticated or disappeared in the region (33–34).

In times of a generalized historic and cultural amnesia and in light of the disappearances caused by the Argentine dictatorship, Futoransky's poetic locations acquire a distinct feminist perspective. Written from the standpoint of a female poet who perceives global mobility as an illusion or, better yet, as a perverse form of domesticating memory and oblivion, her works engage in a steep criticism of the perverse market logic that dominates our contemporary global reality. In "Cartulina de Ljubljana," references to cultures sold in a market as global goods embody the artificiality of a touristic postcard conveyed by the title: Bolivians selling their cultural identities as merchandise comparable to big peppers and ripe bananas (38). As in her previous narrative works, Futoransky's postmodern aesthetic of collage and linguistic playfulness signals her versatility to move around different cultural traditions. In her essay "Prender de gajo," she states that her "patchwork style" is like a fragile citadel made of "retazos" [remnants] of lived experiences and literary references, an endless "circunloquio" [circumlocution] (123–24). The compelling metaphor of "Prender de gajo" describes her identity as a deterritorialized subject, "transplanted" like the violently uprooted old tree in the Francis Bacon expressionist painting, *Portrait of Van Gogh,* which Futoransky acknowledges as the best visual representation of her condition as an expatriate (125). In her scattered poetic geographies, memory is the force infusing transnational connections between languages and places, the memory of the poet nomad connecting experiences of displacement and the painful and slow mobility of those displaced in global networks. In fact, "Con el escorpio puesto" describes this memory as a "abigarrado mercado de pulgas" [motley flea market] (*Seqüana barrosa* 72). *Prender de gajo* reinforces the notion of poetry as a "testimonio," or what Tamara Kamenzsain describes as the "mouth of testimonio," because poetry reveals, with the force of a live utterance, those discourses that have disappeared by bringing them back to life, as if we were experiencing in each poetic connection the "breath of the other's mouth" (*La boca* 12). Such is the experience of communication that Futoransky's poetry asserts: voices and discourses that in the present temporality that characterizes poetry "make real" languages and subjectivities that have been erased in discourses on globalization. In Jill Kuhnheim's words, poetry and, in particular, poetry from a woman's perspective, augments anarchy by exasperating difference; as a challenging discourse, it disrupts the apparent univocality of the institutionalized word (*Gender* 77). Dialogic, humoristic, and composed by a myriad of voices resonating in the global sphere, the labyrinths in Futoransky's works demonstrate the endless possibilities for remaking global space through the virtual cartographies of poetry.

Within this scenario of global relationships, *Prender de gajo* also addresses the search for a different kind of memory through the reconstruction of personal genealogies. As she states in the essay "Prender de gajo," hers is a memory that crosses over generations, "una memoria transgeneracional de remotas errancias y nomadismos arquetípicos y primordiales" ["a remote intergenerational memory of wanderings and archetypal and primordial forms of nomadism"] ("Ir volver" 119). Through the lenses of this nomadic memory, Futoransky approaches an estranged connection with her native language. "La lengua natal castra" ["The native tongue castrates"] (Graziano 91) opposes the poetic expression "En esta noche, en este mundo" of Alejandra Pizarnik (239). Similarly, the oral quality of Futoransky's poetry describes a deterritorialized or distanced perspective of national language whereby the poet rejects identifications with national uses of language as expressed in colloquialism. Through word puns that deconstruct codified cultural meanings embedded in language, the poet mixes lyrical and colloquial uses of language, with memory as the main connecting force in the re-creation of the native language as evidenced by the poem "Corte y confección" ["Dressmaking"] wherein she sews up remembrances of childhood words while tracing different stitches in the page: "arroz, calceta, del revés y desmenguado" [rice, knitting, wrong side out, and diminished] (*Inclinaciones* 24). In other instances, nostalgia permeates poetry in a search for a personal memory that recovers a pristine, unmediated relation with childhood language, as in "El patio y los abuelos" ["My Grandparents' Courtyard"] (*Prender de gajo* 16). And along with this poetic search for language, which she characterizes as "fishing" from a universal linguistic memory, there is a quest for the "heart of places." As in her previous collection, *El corazón de los lugares*, *Prender de gajo* explores places as sites for linguistic memory, whereas the poem, a virtual territory or a map, enables a lost connection with seemingly original relations to place and language. However, reconstructing a spatial memory or penetrating the "heart of places" seems to be an unattainable goal in a global reality where such original, unfiltered experiences of space have vanished. The poetic subject is, like the character of Raymond Isidore or "Picassiette," a trash collector with access to the remains of spatial and linguistic memories, fragments and pieces that Picasiette collected at the cemetery. "Picassiette" describes a house built with those remnants, embodying an impossible return that, like the family house in Santos Lugares, describes the unattainable memories and the fleeting languages of childhood. The poem "Picassiette" ends with a somber comment on the vanishing quality of memory: "Cuánto cierzo sopla sobre el olvido, Picassiete." [How much the north wind blows over all that is unremembered, Picassiette] (40).

Seqüana barrosa (2007) similarly explores the dissemination of the poetic subject, the creation of an eccentric self that also characterizes other women poets' production like Pizarnik's. Centered in Paris, where Futoransky had lived for the past twenty years, this collection refers to the Seine and its deity traveling the river in a small boat shaped like a duck. The river, as Reina Roffé states in the foreword, is a universal metaphor connecting the many geographies of Futoransky's poetry: Buenos Aires, Paris, "un río de la lengua y del lenguaje de la mujer nómada" [a river of language, and of the language of the nomadic woman] (10). In Masiello's words, the river's image, common in poetry by Gelman and Futoransky, reflects experiences of migrancy and dislocation, moving "bodies and nations through a river of language, constructing an alternative global map from nomadic wisdom. One's name is the equivalent of a country: it is a map and river, graveyard and air" (*Art* 150). Many poems in this collection describe fluid positions for the poetic self that alternate between representations of the subject as a discursive creation and what Kuhnheim calls the "historical fact of the presence of a writing subject" (*Gender* 14). *Seqüana barrosa* and *Inclinaciones*, published a year earlier in 2006, engage in self-exploratory poetic games that give both of these collections a personal tone. In "Colofón y fin de fiesta" ["Colophon and End of the Party"], the poetic self adopts the form of a literary assemblage of readings; she describes herself as a textual construction of dissimilar lineages and influences: Jorge Luis Borges, Miguel de Cervantes, Julio Cortázar, César Vallejo, Felisberto Hernández, and the Bible. However, other poems such as "Cenizas" ["Ashes"], play with a connection with the authorial subject by creating an acronym with the name "Luisa" and referring to a concrete body, exuberant and dressed in an eaten-away kimono (18). "Nómina" ["Payroll"], a title that refers to a legal term expressing the payroll of a business, is here employed as a list of memories, people, and things that define the life and identity of the textual subject (*Inclinaciones* 49–53). As epitomized by "Atravesares" ["Crossings"], these two collections play with the two identities of the poet as both a discursive and a historical entity. In "Atravesares," the space of the page and that of a mirror collide, allowing the poetic subject to cross over and connect her textual and real identities (32). As a subject migrating positions and identities, the playful subjectivities in Futoransky's poetry embody the fluid geographies described by Masiello, maps and landscapes that the poet crosses over and reverses through her poetic writing. Further, in the poetic tradition of a "de-centered subject" in Pizarnik and Olga Orozco that Kuhnheim associates with a subversion of the universalist, transcendent subject of modernist poetry (*Gender* 15), Futoransky resists and questions authority in the creation of a slippery subject that undermines dominant signifying practices. Echoing Kuhnheim's words, Futoransky's poetic subjects express "her experience of alienation, either directly or by strategically refusing an authoritative speaking position" (17).

Terms such as "exile," "nomadism," and "deterritorialization" are central in feminist theories on location. In Rosi Braidotti's *Nomadic Subjects,* for instance, "nomadism" is both a political instrument and a capacity to produce an epistemological or aesthetic discourse. In contrast to notions such as "exile," "migrant," or "traveler," the nomad has the capacity to oppose hegemonies and a "nomadic" critical practice leading to a radical knowledge consonant with Adrienne Rich's "politics of location." As a "theoretical figure" the nomad both denies fixed categorizations and has "a cohesion engendered by repetitions, cyclical moves, rhythmical displacement" (22). Memory plays a key role in a nomadic consciousness; Braidotti states that feminists as well as other "critical intellectuals... are those who have forgotten to forget injustice and symbolic poverty: their memory is activated against the stream; they enact a rebellion of subjugated knowledges" (25). In Latin American criticism, nomadism is also a key feminist concept. Forcinito's *Memorias y nomadías* states that memory is a battleground for historical interpretation linked to feminist attempts to "deterritorialize" official politics of memory. Within the context of the historical debates on memory in the Southern Cone area, these "subaltern" representations of memory seek to destabilize the affiliation of a masculinist territoriality and the politics of memory described as patriarchal, unilateral, and exclusionary.

As a both political and aesthetic strategy, Futoransky's nomadic poetics rewrites territories and maps as corporeal spaces, as sites of desire and repression, and engages in a critical redefinition of the politics of memory in contemporary societies like Argentina. Written in a period when immigration, neoliberalism, and globalization changed the demographic landscape of many societies, her poetry reveals the dark side of territorial reconfigurations marked by an acute increase of militarization and economic and social injustice. By centering on the politics of memory, her works refer to experiences of authoritarianism and the perverse role of memorials in building univocal narratives of national identity. Futoransky builds a collective body that inscribes female desire as well as social and generic oppression into previous narratives of displacement and location about the "Orient," Paris, and Argentina.[17] Her poetic texts illustrate the apparent contradiction between nomadic mobility and the excruciating awareness of context and positionality. Masiello characterizes the linguistic dislocations and the constant references to translation that are present in Futoransky's works when she states that her subjects are permanently translated by official discourses ("In Search of" 48). By employing a nomadic subjectivity based on incongruities, repetitions, and a polyglot aesthetics, Futoransky questions the "illusory stability of fixed identities, bursting open the bubble of ontological security that comes from familiarity with one linguistic site" (Braidotti 15). This nomadic subjectivity allows for a creation of new forms of political and engendered placement of bodies that circulate through global networks. In this new "poetic economy,"[18] poetry at the end of the twentieth century becomes a deterritorialized expression that reworks economic and political challenges brought about by globalization.

In *Islandia* [*Iceland*], María Negroni similarly engages in reflections on place through the exploration of an "insular poetics" where spatial metaphors of an imaginary island that is both the island of Manhattan and the "Islandia" of Borges conflate. Territories dissolve in Negroni's poetic endeavors, proposing new ways of rewriting space within a feminist poetics of mobility and location that will be explored in the following section.

3. Islandia / Iceland: María Negroni's Insular Poetics

In "Ir volver/de un adónde a un adónde" ["Go Come Back / From A Where To A Where"] Negroni refers to "Islandia" as an imaginary place:

> Los islandeses no habían hecho otra cosa: también ellos se habían alejado de su país de origen (Noruega) en la confianza de que, en el extrañamiento, podrían acceder a ciertas percepciones sutiles y así ser los escribas más veraces, más tenazmente desesperados, de la tierra perdida. Demás está decir que la isla que eligieron para hacerlo coincide con la tierra de la poesía, es decir, con ese territorio ciego, absoluto, encallado en lo imaginario, donde las palabras no tienen más pasión que lo inexplicable.
>
> [The Icelanders too had abandoned their country of origin (Norway), trusting that such estrangement would give them access to certain subtle perceptions, that would make them the most authentic, most tenaciously desperate scribes of their lost land. It goes without saying that the island where they chose to do so corresponds to the land of poetry, that is, with

that blind, absolute territory stranded in the imaginary, where words' only passion is the inexplicable.] (27)

Negroni's works deal with spatial displacements, from the Nordic sagas (*Islandia*) and medieval legends (*El sueño de Úrsula* [*Ursula's Dream*]) to the notion of aesthetic displacement that she connects with the gothic (*El viaje de la noche* [*Night Journey*]). Traveling is an experience of temporal disjunction and aesthetic awe, transporting the reader to new levels of literary perception. As in Futoransky's poetry, Negroni addresses the situation of women's increased and yet paradoxically reduced mobility in globalization by building a site for feminine agency and empowerment: "Iceland," the imaginary land of poetry. Read from the perspective of the "politics of paradoxical space" described by Gillian Rose, her anachronistic poetics intersects multiple levels of spatiality that re-create women's positionalities in the global sphere. From the seemingly reduced and constrained geography of the imaginary island of poetry, Negroni's works connect women from distant geographies and historical periods into a virtual network of fluid relationships. In this section, I focus on her poetry collection *Islandia* (1993) because the topic of feminist geographies is most evident in this book where Negroni combines the narrative discourse of the Nordic saga and the baroque symbols of opacity and illusion to craft a complex "insular poetics." However, I will contextualize my analysis in readings of her poetry collection *El viaje de la noche (*1994) and her two novels *El sueño de Úrsula (*1998) and *La anunciación* [*The Annunciation*] (2007), as they shed light on the rich characteristics of what I designate as Negroni's "insular poetics": the construction of alternative collective alliances for women, the confluence of the epic and the lyric, the influence of the gothic and the melancholic, and the roles of memory and allegory in the postdictatorial scene.

Through allegorical exchanges among characters from different temporalities and places, *El sueño de Úrsula* and *La anunciación* examine the role of memory in contemporary society. In *El sueño de Úrsula,* a German Benedictine visionary from the twelfth century dialogues with Saint Ursula who, according to the legend, embarked in the fifth century upon a pan-European pilgrimage to delay her marriage to a pagan leader, Aetherius. In *La anunciación,* a monk named Athanasius assists the female protagonist, a leftist militant who flew Argentina in the 1970s, in reconnecting with some of her friends—Emma, an artist, and Humboldt, an ex-lover—who disappeared during the dictatorship. In her narratives, Negroni challenges linear temporality; her novels transform into a frozen space, an offsite territory, a lost land, a virtual museum re-creating, through dream appearances and timeless visions, recurrent and interrupted tales of displacement and loss. María Rosa Olivera-Williams interprets this anachronistic structure as a way of building virtual places for women's subjectivity that cannot be reduced to traditional social roles or images or to a marketable product (285, 289). Written in the "untimely present" that characterizes postdictatorial fiction, *El sueño de Úrsula* and *La anunciación* place women as bearers of the difficult role of interweaving a common memory of traumatic loss. Idelber Avelar describes this paradoxical temporality of postdictatorial fiction: "As opposed to the market's perpetual present, where the past must incessantly be turned into a tabula rasa to be replaced and discarded with the arrival of new commodities, the allegorical temporality of mourning clings to the past in order to save it, even as it attempts ultimately to produce an active forgetting of it" (4).

The notion of feminist "paradoxical spaces" is quite relevant here. In both her novels and poetry, Negroni constructs multilayered and paradoxical spaces where female protagonists can imagine themselves outside of what Rose calls the hegemonic "territorialities of masculinism" (159). Women travel through labyrinthlike utopian or virtual places, and such literary displacements are central in a radical poetic and narrative estrangement acquiring multiple representations: the exile of the Vikings to *Islandia*, the surrealist travel to a dream world in *El viaje de la noche*, the pilgrimage of Ursula in *El sueño de Úrsula*, and the political exile in *La anunciación*. Negroni proposes that literary spaces are a complex and virtual chain of signifiers where the worlds of "here" and "there," "home" and "abroad" are blended into paradoxical representations that question spatial and aesthetic dichotomies. Baroque representations of space abound in her works: the exuberant description of medieval dresses and ornaments replicating the intricate scene of the fleet's flags in *El sueño de Úrsula* and the detailed references to the shields, swords, and armor of Nordic warriors in *Islandia* mirroring the sharp geographies of the fiords in Iceland. This baroque aesthetic reflects women's intricate position in social and spatial networks. Located in eccentric positions, her female characters craft weblike fictional narrations that question univocal historical accounts. For instance, Ursula rewrites, along with Isabel de Schonau, the role of women as the dowry of a territorial or religious empire, whereas the female narrator exiled in Rome, along with the disappeared artist, Emma, reshapes the history of the male-dominated leftist groups in 1970s Argentina and their longstanding debate about the paradoxes between social and artistic engagement.

Such spatial representations respond to allegorical readings of history and point to the intricate links between poetry and society. Negroni's works are reflections on the arbitrary connections between meaning and words, signifier and signified, and history and its literary re-creation. Allegory plays a crucial role in Negroni's poetics. As both a system of writing and a means of interpretation, it points to the ambivalence of meaning while it examines cultural processes of symbolization.[19] Walter Benjamin's well-known distinction between symbol and allegory is important to mention here. In *The Origin of German Tragic Drama*, Benjamin explores the origins of the "trauerspiel," or baroque German drama that he contrasts with the tragedy. In his study, Benjamin goes back to medieval Christianity to describe how the "trauerspiel" displays a "damnation registered in a profoundly carnal sense" that opposes the metaphysical and transcendent foundation of tragedy (16). Benjamin associates allegory and "trauerspiel," allegory being at the foundation of the "sorrow-play" that constitutes a "trauerspiel." A literary form that privileges mourning, allegory resists symbolization processes that are crucial, for instance, to the tragic form (166). According to Benjamin, allegories stress the dialectic (and artificial) relation between signifier and signified, and history and art. In times of deep historical loss and melancholia, as the Baroque period, allegory is the preferred expression, as in it "...the observer is confronted with the *facies hippocratica* of history as a petrified, primordial landscape..." (emphasis in the original, 166). As the primary "way of seeing of the baroque," allegory establishes a deep "demarcation between physical nature and significance" (166).

In a comparable analysis, Avelar states that postdictatorial fiction employs allegory to represent mourning practices that build an "allegorical crypt" in literature, which Avelar relates to "the remainder that names the phantasmatic persistence of unresolved mourning work." Moreover, "if post-dictatorial mourning manifests itself in certain semiotic practices as allegory, then it is the possible link between the crypt of a love object buried alive within the ego...and the structure of allegory that must be pursued. For in allegory too the sign undergoes resistance to figuration..." (8). Such "resistance to figuration," or the incorporation of the object of mourning into a signifying practice, characterizes the radical disjunctive structure of allegoric expression. In Negroni's works, this allegoric form is represented as a proliferation of signifiers, as complex networks of artistic objects that question symbolizing practices, and as radical disassociation of physical space from literary representation. For instance, in *La anunciación*, allegorical figures take center stage in the debate over the connections between literature and history. Projections of the narrator's consciousness, these allegorical figures continue the tradition of the "deployment of abstract figures as dramatic characters" that, since the era of ancient Greek drama, illustrates how literary personification and allegorical expression connect (*New Princeton* 32). Such characters, named "the house," "the anxiety," and "the unknown," attempt the practice of mourning through the reenactment of a painful past: they replicate Humboldt's disappearance, the last speeches and populist rhetoric of Peronism, and imaginary dialogues imitating the meetings of the revolutionary group. As aesthetic replicas of historic events, these allegorical characters emphasize the "memory-as-theater." Avelar explains:

> The metaphor of memory-as-theater, as opposed to memory-as-instrument, makes the remembered image condense in itself, as a scene, the entire failure of the past, as an emblem rescued out of oblivion. Trapped between the imperative of memory and a general inability to imagine an alternative future, post-dictatorial fiction maintains an estranged, denaturalized relation with its present. (10)

As parallel worlds, the allegorical scene and the historical theater coexist in *La anunciación,* echoing the tensions of a "creationist" aesthetic that Athanasius cultivates. In a section of the novel, Athanasius conducts an interview with Huidobro in which he stresses the existence of the independent world of poetry. When asked how he relates poetry, beauty, and truth, Huidobro replies: "Un poema es hermoso porque crea situaciones extraordinarias que necesitan del poema para existir en algún lado." [A poem is beautiful because it creates extraordinary situations that can only exist in the poem] (193). *La anunciación* crafts these eccentric places as historic revelation and aesthetic contemplation. In the virtual places of literature, built around the allegorical scene, historic memory is made possible through the voice of those who, coexisting in past and present temporalities, evoke common memories of exclusion.

Islandia transforms such itineraries into a personal and collective search for identity. In this collection, two poetic voices alternate: one inspired by the language of the Nordic sagas, the complex symbolic systems of the *Kenningar,* and the Scald poets of Iceland, the other, identified as feminine, takes on different identities such as "la sosías" [the stand-in] "la náufraga" [the castaway] or "la travesti" [the transvestite], and employs a poetic language with baroque undertones. The quest for identity and the creation of a common genealogy, first referred to through the Vikings' migration to Iceland in the tenth century, are predominant themes. However, the collective search for a common origin is perceived as an artificial creation:

> En la única tarde que recuerdan, la tarde cuando parten, un ruiseñor está cantando. Pero hay también (debe decirse) estruendo en los ojos y adargas en desorden, como si la belleza, cordial, se aviniera a frustrarse. Se dan cuenta que están fraguando un recuerdo. (103)
>
> [On the only afternoon they remember, the afternoon of their departure, a nightingale is singing. But there is also (not to be omitted) thunder in their eyes

and shields in disarray, as if (cordial) beauty consented to a blotch. They realize they are contriving a memory.] (emphasis in the original, Twitty 19).

As in the poem by Borges, cited in one of the opening epigraphs, "Islandia" refers to a poetic genealogy connecting Nordic and baroque traditions. The sections in *Islandia* written in the voice of the Scalds follow aesthetic principles of word composition of the "kenningar," compound phrases that replaced single nouns in Icelandic poetry of the first century. The highly figurative language of the "kenningar" fascinated Borges who, in his study "Las Kenningar," states that such metaphoric use of language was "el primer deliberado goce verbal de una literatura instintiva" [the first intentional verbal pleasure of an instinctive literature"] (368). As a self-referential language, Borges recognizes that expressions such as "alimento de cuervos" ["raven-food"] to name a corpse, or "tempestad de espadas" ["sword-tempest"] to refer to a battle, are complex linguistic games that still captivate the attention of the "former ultraist" that exists in him (380). And in his poetry collection *La moneda de hierro* [*The Iron Coin*], he goes back to Nordic genealogies to refer to the obscurity of symbols concealed in images such as the iron (as a metonymic reference to armor and swords), the war, and the sea. Imagining himself as the successor of such a dynasty of courage, his connection with this genealogy seems to be obscure and yet a powerful influence in his poetic expression: "And finally I allow myself to engage in the cult of my ancestors and that other cult that illuminates my decline: the study of Old English and Icelandic" (*Selected* 371).[20]

In *Islandia*, the "kenningar," "runes," and heraldic symbols characterize the allegorical language of Negroni's "insular poetics." Established as chains of signifiers that resist the process of symbolization, such expressions build an autonomous, self-referential, and "insular" world for poetry. Connected to the obsession of re-creating an "original" world, such "insular poetics" is highly elegiac in tone:

> *Saben poco del amor los escaldas... Están tan lejos del tacto, tan cerca de la atrofia encendida de las kenningar, ese deseo inconfesado de abstraer, terminar algo (no empezarlo)... Al escribir, han entrado en el territorio de los padres, de caballos de Madera y mástil contra el mar, de flotas como fortalezas, leyendas de bravura, en una suerte de necromancia de imágenes... Están solos contra sus propios héroes. En el inmenso rodeo del poema, interminables, se los ve deambular. A veces un suspiro, el corazón reducido a cenizas. ¿Hasta cuándo reemplazarán la patria con palabras rojas?* (153)
>
> [*The Skalds know little of love... They are so remote from touch, so near the ardent atrophy of the kenningar, that unconfessed desire for abstraction,*

for concluding (not beginning) something… In writing, they have entered the territory of the fathers, of wooden horses and masts against the sea, of flotillas like fortresses, legends of bravery, in a sort of necromancy of images… They stand alone against their own heroes. In the vast corral of the poem, interminable, they seem astray. Once in a while a sigh, the heart burnt to ashes. How long will they continue to attempt a homeland out of redhot words?] (emphasis in the original, Twitty 69)

As her poetic counterpart, the Scalds, the woman poet "la sosías" searches for an identity in a complex world of fleeting images, global journeys, and international airports. Like the Scalds, she embarks upon an itinerary leading to an island of reduced dimensions, the place where she looks for a poetic self disguised under layers of theatrical images:

Hacia el oeste (que en los mapas planos
es el este), la sosías buscará su isla
milimétrica, galerías bajo cuerda
que pudieran conducirla al camouflage,
el facsímil ma non troppo de sí misma. (97)
[Westerly (which on flat maps is east),
the stand-in seeks her millimetric isle,
clandestine galleries fit to conduct her to the camouflage,
to facsimile ma non troppo of herself"] (Twitty 13).

In Negroni's "soliloquio de viajera" ["soliloquy of traveler"] (Twitty 17), structured as an internal dialogue expressed through the recurrent use of the apostrophe,[21] she replicates the Scalds' epic language. Negroni's poetic language, filled with uses of hyperbaton, along with lexical expressions from the sixteenth and seventeenth centuries and baroque ideas on artifice and visual opacity, reinforces the notion of identity (and subjectivity) as an artificial construct. The autonomous world for poetry, the archipelago, the islands that "podrían repetirse, en el futuro, al infinito…(105) ["in the future, reproduce themselves interminably…"] (Twitty 21), emerges from under the multiple layers of the poet's expression as she navigates through a complex geography of fjords and rocky coasts:

A Islandia no se llega atravesando
fiordos sino membranas de espacio:
dalias, lamés en demasía
y una fanfarria de aeropuertos
cuyas luces, con franjas de espuma

pudieran confundirse o vanagloria.
¿Laborioso derroche de soportes
o escritura flagrante
de lágrimas cansadas? (94)
[Islandia is not won by fording
fjords, but piercing pellicles of space:
dahlias, inordinate lamé,
fanfare of landing fields
whose lights for seafroth could be
misconstrued, or for vainglory.
Strenous squandering of props,
or flagrant scribble
tiring of tears?] (Twitty 10)

Cast away in this hidden refuge, the land of poetry, "la sosías" and the Scalds seek to establish the memory of a lost genealogy. As a collection characterized by the experience of dislocation and grief, the search for a lost homeland amid experiences of exile and deterritorialization is a central topic in *Islandia*. As in Negroni's narrative works, the lyric and the narrative are blended in order to question the creation of a common origin in epic narrations. In *Islandia*, the female poetic voice of "la sosías" deconstructs the discourse of the Nordic saga and points to the artificial links of territories and historic identities. By transforming "Islandia" into the autonomous world of poetry, the lost homeland becomes a site for virtual remembrances that take place outside the narrative frame of history.

In *Museo negro* [*Black Museum*] (1999), Negroni explores different lines of a gothic aesthetic that she associates with poetry. Claustrophobic mansions, ghosts and cemeteries, the cult of necrophilia, and the golem are some of the topics that since the eighteenth century have structured what Negroni perceives as the "dark aesthetic" of poetry. Connected to a cult of melancholy and death, poetry can be said to be an island or dark castle, a besieged medieval city or refuge for an aesthetic pulse that responds to the totalitarian discourse of realism.[22] As in *Islandia*, this poetic space is described as enclosed and autonomous ("The world created by art is... claustrophobic and perversely circular," states Negroni, invoking the words of Pizarnik [*El testigo lúcido* 143]) or as a melancholic island where the symbolic order is disrupted:

> Al obedecer a un ritmo hecho de súbitos detenimientos, cambios de dirección y nuevas inmovilizaciones, el poema actúa precisamente una imposibilidad: la de condensar significado y significante. Una y otra vez,

la isla heróica de la melancolía...insiste en la experiencia material y fracasa. Este fracaso es espléndido...porque, con él, se pone de manifiesto lo construido (lo falso) de la verdad simbólica, dando lugar a un mundo donde la jerarquía de una visión coherente de lo real no se sostiene. [By obeying a rhythm made of sudden halts, changes in direction, and further interruptions, the poem performs an impossibility: it condenses the signifier and the signified. Time after time, the heroic isle of melancholy...insists on [representing] material experience, and fails. This failure is splendid...because it makes evident the constructed (false) nature of symbolic truth, and allows for [the creation of] a world where the hierarchy of a coherent vision of the real cannot be sustained.] (28)

Examples of claustrophobic spaces abound in Negroni's collection *El viaje de la noche*. The forest, the diminutive house or its gardens, the submerged or the walled European cities, the cage, and the underworld are examples of how enclosed spaces shape Negroni's gothic poetics. Paradoxically, the subject trapped in these sites is able to experience the mobility of dreaming and imagination and embarks upon a "night journey," or quest for alternative worlds for the self and its poetic representation. *El viaje de la noche* associates this poetic searching with a female subject who, secluded in societies' attics and dark basements, pays the price of isolation in order to create her own poetic words. As in "El padre" ["The Father"], which reconstructs the mythic patricide of Orpheus by the Maenads, or in "Casandra," where the prophetess announces the apocalyptic end of the world while trapped on an island about to sink, women are the exiles who proclaim from the dark corners of such surreal places a discourse that is prophetic of the world of poetry yet to come. The title of this collection refers to both the journey that women embark upon as poets and, in the tradition of surrealism, an invitation to the reader to rethink the borders dividing the real and the imaginary. Following baroque and surrealist traditions, *El viaje de la noche* employs visual delusion to challenge the subject's homogeneity, internal dialogues, and apostrophes, displaying imaginary exchanges between the poet and different representations of her consciousness. The absurd and the fantastic are additional poetic strategies that bring about the eruption of the unexpected, the "dark drive" characteristic of Negroni's poetry. Many of the poems focus on the in-between spaces that separate reality from the imagination, the wall being a central metaphor of how the self and society at large leave out what is feared. Most important, the wall is an obstacle for attaining the aesthetic contemplation that takes place only on the "other side" of poetry, of which "Los dos cielos" ["The Two Heavens"] is an excellent example. Here, a girl is trapped by the fear of crossing the border, of jumping over the wall that divides a fantastic space described as double (as in the poem's title, the "two heavens"):

> Ella teme saltar. Teme la tenue lámina del agua, es
> decir el borde agudo de sí misma y ese vaho sobre
> la superficie, esa duplicación de cielos. Teme saltar,
> como si la esperara un país neurótico, resurrecciones,
> islas cantadas y vacías como fotografías de algo que
> no existe. En su corazón sopla un viento tan rojo. (60)
> [She is afraid to jump. Afraid of the tenous blade of
> Water, that is, the sharp edge of herself and that
> Vapor hovering on its surface, that duplication of
> Havens. She is afraid to jump, as if a neurotic
> Country awaited her, resurrections, islands epic and
> Empty as photographs of the nonexistent. In her
> Heart such a red wind is blowing.] (Twitty 61)

El viaje de la noche locates the realm of poetry in this liminal site, the "thin leaf," the "sharp edge" that opens the experience of reading to fantastic or surreal dimensions. Although evoked as a site on the brink of disintegration, the world of childhood and its fairy tales and dialogues with imaginary friends occupies a central representation of this liminal poetics. In "Sleeping Beauty," the traditional fairy tale is rewritten as an imaginary exchange between the woman poet and her corpse; at the end, references to necrophilia establish the confusion between real and imaginary selves:

> Te veo dormir, sentada en un bosque
> azul, tridimensional, fabulosamente estático. Como
> no sé despertarte, decido volver a mi casa del otro
> lado del mar. Pero mi casa no existe, no es mía, son
> otros los que allí dan órdenes. Ah ¿cuántas millas
> antes de tu despertar? ¿Cuál de las dos está viva?
> ¿Quién me libra de tu sueño poderoso? (78)
> [... I see you
> Sleeping, seated in a blue, three-dimensional,
> Fabulously ecstatic forest. As I don't know how to
> Wake you, I decide to return to my house on the
> Other side of the ocean. But my house does not exist,
> It isn't mine; others give the orders there. Ah, how
> Many miles before you wake? Which of us is alive?
> Who will free me from your compelling dream?] (Twitty 79)

In *Technologies of Gender,* Teresa de Lauretis addresses the issue of gender as represented by filmic space. She proposes that the "subject of feminism" is built on "heteronomous spaces" that move back and forth "between the representation of gender (in its male-centered frame of reference) and what that representation leaves out or, more pointedly, makes unrepresentable." In what she describes as a "contradictory" place, feminist practices move "between the (represented) discursive space of the positions made available by hegemonic discourses and the space-off, the elsewhere, of those discourses: those other spaces both discursive and social that exist...in the margins (or "between the lines," or "against the grain,") of hegemonic discourses and in the interstices of institutions, in counterpractices and new forms of community" (26). Negroni's "insular poetics" thoroughly exemplifies such places of feminist resistance. Her aesthetics of baroque and surrealist undertones continues the poetic tradition, going back to what Negroni characterizes as the "somber poetics" of authors such as Alejandra Pizarnik, Susana Thénon, Osvaldo Lamborghini, and Néstor Perlongher (*El testigo* 18). Negroni's "insular poetics" rewrites oppressive social spatialities for women in building off-spaces located in the realm of literary imagination. As the fluid cities she describes in *El sueño de Úrsula,* contrasting with the walled medieval city where her women characters are entrapped, the virtual spaces of her poetic and narrative texts establish new sites where women can imagine new creative dialogues in the interstices of hegemonic spatialities. As the baroque city described by Angel Rama in *The Lettered City,*[23] this city is a virtual labyrinth of symbols; however, this literary virtual space is not the realm of hegemonic practices of control and domination but rather a poetic crossover, a tapestry of endless poetic possibilities, a "nomadic city":

> Veo que la ciudad se acerca y pasa por delante como
> si fuera un río. Una novia clara. Transcurre, de
> izquierda a derecha, lentamente, con su perfil de
> almenas y de lumbre. Alborozada, me pregunto por dónde he de
>   cruzarla. (24)
> [I see the city approaching and flowing past me like
> a river. A lucedent bride. It transpires from left to
> right, slowly, its profile of parapet and light. Elated,
> I wonder where to cross.] (Twitty 25)

As imaginary geographies where literature trespasses boundaries and frontiers, Negroni's works are prophecies, "annunciations" of a world yet to come. Bellessi, Futoransky, and Negroni create eccentric geographies that recover those voices excluded in hegemonic spatialities of the last decades in

Argentina. The postdictatorial scene has a direct impact on this geopolitical decentering: memory and allegory are central mechanisms in crafting paradoxical spaces that establish imaginary dialogues with the historical subjects erased from the national space. The presence of what Alicia Genovese calls the "double voice" in women's poetry (15–16) underscores the self-reflexive traits of their poetry. The rich, labyrinthlike spaces in their works point to the complexities of social location that women and other underrepresented groups experienced in a period when neoliberalism and redemocratization produced new and more perverse forms of social exclusion. The virtual geographies analyzed here establish a series of poetic crossovers that communicate multiple temporalities: painful memories of past exclusion and a future when new levels of social agency can be built. As an archeological site in Bellessi, a postmodern collage in Futoransky, or as an insular landscape in Negroni, spaces are depicted as elaborate sites for virtual exchanges. Poetry is, therefore, a path to a utopian land of possibilities where women can unmake the world, according to Negroni.

> "Hay una marca genérica porque la idea de territorio es un sinónimo de orden. Y esto es lo contrario de lo que estoy tratando de hacer con la escritura. La idea de territorio implica frontera, legalidad, homogeneidad, nación, comunidad. En cambio los espacios que yo creo y que crean las mujeres en general son corrosivos, son pústulas que aparecen en el medio de este orden para desarticularlo. Es como una comunidad de refugiados." [The notion of territory is marked by gender because territory is synonymous with order. And this is the opposite of what I am trying to do in my writing. The notion of territory implies frontiers, legality, homogeneity, nationhood, community. But the spaces I create, and that women in general create, are corrosive, they are pustules that appear in the midst of this order for the purpose of dismantling it. (Women writers) are like a community of refugees" (personal interview).

The paradoxical spaces of authors Bellessi, Futoransky, and Negroni are compelling examples of poetic lands where women authors seek to create, at the turn of the twenty-first century, a new "community of refugees," unmaking and creating new forms of social space.

Notes

1 Displacing Domesticity: Cosmopolitanisms, Travel Writing, and Narratives of the Home

1. Ocampo explains how her great-grandfather, Manuel Hermenegildo de Aguirre first traveled to England to buy books for a public library under the request of the principal of the Colegio de San Carlos, Luis José de Chorroarín. Years later, in 1817, he embarked upon a diplomatic trip to request that the then U.S. president, James Monroe, acknowledge the recently declared independence of the provinces of South America. Aguirre was also tasked with buying weapons and ships to help the liberation of Perú. Ocampo concludes a preface to the first volume of her autobiography by saying, "Y como don Manuel Hermenegildo se trajo de Norteamérica el Horacio y el Curiacio, y armas que le costaron tantos dolores de cabeza, yo soñé con traer otros veleros, otras armas, para otras conquistas. Y viviendo mi sueño traté de justificar mi vida. Casi diría de hacérmela perdonar." [And just as Mr. Manuel Hermenegildo brought the *Horacio* and the *Curiacio*, and armaments from North America which caused him great trouble, I dreamt of bringing other ships, other armaments, to engage in other conquests. And by living my dream, I sought to justify my life. I would almost say, to ask forgiveness for it] (*I* 24).
2. The notion of "space as a text" is defined by Henrietta Moore: "To treat the organization of space as analogous to a text is to begin with the assumed interdependence of parts with the whole, of sense with reference, and of structure with action. This assumption permits a text to be approached in two ways; either it can be analyzed and explained in terms of its internal relations (langue, sense) or it may be interpreted as process, as the actualised product of social actors in a particular context (parole, reference)" (80).
3. In her study *Women, Feminism, and Social Change in Argentina, Chile, and Uruguay 1890–1940*, Asunción Lavrin explains that the reforms of social codes accomplished in Argentina in 1926 represent only "evolutionary steps" in social change. However, they were helpful in relation to two issues in family law that affected women: "whether the home should have an incontestable male head controlling the property and behavior of wife and children, and whether the

hypocrisy implied in the social cult of motherhood and the reality of mother's lacking any jurisdiction over their own children should be allowed to remain unchanged" (11).
4. In Masiello's words: "By the twentieth century, woman in the public sphere was marked by the unmistakable impulses of barbarism. As the outsider she set the boundaries between intelligibility and irrationality; she defined the limits between high and low cultures, between elite and popular responses; and, finally, she allowed men to mark the difference between civilization and savagery" (*Between Civilization* 9).
5. There is an abundant critical bibliography on Lange and Ocampo's works. Nora Domínguez analyzes Lange's descriptions of family dynamics in the light of her public role in *Martín Fierro*. Elizabeth Marchant proposes that Ocampo holds a position of cultural critic that is based on her public role and the intimate representations of her autobiography. Masiello explains how Lange and Ocampo "bridge" the public and private spheres in a period of modernism and nationalistic revival. Molloy conducts a brilliant analysis of the autobiographies by Lange and Ocampo and establishes how they both embody gender tensions of the period. Last, Unruh states how the negotiation of the public and the private is linked to a literary performance that enacts new social roles for women. For further reference, see Domínguez; Marchant; Masiello, *Between Civilization*; Molloy; and Unruh.
6. In Amy Kaminsky's words: "The points from which Argentina is perceived, from inside and from without, do not merely rest inertly side by side, but rather interact with each other in the creation of the multiple, conflicting, interdependent yet mutually destabilizing notions of Argentina as a place and a culture" (*Argentina* 7).
7. Felski proposes that instead of characterizing women's writing based on their textual transgressions, literary criticism should estimate the value of innovative paradigms within the context of social change and women's transformation of the public sphere. In Felski's words, "I suggest in contrast that it is impossible to speak of 'masculine' and 'feminine' in any meaningful sense in the formal analysis of texts; the political value of literary texts from the standpoint of feminism can be determined only by an investigation of their social functions and effects in relation to the interests of women in a particular historical context and not by attempting to deduce an abstract literary theory of 'masculine' and 'feminine,' 'subversive' and 'reactionary' forms in isolation from the social conditions of their production and reception" (*Beyond Feminist Aesthetics* 2).
8. Unless otherwise specified, Cindy Schuster has been in charge of all translations.
9. For more information about the naturalization of motherhood and the impact of medicine on it, see Nari's chapter, "La maternalización de las mujeres" in *Políticas*, 101–70.
10. Storni's journal articles are filled with references to women immigrants and the complexities of the gender realities of the period. See, for instance, the compilation *Nosotras... y la piel. Selección de ensayos de Alfonsina Storni*.

11. Sidonie Smith examines at length the implications of this generic contract for the woman writer. In addition, Smith provides an excellent definition of this doubling by defining autobiography as "a written or verbal communication that takes the speaking 'I' as the subject of the narrative, rendering the 'I' both subject and object" (19). For a detailed discussion on the theoretical considerations around the process of autobiographical doubling, see her chapter "Woman's Story and the Engenderings of Self-representation" in *A Poetics*.
12. *Ultraísmo* is a literary movement born in Spain in 1918 in which both Jorge Luis Borges and González Lanuza participated. González Lanuza published *Prismas* [*Prisms*] in 1924, in which he explored the traits of ultraist poetics, as influenced by Vicente Huidobro's *Creacionismo* [*Creationism*]. Characteristics of ultraist poetry include evocative imagery, references to the culture of modernity, elimination of rhyme, and creative graphic treatment of the layout of poetry in print. In "Anatomía de mi ultra" ["Anatomy of My Ultra"], Borges summarizes ultraist goals as the cultivation of rhythm and metaphor in order to create deep emotions in the reader. He further states that image reflection is central in modern poetry, as expressed by the "active aesthetic of *prismas*" (83).
13. In a previous essay, I study in depth the link between modern technologies of visual reproduction, such as photography and Lange's works. See Sierra, "Oblique Views."
14. See Caws, "Doubling."
15. In her speech to "Oliverio Girondo," Lange states, "El *gran simpático* de Oliverio Girondo ya nos obligó a deambular satisfactoriamente, hace catorce meses, en parecida obsesión marina, rememorada en anterior monólogo y que respondió al nombre de 'Bergantín Martín Fierro'" [The *most charming* Oliverio Girondo has already obliged us to wander satisfactorily, fourteen months ago, in a similar marine obsession, recalled in a previous monologue called 'The Brigantine Martín Fierro'"] (emphasis in the original, *Estimados Congéneres* 50).
16. In Unruh's words, Ingrid's superior linguistic knowledge and her role as a language teacher and translator "conforms to the social motherhood agenda of Buenos Aires feminism that posited a requisite utility for modern women in the changing social order" (81).
17. Beatriz Sarlo illustrates the redefinition of literary nationalism in her "Introduction" and "A Landscape for Borges" in *A Writer on the Edge*, 1–19).
18. For instance, Ingrid states, "En mi país existe el prejuicio por lo nacional. Ahora comienza a sacudirse un poco, y ya el público sonríe ante una edición barata de Elinor Glyn, aunque la compra luego, cuando nadie lo mira." [In my country there is a prejudice for the national. We are beginning to get away from it a little, and now the public smiles before a cheap romance novel by Elinor Glyn, even though they buy it later, when no one is looking] (32).
19. Griselda Pollock studies artistic representations of the role of women in the modernist city. For further reference, see her chapter "Modernity and the Spaces of Femininity," in *Vision and Difference*. Elisabeth Wilson explains, for instance, how department stores or restaurants offer European women spaces for a new freedom and self-definition (10). See "The Invisible Flâneur" in *The*

Contradictions of Culture. In Argentina, Sarlo comments in her study "Buenos Aires, ciudad moderna" that modern changes in the city affected urban customs, in particular in relation to women. See Sarlo, *Buenos Aires.*
20. To illustrate, Stevenson's tale of his old aunts who live an isolated existence in a house crowded by ornaments and family relics is very relevant to the association between femininity and domesticity. The gothic traits of the story, especially with regard to the enclosed and ghostly space of the house, relate to Lange's later narratives of the home, where women are also trapped by family traditions they cannot escape.
21. See Prebisch, "Precisiones de Le Corbusier."
22. See Facio, *Victoria Ocampo en fotografías* [*Victoria Ocampo: Photographs*], 44–45.
23. In *Victoria Ocampo en fotografías,* Sara Facio transcribes some comments Ocampo made about Rufino de Elizalde's house: "La arquitectura moderna me fascinaba. Tenía hambre de paredes blancas y vacías. Era una nueva manera de vivir. Fue una gran satisfacción que cuando vino Le Corbusier le gustara la casa y la decoración." [Modern architecture fascinated me. I was hungry for white, empty walls. It was a new way of living. It was a great satisfaction when Le Corbusier visited the house and admitted he liked it] (44). And later, when talking about the furniture, she states, "Yo estaba enamorada de la casa... Todo tenía sentido, nada librado a la improvisación." [I was in love with the house... Everything had a meaning; nothing was open to improvisation] (45).
24. Later texts also reflect her interest in furniture and decoration as cultural manifestations. For instance, in her commentary on Anna de Noaille's poetry, she devotes an important part of her *testimonio* to describing the crammed interiors of her home ("Anna de Noailles" 14). In *Autobiografía,* she refers to the modern simplicity of the apartment in Paris where she is introduced to Drieu La Rochelle. When meeting with Benito Mussolini, she carefully depicts the "laconic" interiors of the "Palacio Venecia" [Venetian Palace] as a symbol of fascism's masculine aesthetics. Following her description, she transcribes a passionate exchange with Mussolini about the female character roles in *The Divine Comedy* and in her *De Francesca a Beatrice.* According to Ocampo, fascism's architectural style replicates its male authoritarianism ("La historia viva" ["Living History"] 11).
25. In *La literatura autobiográfica argentina,* Adolfo Prieto explains that the nineteenth-century independence wars made the autobiographical genre in Argentina into an example of public political debate. Additional causes for autobiographical writing are wealth, power, or prestige (21). Ocampo felt compelled to write her *Autobiografía* partially because of these motives.
26. The significant competition of other publishing houses founded by exiled Spanish intellectuals is important to bear in mind in this changing scenario of cultural relations. Among others, it is worth mentioning Antonio López Llausás's creation of Sudamericana, Mariano Medina del Río y Álvaro de las Casas's founding of Emecé, and in 1939, Gonzalo Losada's founding of Losada. For an overall description of this period's editorial activities, see José Luis de Diego, *Editores y políticas editoriales.*

27. One important drive of the "gendering of modernity" is, according to Felski, the historic nostalgia that she associates with images of pre-Oedipal motherhood. In this context, gender representations in modern culture are shaped into an identification of women and nature and the "construction of a redemptive realm of the maternal" (39). The growing demarcation between private and public worlds resulted in the emergence of the nuclear family and an idealization of the role the mother played in it.
28. She used her homes for intellectual functions. In 1923, she hosted Rabindranath Tagore at her home in San Isidro, which became a cultural center for the time the Bengali poet stayed there (*II* 138–39). The most radical transformations took place at Villa Ocampo when she returned to live there. She remodeled the house completely according to her modernist taste and eventually donated the estate to UNESCO.
29. The publication of her commentary on *The Divine Comedy* signifies, according to Sylvia Molloy, the exposing of the body to the public, as the passion Ocampo describes in her autobiography echoes the passions in Dante's text (95). In fact, *De Francesca a Beatrice* is a ciphered text, dedicated to her lover and filled with references to their troubled affair, as confessed in detail in the second volume of *Autobiografía*. Ocampo conducts literary criticism by negotiating gender tensions and masking her feminist claims in the textual commentary. In other words, she annotates her life through texts (Molloy 95).
30. In *Cosmopolitanisms and Latin America,* Jacqueline Loss proposes moving beyond the international definition of the term that was popularized in Latin America since the *modernista* movement because this perspective only foregrounds the participation of intellectuals in a modern, universal culture. Contrary to that idea, Loss proposes redefining cosmopolitanism as a complex process, similar to James Clifford's conceptualization of "discrepant" cosmopolitanisms as productive sites of cultural crossing. See "Cosmopolitanisms between the Americas."
31. By the end of the nineteenth century, domesticity and masculinity began to be considered oppositional, with the motherhood ideals of intimacy, nurturing, and comfort as characteristic of the domestic. As Heynen demonstrates, such redefinition of domesticity posed serious problems to patriarchal authority, especially in England. There was a "male revolt against domesticity" that later pervaded the antidomestic trait of certain modernist discourses (8–9).

2 "Of Other Spaces": Staging Repression in Griselda Gambaro and Diana Raznovich

1. Unless otherwise specified, Cindy Schuster has been in charge of all translations.
2. On the figure of the joker, see Mady Schutzman's "Jok(er)ing. Joker runs wild" (Popen 133–45). Besides being a polyvalent figure, Schutzman states that the joker interjects disorientation and incongruity into the stories, a role

similar to that held by the "guides" in Gambaro's play. One important trait of the joker is the use of laughter as an ethical instrument that places the spectator in a "dangerous in-between" and challenges our sense of "location," the attachment to certain ideas or judgments (140). *Información para extranjeros* similarly employs humor as a means of shattering the foundations of social concepts. As the guides "invite" the audience to gradually move through different and increasingly violent itineraries, their humorous interventions prompt us to revise our position as spectators and our attachment to preconceived ideas.

3. "Chupado" is one of the terms listed by Marguerite Feitlowitz in her "lexicon of terror," a compilation of euphemisms that the dictatorship used during its regime: "*Chupado* (past. part. of *chupar*); n. *chupado/a*, someone who has been sucked up, i.e., disappeared). 'You're lucky that we were the ones to suck you up *(que te chupamos nosotros)*. You'll get bashed around, but you'll live. We're the only branch of the military that doesn't kill its *chupados* anymore. [A lie]. The country can no longer afford the luxury of losing strong arms.' This was systematically repeated by all the interrogators." (Oscar Alfredo González and Horacio Guillermo Cid de la Paz in Feitlowitz, *Lexicon* 54).

4. Marta Morello-Frosh explains that a number of literary works dealing with the influences of Peronismo on Argentine history reflect tensions in the cultural field during the 1950s and 1960s. Fictional works by Julio Cortázar, Jorge Luis Borges, Delmiro Sáenz, David Viñas, and Germán Rozenmacher explore the relationship between hegemonic and marginal groups in Argentine history and the changes in the social landscape of the period. Morello-Frosh compares, for instance, the trope of "invasion" in Cortázar and Rozenmacher. "Casa Tomada" ["House Taken Over"] by Cortázar and "Cabecita negra" ["Little Black Head"] by Rozenmacher both deal with the image of the mestizo "cabecita negra," a new political class emerging during the Peronista years (1946–1955). Written in the 1950s, Cortázar's story represents the social space of the nation as a house taken over by invisible invaders. In the case of Rozenmacher, the invaders have the faces of two migrants from the provinces, a woman and her brother, a police officer. As Morello-Frosh explains, the trope of invasion has different characteristics in both authors: whereas Cortázar depicts the fears of rural oligarchies facing the rise of Peronism, Rozenmacher's story embodies the fears of the emergent middle classes who during the Peronista years also gained new social representation and feared being displaced by the new political importance of the "cabecitas negras." In both stories, the house is either left closed (Cortázar) or open (Rozenmacher), signaling the differences in political climate and the possibilities for social alliances between hegemonic and marginal groups. See Morello-Frosh, "La ficción."

5. Gambaro has acknowledged in an interview the relation of *Del sol naciente* to the Falklands War: "The project that I'm most interested in is a play I wrote last year, *Del sol naciente* [*From the Rising Sun*]. In Argentina we call Japan "the rising sun." It's a play that began as a dream. I dreamt that I had written a perfect play, with a Japanese ambiance. When I woke up, I thought, "Why not?" I

wrote a play with a Japanese setting, but the theme is related to the Falklands War" (*Interview* 1987).
6. Examples of women's testimonials about their experiences in clandestine detention centers in Argentina include *Pasos bajo el Agua* [*Steps Under Water*, Kozameh, 1987], *La Escuelita. Relatos Testimoniales* [*The Little School. Tales of Disappearance and Survival in Argentina*, Partnoy, 1998], and *Una sola muerte numerosa* [*A Single Numberless Death*, Strejilevich 1997].
7. The intentions of the military were several. While the admiral, Jorge Isaac Anaya, had wanted for years to establish a military base in the islands to protect the military from the Chilean army, Galtieri needed a triumph for the discredited army in a moment when the economic situation of the country—an inflation of 150 percent in 1982—was also rapidly deteriorating (Puga 190). The war only lasted about two months but yielded about seven hundred deaths and one thousand wounded for the Argentine army, mostly young men who were drafted in a compulsory enrollment to the armed forces.
8. The expression refers here to Taylor's chapter on the Madres de Plaza de Mayo and the play by Gambaro, *Antígona furiosa*—"Trapped in Bad Scripts: the Mothers of the Plaza de Mayo,"—in which Taylor examines in great detail the paradoxes in the Madres's movement from the perspective of Gambaro's play. The main contradiction, as Taylor summarizes, resides in the fact that while the Madres were able to gain key political aims, such as bring the Argentina junta to trial and damage its legitimacy and credibility, they were "trapped" in traditional gender roles that left the sexual differentiation at the core of the regime pretty much untouched (*Disappearing Acts* 190–93).
9. In her study on the supernatural in Gothic fiction, Margaret Carter explains that the Gothic is a genre that bears similarities to the "uncanny," a term used by both Tzvetan Todorov and Sigmund Freud to describe psychological and literary examples of a "dissonance produced by the intrusion of strange events into a familiar, realistic genre" (9). In all cases, the supernatural elements of the Gothic, in particular in those cases where there is a mediated narrative and a limited perspective, invite the reader to identify with the protagonist's uncertainty. The supernatural allows speculation about the "nonmaterial dimensions of existence without demanding a positive act of either acceptance or rejection" (3). See Carter, *Specter or Delusion? The Supernatural in Gothic Fiction*.
10. There are a number of cultural geographers who address this idea, starting with David Harvey's foundational text, *Social Justice and the City*. The spatial turn in the social sciences and the cultural turn in geography both relate to a more complex understanding of space as a social and historical reality. Such notions are also at the core of Edward Soja's ideas on a "third space," a space that disrupts hegemonic spatialities and allows for strategic political alliances among those who had otherwise remained invisible in a social structure deprived of political power. As I summarize in the introduction, feminist critics and geographers have also theorized about the appropriation of social space as a form of feminist resistance. See, for instance, Harvey, "The Social Construction"; Soja, "Thirdspace."

11. In Antígona's words: "Y en esta cadena de los vivos y los muertos, yo pagaré sus culpas" (201) ["And in this chain of the living of the death, I will pay for their wrongdoings"] (Feitlowitz, *Information* 141).
12. My own translation.
13. The term "capucha" [hood] in English refers to both a prisoner's situation of being "hooded" and to the section of the attic in the *casino de oficiales* in the ESMA, where hooded prisoners were kept in complete isolation.
14. "Una clase de historia" ["A History Lesson"], *Página 12*, October 22, 1995. Cited in Feitlowitz, *A Lexicon of Terror*, 174.
15. This description follows the information I obtained during a visit to the ESMA in June of 2007 and the accounts of survivors compiled by Marguerite Feitlowitz. See Feitlowitz, *A Lexicon of Terror*.
16. Andreas Huyssen's *After the Great Divide* explores the volatile and problematic relationship between high art and mass culture in different literary and artistic movements in the twentieth century and the identification of women with mass culture as one of the many ways in which the culture of modernity built an artificial "great divide" between these two ideas.
17. As Hortiguera and Rocha point out, the years between 1989 and 2001 represent the rise and fall of neoliberalism in Argentina. "Every cultural field—narrative, music, film—was influenced by the prioritization of market forces and rules" (9).
18. In her study, Masiello mentions different genres, such as chronicles by anarchists, serial novels, narrations by Italian immigrants, and the feminist novellas, as manifestations of how subaltern groups confront official discourses. She also analyzes examples of Afro-Argentine publications, such as *La Broma* (1876–1885), which abounds in examples of critical views on Argentine modernization. According to Masiello, these publications depict private space as a place of confusion of categories and challenge the order of public values defended by nationalist rhetoric ("Estado" 143).
19. For more information about the naturalization of motherhood, see the chapter "La maternalización de las mujeres," in *Políticas*.
20. In Susan Sontag's words: "Photography is acquisition in several forms. In its simplest form, we have in a photograph surrogate possession of a cherished person or thing, a possession which gives photographs some of the character of unique objects. Through photographs, we also have a consumer's relation to events, both to events which are part of our experience and to those which are not—a distinction between types of experience such as habit-forming consumer blurs. A third form of acquisition is that, through image-making and image-duplication machines, we can acquire something as information (rather than experience). Indeed, the importance of photographic images as the medium through which more and more events enter our experience is, finally, only a by-product of their effectiveness in furnishing knowledge disassociated from and independent of experience" ("The Image" 351).
21. In *Regarding the Pain of Others,* Susan Sontag comments on the many effects of war photographs on the spectator. For instance, she explains that they can create

a detached form of perception leading to rationalization: "To photographic corroboration of the atrocities committed by one's own side, the standard response is that the pictures are a fabrication, that no such atrocity ever took place, those were bodies the other side had brought in trucks from the city morgue and placed about the street, or that, yes, it happened and it was the other side who did it, to themselves" (11).
22. In Artaud's words: "We want to make theatre a believable reality inflicting this kind of tangible laceration, contained in all true feeling, on the heart and the senses. In the same way as our dreams react on us and reality react on our dreams, so we believe ourselves able to associate mental pictures with dreams, effective insofar as they are projected with the required violence. And the audience will believe in the illusion of theatre on condition they really take it for a dream, nor for a servile imitation of reality. On condition it releases the magic freedom of daydreams, only recognizable when imprinted with terror and cruelty" (27).
23. In her study on the role of mechanical reproduction in the conservation of Lenin's memory, Leah Dickerman describes the contradictory relationship between the attempts to memorialize Lenin and the loss of his importance as a public figure in the process: "As Benjamin suggested, mechanical reproduction lessens one sense of monumentality: it reduced the size and scale of the image so that it was no longer experienced by the viewer as an overwhelming power. Yet through pervasive dissemination of mass-produced images to individuals and throughout the spaces of daily public life, a kind of alternate monumentality was created for Lenin, one peculiarly modern in its horizontal array" (81).
24. Operativo Independencia was the code name of the military operation in the Tucumán Province started by the military in 1975. Its goals were to crush the forces of Montoneros and ERP (Ejército Revolucionario del Pueblo) guerrillas hiding in the towns of Santa Lucía, Los Sosa, Monteros, and La Fronterita in the south of the province.

3 Global Patagonia: Rewriting the National Space

1. As Hortiguera and Rocha point out, the years between 1989 and 2001 represent the rise and fall of neoliberalism in Argentina. This is the period when President Carlos Menem deregulated the Argentine economy and privatized the country's major assets and primary services, such as transportation, gas, and telecommunications. In 1995, after Menem's reelection, neoliberalism consolidated as the predominant economic and social force in the country. Toward 1999, when Fernando de la Rúa was elected to the presidency, the neoliberal model was collapsing, and 13 million Argentines found themselves living in conditions of poverty. In 2001, the signs of the crisis became acute, and the socioeconomic situation of the country deteriorated. Because of the social and financial meltdown, de la Rúa was forced to resign, and the country sank into an institutional crisis; five interim presidents were named in the short time span of only a couple months. The social legacies of this turbulent period in

Argentina are the disintegration of social relations and the deregulation and privatization of culture (8). The market became a central force in regulating cultural production. As Hortiguera and Rocha explain, "every cultural field—narrative, music, film—was influenced by the prioritization of market forces and rules" (9).
2. In "La muralla china cabeza abajo" ["The Great Wall of China Upside Down"], Blengino summarizes the debate that took place in Buenos Aires around the time of the construction of the ditch. As he explains, most of the criticism came about because of Alsina's pacifist strategy; in fact, Blengino claims that the ditch was built mainly as a defense strategy looking to create a porous frontier that would enable social exchanges among people living on both sides of this border (53). The ditch proved to be impractical and inefficient in trying to contain the *malones;* Blengino quotes a testimony by Alfred Ebélot, the French engineer in charge of the construction, in which he describes how a *malon*, commanded by the infamous Chief Catriel, crossed over it after forcing a herd of sheep into the ditch (45). See Blengino, "La muralla," 29–61.
3. Key historic dates in the territorial formation of Patagonia are: in 1879, the creation of the national territory of Patagonia; the Boundary Treaty in 1881 that delineated the entire frontier between Argentina and Chile after a number of territorial disputes that centered mainly on the Strait of Magellan (Chile had founded Punta Arenas in 1845, which had threatened Argentina's claims to Patagonia); an Argentine law in 1884 divided Patagonia into five national territories that included the area of the Strait of Magellan, the same year that president Avellaneda conducted the last campaign of the Conquest of the Desert; and the creation in 1895 of a penal colony in Tierra del Fuego after being moved from Staten Island.
4. Andermann explains that the writing of this national space is connected to a systematic effort to transform it into a national territory, as evidenced in *Una excursión a los indios Ranqueles* by Lucio V. Mansilla and *Viaje a la Patagonia Austral* [*Journey to Southern Patagonia*] by Francisco P. Moreno. Later textual representations reworked this image, as in Roberto J. Payró's *La Australia Argentina* [*The Argentine Australia*] and *Aguafuertes Patagónicas* by Roberto Arlt. Contrary to the nationalistic tone of the former examples, Payró and Arlt employ ironic, triumphal tones that brings to the fore the modern complexities of Patagonia as a textual representation of the last frontier.
5. During this period, a number of movies were also produced in relation to Patagonia, for example, *La nave de los locos* [*Ship of Fools*] by Ricardo Wülicher (1995); *El viaje* [*The Journey*] by Pino Solanas (1990); *Mundo Grúa* [*Crane World*] by Pablo Trapero (1999); and *Caballos Salvajes* [*Wild Horses*] by Marcelo Piñeyro, (1995). Besides the novel by Iparraguirre, another fictional account of the history of Jemmy Button and the Yahgans captured by Fitz Roy was written in the 1990s, *Fuegia* (1991) by Eduardo Belgrano Rawson. Additionally, *Inglaterra* [*England*] (1999) by Leopoldo Brizuela is a historical novel taking place in Tierra del Fuego at the end of the nineteenth century.

6. In a recent interview, Iparraguirre explains that the novel is set in the 1990s to show the "other face" of the Menem years, the face of poverty that pushes a vast sector of the population into extreme levels of marginalization. The novel's main character is a seventeen-year-old, Cristóbal, who wanders the streets of Buenos Aires trying to sell plastic novelties imported from Taiwan. As Iparraguirre explains in the interview, setting the novel in 1995 refers both to the local market opening its doors to Taiwan's imports and to the changes in Argentine society during the implementation of the neoliberal policies of the Menem years. See Iparraguirre, "Quise contar."
7. The article by Juan Pablo Neyret further contends that Iparraguirre's metatextual reflection follows a literary model described by Adolfo Prieto in *Los viajeros ingleses y la emergencia de la literatura Argentina, 1820–1850*, that is based on intertextual references in travel writing. Iparraguirre, like many writers of nineteenth-century Argentina, establishes a dialogue among canonical writers such as Domingo Faustino Sarmiento, with his ideas on civilization and barbarism, and English travel writers such as Herman Melville. The novel begins with two epigraphs by Sarmiento and Melville, and as Neyret and later Perkowska state, these epigraphs show a conscious effort by Iparraguirre to locate her fiction at the intersection of two cultural paradigms provided by England and Argentina. See Neyret, "De alguien a nadie"; Perkowska, "Rememoración y reescritura"; and Prieto, "Viajeros ingleses."
8. The "object book" has gained importance in Spain and Latin America in recent years. Chilean writer Pía Barros is a strong believer in the format. She states that object books challenge the notion of "sacred" text and reject massive commercialization since they are published in small numbers; they resemble a craft and establish a more personal and intimate relationship with the reader. Pía Barros preferred the format because it sheltered her literary creations during the dark years of the Pinochet regime (personal interview, June 3, 2007).
9. In an interview, Iparraguirre explains that Total Austral, an oil company based in Patagonia, commissioned her work. She wanted not only to "honor" Tierra del Fuego (the photographs by Von Der Fecth clearly fulfill that role), but also to memorialize the cruel history of the area. Therefore, she organized the book into four sections: tributes to the aboriginal Yahgan and Selk'nam people and histories on "legendary sailors" and the missionaries of Tierra del Fuego (personal interview, June 26, 2008).
10. *Journal and Remarks*, the first version of Darwin's journal, was published in 1933 by his granddaughter, Nora Barlow. The second version, which was expanded and included a longer account of the Jemmy Button and the other Fuegian Indians, was known earlier under the title of *The Voyage of the Beagle;* this is the version considered here (96).
11. Sylvia Molloy states that autobiographies are characterized by a "textual self confrontation"; the author believes he or she is the topic of his or her book, contrary to those texts wherein there is only a preoccupation with self-representation but the main finality is not autobiography. See "Introducción," *Acto de presencia*, 11–22.

12. The basic facts are as follows: A mission had been established on Keppel Island where Reverend Despard was in charge. He had hired a group of sailors to help him organize the logistic details of the mission. Parker Snow, a sailor employed by the mission as the man in charge, had gone to Port Stanley for Despard to communicate Despard's intentions to the island's governor. The ship that the mission used to abduct Yahgans and bring them to the mission, the *Allan Gardiner,* was captured and its crew killed.
13. The editor's note reads: "A copy in English of the minutes was affixed to the seven sections of Guevara's account. How they came into his hands is not known. The testimonies of Smyley, Coles, and Jemmy Button are textual. We have no record, however, that Rev. Despard, his wife, and Parker Snow were present at the trial. Nevertheless, the words attributed to them by Guevara conform almost point for point to letters and documents of the Public Record Office, in London" (*La tierra* 156). In an interview, Iparraguirre stated how she personally read those documents in the Public Record Office in England, and how the long-lasting impression they made motivated the writing of the novel's last scenes (personal interview, June 26, 2009).
14. The term "postcolonial" is appropriate here since, as Homi Bhabha states, the postcolonial perspective seeks more complex ways of understanding the intricate relation between the so-called "first" and "third" worlds by making evident the presence of those voices previously marginalized in the colonial order (173).
15. In *Between Civilization and Barbarism: Women, Nation, and Literary Culture in Modern Argentina,* Masiello explains that there is a robust tradition of literary women who initiated their writing in the domestic sphere and who were able to carry out a critical project of the Argentine state in the nineteenth century. Juana Manuela Gorriti, Eduarda Mansilla de García, and Juana Manso were critical of the Rosas regime, the program of expansion in the Pampas, and the absence of any proper education to train future citizens (11). Masiello also states that they were able to reflect upon the heterogeneity of language (12), a trait that also connects *La tierra del fuego* with this tradition of Argentine women's writing.
16. I use "Pampas" and "Patagonia" as two interchangeable terms here because they are synonyms in Guevara's description of the area where his story takes place. The nineteenth-century geographical imagination of Argentina tends to render the two identical; the Pampas as a deserted land, a frequent representation in Sarmiento's *Facundo,* is a representation that will later justify Roca's "Conquista del Desierto," the military campaign that took place in northern Patagonia and that sought to push the southern borders of Argentina even further south to the rivers Negro and Neuquén. The novel clearly identifies the image of the Pampas as an empty land with the colonization of Tierra del Fuego and Patagonia.
17. Unless otherwise noted, Cindy Schuster has been in charge of all translations for this chapter.
18. I employ here the term "spatialities" instead of "space" intentionally. In Edward Soja's words, it is necessary to make a "space per se, space as a contextual given,

and socially-based spatiality, the created space of social organization and production" (79). As analyzed here, Gache's works explore the construction of such spatialities as territorial and textual entities.

19. I am referring here to the texts by: Diana Bellessi, *Sur* (1998); Eduardo Belgrano Rawson, *Fuegia* (1991); Sylvia Iparraguirre, *La tierra del fuego* (1998); Clemente Riedemann, *Karra Maw'n* (1984); and Juan Pablo Riveros, *De la tierra sin fuegos* (1986), all of which address the process of colonization of the southern areas of Argentina and Chile. From the perspective of the narrative or poetic discourse, these authors address how original populations such as the Selk'nam, Yahgans, or Mapuche were exterminated at the turn of the nineteenth century. They describe the issue of colonization as both a process of territorial displacement and a violent cultural and linguistic conflict.

4 Poetic Crossovers: The Paradoxical Spaces of Women's Poetry

1. Unless otherwise noted, Cindy Schuster has been in charge of all translations.
2. As Foucault comments in "Of Other Spaces," heterotopias reflect and contrast society's utopias by distorting ideals of spatial order. Heterotopias are both real and unreal: "Starting from this gaze that is, as it were, directed toward me, from the ground of this virtual space that is on the other side of the glass, I come back toward myself. I begin again to direct my eyes toward myself and to reconstitute myself where I am" (24).
3. Bellessi comments at length on her role as the interpreter of collective and anonymous voices. In an interview with María Claudia André, she explains that the characters in her poetry are "real people" who whisper in her ear so she can write and that her skills come from her own popular background, illiterate people who sang and told stories in that broken language. She describes herself as the "lost daughter" of that lineage (28).
4. Women were the first to conduct this mythical ceremony of initiation, the Hain, in Selk'nam society. According to the myth described by Anne Chapman and previously by Father Martin Gusinde, women, led by Moon (Kreeh), held the Hain ceremony and guaranteed the ruling of women or the matriarchal system for centuries. Men feared women because of the supernatural powers they supposedly displayed while the Hain was taking place and were forced to all sorts of servile tasks to guarantee the subsistence of women and other members of the group. According to different accounts by Chapman and Gusinde, men eventually found out the truth and murdered Moon and the rest of the women. A patriarchal system where men conducted the Hain was established, and women were forbidden from participating in the ceremony (Chapman, "The Ideology," 66–77).
5. Pratt deconstructs the notion of a "flux metaphor" prevalent in discourses that legitimize globalization and states that the term is not neutral, but rather connected to certain ethical dimensions of global processes. The notion of global mobility does not acknowledge the dark side of globalization, such as

the duplication of labor hours, children's and women's exploitation, infanticide ("¿Por qué la virgen" 39–40). On the contrary, according to Pratt, contemporary literature in Latin America mitigates such metaphors by proposing narratives of survival that, locked in interior spaces, deny any form of mobility, as shown by Bellessi's *Sur* (40).

6. I am using here the translation by Daniel Balderston and Marcy Schwartz of Bellessi's "Género y traducción," originally published in *Lo propio y lo ajeno*. Other examples from *Lo propio y lo ajeno* cited in this chapter are Cindy Schuster's translations.

7. Caren Kaplan states that a "politics of location" is "a critical practice" that "identifies the grounds for historically specific differences and similarities among women in diverse and asymmetrical relations" ("Becoming Nomad" 183–84). In her chapter on "Postmodern Geographies," she analyzes different ways in which Euro-American feminisms of the 1980s and 1990s critique both modern and postmodern concepts of "location" (146). Kaplan redefines this concept by reasserting gender as a key component in postmodern definitions of spatiality by Marxist geographers, such as Harvey or Soja, and by redefining location as an axis rather than a place, in the way Chandra Mohanty uses the term in studies on third-world women.

8. Kaplan examines how new technologies and the fragmentation of mobility in post-Fordist conditions transform the notion of the "local": "One could say, then, that 'the local' is not really about a specific intrinsic territory but about the construction of bundles or clusters of identities in and through the cultures of transnational capitalism. Whether the 'local' is seen to be fluid and relational or fixed and fundamentalist depends upon one's position or enunciatory situation vis-à-vis economic, political, and cultural hegemonies. This is, perhaps, one of the greater paradoxes of the global-local nexus: The local appears as the primary site of resistance to globalization through the construction of temporalized narratives of identities (new histories, rediscovered genealogies, imagined geographies, etc.), yet that very site prepares the ground for appropriation, nativism, and exclusions" ("Becoming Nomad" 159–60).

9. Marjorie Perloff states that collage plays a central role in postmodernism's "return to radical *artifice*" ("Avant-Garde" 26). Quoting critics such as Donald Davie and Frederic Jameson, Perloff explains that the collage is a figure that questions mass production and the rising importance of the media in postmodern societies. See "The Invention of Collage" and "Avant-Garde or Endgame?"

10. "*De Pe a Pa* disproves the guarantees of cultural integration and artistic success for expatriates that the Latin American construct of Paris has maintained. Laura's desperate attempts to pursue literary recognition are based on the Paris she believed in from afar. As in Proust and in Bryce Echenique, the anticipated place rarely materializes like the illusions promise. Nevertheless, daily experience in the place does not eliminate the persistent ghosts. Laura, like Martín Romaña, takes on the often excruciating task of simultaneously living in the current Paris and the textual Paris" (Schwartz, "Paris" 126).

11. Julio Cortázar in "América Latina: exilio y literatura" ["Latin America: Exile and Literature"] states that a "cultural" form of exile affects writers in Latin America (164) and that a "condition of being exiled" can be turned into an aesthetic form of exploration for those writers. In addition, he advocates for literary resources such as humor to rewrite a "nostalgic" trait of the literature of exile (169). However, as Amy Kaminsky and other critics propose, exile conditions are more complex for women writers because "as writers, women and exiles have both been rendered invisible, though in different ways" ("The Presence" 29). As Marcy Schwartz demonstrates in her study, "Futoransky's feminist mission calls upon women to transgress their alienating gender categorization, an implicit form of exile, as well as official dogma and the exile of expatriation, by embracing their sexuality and eroticism" ("Paris" 122). Therefore, Futoransky rewrites the exile tradition in Latin America by a material parody wherein social and generic conditions impose geographical constraints that previous male writers belonging to Cortázar's generation did not experience.
12. Studies by Araceli Tinajero and Julia Kushigian describe Latin American "Orientalisms" as more embracing of the cultures of the Orient than European "Orientalism," defined by Said as fundamentally ethnocentric. However, as Tinajero states, the Orient in *modernista* works in Latin America is a reaction against the riveting positivism and materialism of the rising middle classes in their countries (16). In *modernismo*, the Orient became a symbol of collective spiritualism, a trait that is absent in the postmodern vision of the Orient characteristic of Futoransky's works. In her works, the awareness that Eastern spirituality has become touristic merchandise replaces the search for transcendent answers in the Orient. In relation to this topic, see Schwartz's comments on Futoransky's narrative works ("Paris" 139).
13. Roy Bridges states in "Exploration and Travel outside Europe (1720–1914)" that by 1800, the travel log or journal was established (56–57). Starting in the eighteenth century, these travelogues were instruments of territorial surveillance at the basis of European colonial expansion. As Mary Louise Pratt analyzes in *Imperial Eyes,* the subjectivity of the European traveler built upon such journals allowed for a "reinvention" of colonized territories, such as Humboldt's reinvention of America for European audiences. However, Futoransky's deterritorialized travel journal embodies a postmodern reading of mobility and location; her narrative "reinvents" Paris and the Orient from the perspective of the woman writer's postmodern travelogue.
14. Doreen Massey defines the "dynamic simultaneity" of space as follows: "The view of place advocated here, where localities can in a sense be present in one another, both inside and outside at the same time, is a view which stresses the construction of specificity through interrelations rather than through the imposition of boundaries and the counterposition of one identity against another" (7).
15. Caren Kaplan defines the local as a positionality ("Postmodern Geographies" 160).

16. Implied in her definition of a "poetic economy" is the reorganization of the social space of a city like Lima, as her analysis of poetry by Peruvian writers José Cerna Bazán and Marita Troiano attests: "Poetry, like the city itself, is a system, a framework of rhetorical traditions and conventions, which these poets manipulate...Poetic economy often means brevity, but 'economy' can also mean management" (from the Greek *oikonomia*, or "household management"). I use the term in this latter sense, thinking of organization rather than supervision or corporatization, for we have seen how these authors loosen some of poetry's formal elements in order to reorganize their visions of Lima" (112).
17. Marcy Schwartz states, referring to her fiction, that "Futoransky contests gender politics both at home and abroad. Her protagonist, Laura, clearly pursues an erotic agenda, as a form of resistance to state-sponsored terrorism in Argentina as well as a response to sexual repression in China and sexist exclusion of women in Latin America's imagined Paris" ("Paris" 121).
18. Kuhnheim links notions of "generic memory" and "poetic economy" to the "recycling urban poetry" that takes place at the end of the century in South America. She studies how poets such as Nicanor Parra in Chile question the concept of society as a whole and break down the differences between high and low culture in a poetic form that emphasizes the spectacle. Such postmodern poetics also shape Peruvian poetry of the period characterized by new ways of "managing" poetic resources.
19. According to *The New Princeton Encyclopedia of Poetry and Poetics*, "western allegory" is a "term that denotes two complementary procedures: a way of composing literature and a way of interpreting it. To compose allegorically is to construct a work so that its apparent sense refers to an "other" sense. To interpret allegorically...is to explain a work as if there were an "other" sense to which it referred" (31).
20. In *La moneda de hierro,* poems such as "En Islandia el alba" [In Iceland the Dawn"], "Einar Tambarskelver," and "991 A.D." have close references to the Nordic tradition. As in many other works, Borges employs metaphors of visual delusion, in this case the opacity of iron, to delve into connections between the individual and the universal, a linear and circular perception of time, and the idea and projections of eternity in artistic forms.
21. It is relevant here to point to the definition of "apostrophe," as it appears in *The New Princeton Encyclopedia of Poetry and Poetics*: "A figure of speech which consists of addressing an absent or dead person, a thing, or an idea as if it were alive or present" (82). Negroni employs this trope extensively in *Islandia* to convey an allegorical and elegiac tension in the fictional dialogues it re-creates.
22. In Negroni's words: "Así, entre la actividad riesgosa del exilio y la tentativa de edificar una casa humana entre la Nada y lo Absoluto, el castillo gótico cierra al mundo un centro de gravedad negro para abrirlo sólo a la noche interior y, en ese sentido, se identifica con la poesía o mejor, es su devenir lírico transformado en interrogación. Su insumisión espectacular ante lo literal lo lleva a desmantelar el orden de los principios (es decir del sujeto y la voluntad), y

a tramar un territorio de preguntas, encallado en la experiencia, los objetos y la sensibilidad, conquistando el vacío que funda y niega, al mismo tiempo, lo impensable. Contra lo noble o ejemplar del ser humano, la poesía, igual que el castillo gótico, opone la violencia de un movimiento que, una y otra vez, es fiel a sus tristezas." [Between the perilous activity of exile and the attempt to build a human home amidst Nothingness and the Absolute, the gothic castle keeps a dark center of gravity hidden from the world, revealing it only to the interior night, and in this sense, it can be identified with poetry or, better yet, with (poetry's) lyric transformation into interrogation. (The gothic castle's) dramatic insubordination in the face of the literal leads it to dismantle the order of principles (that is, the subject and his will), and to chart a territory of questions, grounded in experience, objects and sensibility, which conquers the emptiness that creates, and at the same time negates, the unthinkable. Against the noble and exemplary qualities of the human being, poetry, like the gothic castle, opposes the violence of a movement that, once and again, is faithful to its sorrows.] (*Museo negro* 22).
23. Angel Rama proposes in *The Lettered City* that the cast of "letrados" [learned men] who shaped the culture of Latin America "produced"—to use the term coined by Henri Lefebvre in his foundational text, *The Production of Space*—a "lettered city," a written reproduction of the "real city" that performs cultural functions in favor of a cast of intellectuals who maintains the colonial order through a symbolic and real domination of space (24–25).

Bibliography

Anderson, Elizabeth, et al. *Memory, Mourning, Landscape.* Amsterdam: Rodopi, 2010.
Aguilar, Gonzalo. "El cuerpo y su sombra. Los viajeros culturales en la década del 20." *Punto de Vista.* 59 (1997): 30–34.
Aguilar, Gonzalo and Mariano Siskind. "Viajeros culturales en la Argentina (1928–1942)." *Historia crítica de la literatura argentina. El imperio realista.* Ed. María Teresa Gramulio. 11 vols. Buenos Aires: Emecé Editores, 2002. 367–91.
Alexander, Jacqui, and Chandra Mohanty. "Cartographies of Knowledge and Power. Transnational Feminism as Radical Praxis." *Critical Transnational Feminist Praxis.* eds. Amanda Lock Swarr and Richa Nagar New York: State U of New York P, 2010.
———, eds. Introduction. *Feminist Genealogies, Colonial Legacies, Democratic Futures.* New York and London; Routledge, 1997. xiii–xlii.
"Allegory." *The New Princeton Encyclopedia of Poetry and Poetics.* 1993 ed.
Altamirano, Carlos, and Beatriz Sarlo. "The Autodidact and the Learning Machine." *Sarmiento. Author of a Nation.* eds. Tulio Halperín Donghi, Iván Jaksic, Gwen Kirkpatrick, and Francine Masiello. Berkeley: U of California P, 1994. 156–68.
Andermann, Jans. *Mapas del poder. Una arqueología literaria del espacio argentino.* Rosario, Argentina: Beatriz Viterbo, 2000.
———. *The Optic of the State. Visuality and Power in Argentina and Brazil.* Pittsburgh: U of Pittsburgh P, 2007.
Arambel–Guiñazú, Maria Cristina. *La escritura de Victoria Ocampo: memorias, seducción "collage."* Buenos Aires: Edicial, 1993.
"Apostrophe." *The New Princeton Encyclopedia of Poetry and Poetics.* 1993 ed.
Artaud, Antonin. "Theatre and Cruelty." *The Twentieth-Century Performance Reader.* Trans. M.C. Richard, eds. Michael Huxley and Noel Witts. New York: Routledge, 1996. 25–29.
Avelar, Idelber. Introduction. *The Untimely Present. Postdictatorial Latin American Fiction and the Task of Mourning.* Durham, London: Duke UP, 1999. 1–21.
Barrancos, Dora. *Mujeres, entre la casa y la plaza.* Buenos Aires: Editorial Sudamericana, 2008.

Bartra, Roger. "Allegories of Creativity and Territory." trans. Dierdra Reber. PMLA 118.1 (2003): 114–19.
Batticuore, Graciela, et al. "Aventura y relato. Apuntes para una historia literaria de la frontera." Comp. Graciela Batticuore, Loreley El Jaber, and Alejandra Laera. *Fronteras escritas. Cruces, desvíos y pasajes en la literatura argentina*. Rosario, Argentina: Beatriz Viterbo, 2008.
Baydar, Gülsüm. "Figures of Wom/man in Contemporary Architectural Discourse." *Negotiating Domesticity*. eds. Hilde Heynen and Gülsüm Baydar. 30–46.
Bellessi, Diana. *El jardín*. Rosario-Buenos Aires: Bajo la luna nueva, 1992.

———. "Entrevista y selección de poemas." *Antología de escritoras argentinas contemporáneas*. ed. María Claudia André. Buenos Aires: Editorial Biblos, 2004. 22–40.

———. "Gender and Translation." trans. Daniel Balderston and Marcy Schwartz. *Voice-overs. Translation and Latin American Literature*. Albany: State U of New York P, 2002.

———. *La edad dorada*. Foreword Jorge Monteleone. Buenos Aires: Adriana Hidalgo Editora, 2003.

———. *Lo propio y lo ajeno*. Buenos Aires: Feminaria Editora, 1996.

———. *Mate cocido*. Buenos Aires: Nuevo Hacer, Grupo Editor Latinoamericano, 2002.

———. Personal interview, June 27, 2007.

———. *Tener lo que se tiene. Poesía reunida*. Buenos Aires: Adriana Hidalgo editora, 2009.

Benítez-Rojo, Antonio. "Introducción: la isla que se repite." *La isla que se repite. El Caribe y la perspectiva postmoderna*. Hanover: Ediciones del Norte, 1998. i–xxxviii.
Benjamin, Walter. *The Origin of German Tragic Drama*. Intro. George Steiner. trans. John Osborne. London, New York: Verso, 1996 ed.

———. "The Work of Art in the Age of Mechanical Reproduction." *Illuminations*. Hannah Arendt, introduction and edition. Trans. Harry Zohn New York: Schocken Books, 1969. 217–51.

Beverly, John. "The Margin at the Center: On Testimonio." *The Real Thing. Testimonial Discourse and Latin America*. ed. Georg M. Gugelberg. Durham and London: Duke UP, 1996. 23–57.
Beverly, John, and José Oviedo. Introduction. *The Postmodernist Debate in Latin America*. eds. John Beverly, José Oviedo, and Michael Aronna. Durham, London: Duke UP, 1995. 1–17.
Bhabha, Homi. *The Location of Culture*. London and New York: Routledge. 2nd ed. 1995.
Bienal del Fin del Mundo. www.finaldelmundo.org-BienalFindelMundo
Blengino, Vanni. *La zanja de la Patagonia. Los nuevos conquistadores: militares, científicos, sacerdotes y escritores*. Buenos Aires: Fondo de Cultura Económica, 2005.
Blunt, Alison. *Domicile and Diaspora. Anglo-Indian Women and the Spatial Politics of Home*. Australia: Blackwell Publishing, 2005
Blunt, Alison and Robyn Dowling. *Home*. London, New York: Routledge, 2006.

Blunt, Alison, and Gillian Rose. *Writing Women and Space. Colonial and Postcolonial Geographies*. New York, London: Guilford Press, 1994.
Borges, Jorge Luis. "Anatomía de mi ultra." *Manifiestos, proclamas y polémicas de la vanguardia literaria hispanoamericana*. ed. Nelson Osorio T. Caracas, Venezuela: Biblioteca Ayacucho, 1988. 83.
———. "El escritor argentino y la tradición." *Obras Completas (1923–1949)*. Buenos Aires: Emecé Editores, 1996. 267–74.
———. "Las Kenningar." *Obras Completas*. Vol 1. Barcelona: Alianza Editorial, 1996. 368–81.
———. "Prólogo." *La moneda de hierro. Obras completas*. vol 3. Barcelona: Emecé Editores, 1996. 121.
———. Borges, Jorge Luis. *Selected Poems*. ed. Alexander Coleman. New York: Penguin, 1999.
Boyle, Catherine M. "Griselda Gambaro and the Female Dramatist: The Audacious Trespasser" *Knives and Angels. Women Writers in Latin America*. ed. Susan Bassnett. London and New Jersey: Zed Books, 1990. 145–57.
Braidotti, Rosi. Introduction. "By Way of Nomadism." *Nomadic Subjects. Embodiment and Sexual Difference in Contemporary Feminist Theory*. New York: Columbia UP, 1994. 1–39.
Bridges, Roy. "Exploration and Travel outside Europe (1720–1914)." *The Cambridge Companion to Travel Writing*. 53–86.
Butler, Judith. *Bodies that Matter. On the Discursive Limits of Sex*. New York, London: Routledge, 1993.
Calinescu, Matei. *Five Faces of Modernity. Modernism, Avant-garde, Decadence, Kitsch, Postmodernity*. Durham, London: Duke UP, 2007.
Cárcamo-Huechante, Luis, and José Antonio Mazzotti. "Presentación. Dislocamientos de la poesía latinoamericana en la escena global." *Revista de Crítica Literaria Latinoamericana*. 29.58 (2003): 9–21.
Carlson, Marifran. *¡Feminismo! The Woman's Movement in Argentina from Its Beginnings to Eva Perón*. Chicago: Academy Chicago, 1988.
Carter, Margaret L. *Spectre or Delusion? The Supernatural in Gothic Fiction*. Ann Arbor: UMI Research Press, 1987.
Castillo, Debra. "http://www.LAlit.com." *Latin American Literature and Mass Media*. eds. Edmundo Paz Soldán and Debra A. Castillo. New York, London: Garland, 2001. 232–45.
Caws, Mary Ann. "Ladies Shot and Painted: Female Embodiment in Surrealist Art." *The Female Body in Western Culture. Contemporary Perspectives*. eds. Susan Rubin Suleiman. Cambridge: Harvard UP, 1985. 262–87.
———. "Doubling: Claude Cahun's Split Self." *The Surrealist Look. An Erotics of Encounter*. Cambridge, MA: MIT P, 1999. 95–119.
Chapman, Anne. *Drama and Power in a Hunting Society: the Selk'nam of Tierra del Fuego*. Cambridge, New York: Cambridge UP, 1982.
Colombi, Beatriz. "Camino a la meca: Escritores hispanoamericanos en París (1900–1920)." *Historia de los intelectuales en América Latina. La ciudad letrada,*

de la conquista al modernismo. ed. Jorge Myers. dir. Carlos Altamirano. 2nd vol. Madrid: Katz Editores, 2008. 544–66.

———. *Viaje intelectual. Migraciones y desplazamientos en América Latina (1880–1915)*. Rosario, Argentina: Beatriz Viterbo editora, 2004.

Cornejo Polar, Antonio. Introducción. "Piedra de sangre hirviendo: los múltiples retos de la modernización heterogénea." *Escribir en el aire. Ensayo sobre la heterogeneidad socio-cultural en las literaturas andinas*. Perú: Editorial Horizonte, 1994. 11–24, 159–233.

Cortázar, Julio. "América Latina: exilio y literatura." *Julio Cortázar. Obra crítica/3*. Edición de Saúl Sosnowski. Buenos Aires, México: Alfaguara, 1994. 161–80.

Darwin, Charles. *The Voyage of the Beagle*. New York: Collier, 1909.

Deleuze, Giles, and Félix Guattari. "What is a Minor Literature?" *Kafka. Toward a Minor Literature*. trans. Dana Polan, foreword Réda Bensmaïa. Minneapolis: U of Minnesota P, 1986. 16–27.

———. Introduction. "Rhizome." *A Thousand Plateaus. Capitalism and Schizophrenia*. trans. and foreword Brian Massumi. 7th ed. Minneapolis, London: U of Minnesota P, 1998.

De Diego, José Luis. *Editores y políticas editoriales en Argentina 1880–2000*. Buenos Aires: Fondo de Cultura Económica, 2006.

De Lauretis, Teresa. *Alice Doesn't. Feminism, Semiotics, Cinema*. Bloomington: Indiana UP, 1984.

———. "The Technology of Gender." *Technologies of Gender. Essays on Theory, Film, and Fiction*. Bloomington: Indiana UP, 1987.

De Man, Paul. "Autobiography as De-Facement." *MLN* 94.5 (1979): 919–30.

De Marinis, Marco. "El espacio escénico en el teatro contemporáneo: La herencia del siglo XX." Trans. Silvina Díaz. *Teatro, memoria y ficción*. ed. Osvaldo Pelletieri. Buenos Aires: Galerna, Fundación Roberto Arlt, 2005. 75–83.

Derrida, Jacques. *Spectres of Marx. The State of the Debt, the Work of Mourning and the New International*. trans. Peggy Kamuf. Introduction by Bernd Magnus and Stephen Cullenberg. New York and London: Routledge, 1994.

Dickerman, Leah. "Lenin in the Age of Mechanical Reproduction." *Disturbing Remains: Memory, History, and Crisis in the Twentieth Century*. eds. Michael S. Roth and Charles S. Salas. Los Angeles, CA: Getty Research Institute, 2001. 77–110.

Domínguez, Nora. "Literary Constructions and Gender Performance in the Novels of Nora Lange." *Latin American Women's Writing: Feminist Readings in Theory and Crisis*. eds. Anny Brooksbank Jones and Catherine Davies. New York: Oxford UP, 1996. 30–45.

Dolan, Jill. *The Feminist Spectator as Critic*. Ann Arbor, London: University of Michigan Research Press, 1988.

Echeverría, Esteban. *La cautiva*. Buenos Aires: Editorial Sopena. 3rd ed. 1944.

Estrella Gutiérrez, Fermín. Preface. *45 días y 30 marineros*. 4.

Facio, Sara. *Victoria Ocampo en fotografías*. Buenos Aires: La azotea, 2006.

Fara, Luis. "Luchas reivindicativas urbanas en un contexto autoritario. Los asentamientos de San Francisco Solano." *Los nuevos movimientos sociales*. 270–94.

Feijóo, María del Carmen and Mónica Gogna. "Las mujeres en la transición a la democracia." *Los nuevos movimientos sociales*. 41–82.

Feitlowitz, Marguerite. *A Lexicon of Terror. Argentina and the Legacies of Torture*. New York, Oxford: Oxford UP, 1998.

———. "Crisis, Terror, Disappearance: The Theatre of Griselda Gambaro." *Information for Foreigners*, 1–11.

———. *Information for Foreigners. Three Plays by Griselda Gambaro*. Edited and translated by Marguerite Feitlowitz. Afterword by Diana Taylor. Illinois, Northwestern UP, 1992.

Felski, Rita. *The Gender of Modernity*. Cambridge, MA: Harvard UP, 1995.

———. *Beyond Feminist Aesthetics. Feminist Literature and Social Change*. Cambridge, MA: Harvard UP, 1989.

Fernández Bravo, Álvaro. Introducción. *Mi fe es el hombre. María Rosa Oliver*. Buenos Aires: Colección Los Raros, Biblioteca Nacional, 2008. 9–49.

———. *Literatura y frontera. Procesos de territorialización en las literaturas argentina y chilena del siglo XIX*. Buenos Aires: Editorial Sudamericana-Universidad de San Andrés, 1999.

Fondebrider, Jorge. "Una genealogía de la poesía argentina actual." *Cuadernos Hispanoamericanos*. 718 (2010): 21–42.

Forcinito, Ana. *Memorias y nomadías: géneros y cuerpos en los márgenes del posfeminismo*. Chile: Editorial Cuarto Propio, 2004.

Forns-Broggi, Roberto. "El eco-poema de Juan L. Ortiz." *Anales de Literatura Hispanoamericana*, 33 (2004): 33–48.

Foucault, Michel. *Discipline and Punish*. New York: Vintage Books, 1995.

———. "Of Other Spaces." *Diacritics*, 16.1 (1986): 22–27.

Franco, Jean. *An Introduction to Spanish-American Literature*. New York: Cambridge University Press, 1994.

———. "Marcar diferencias: cruzar fronteras." *Las culturas de fin de siglo en América Latina*. ed. Josefina Ludmer. 34–43.

———. *Plotting Women: Gender and Representation in Mexico*. New York: Columbia UP, 1989.

Frank, Waldo. *América Hispana: South of Us*. New Jersey: Garden City, 1940.

Freud, Sigmund. "The Uncanny." *The Complete Standard Edition of the Complete Psychological Works of Sigmund Freud*. Trans. and eds. James Strachey, Anna Freud, Alix Strachey and Alan Tyson. London: Hogarth Press and Institute of Psycho-analysis. 5th ed. 1971. 219–56.

Friedman, Alice. *Women and the Making of the Modern House: A Social and Architectural History*. New York: Abrams, 1998.

Friedman, Susan Stanford. *Mappings: Feminism and the Cultural Geographies of Encounter*. Princeton: Princeton UP, 1998.

Futoransky, Luisa. *Babel, Babel*. Buenos Aires: Ediciones La Loca Poesía, 1968.

———. *De Pe a Pa o de Pekin a Paris*. Barcelona: Editorial Anagrama, 1986.

———. "Elogio del olvido." Lecture at Kenyon College, 7 Nov. 2007.

———. *Inclinaciones*. Buenos Aires: Leviatán, 2006.

———. *Partir, digo.* Sarli E. Mercado, Intro. Madrid: Libros del Aire, Colección Jardín Cerrado, 2010.
———. *Prender de gajo.* Madrid: Calambur, 2006.
———. "Prender de Gajo." *Poéticas de la distancia: Adentro y afuera de la literatura argentina.* Trans. Sylvia Molloy and Mariano Siskind. Buenos Aires: Grupo Editorial Norma, 2006.
———. *Seqüana barrosa.* Jerez, Spain: EH Editores, 2007.
———. *Son cuentos chinos.* Buenos Aries: Planeta, 1991.
Gache, Belén. *Diario de la luna caníbal.* Usuhaia, Argentina: I Biennial of the End of the World, 2007.
———. *El libro del fin del mundo.* Buenos Aires: Fin del Mundo Ediciones, 2002.
———. *Escrituras nómadas. Del libro perdido al hipertexto.* Gijón, España: Ediciones Trea, 2006.
———. *Luna india.* Buenos Aires: Planeta, 1994.
———. *Noches eléctricas para una noche sin luna.* Buenos Aires: Editorial Sudamericana, 2004.
———. *Word Toys.* www.findelmundo.com.ar/wordtoys.
Gambaro, Griselda. *Bad Blood (La malasangre).* Trans. Marguerite Feitlowitz. Woodstock, IL: Dramatic Publishing, 1994.
———. *Información para extranjeros. Teatro 2.* Buenos Aires: Ediciones La Flor, 4th edition, 2008.
———. Interview. *Interviews with Contemporary Women Playwrights.* eds. Kathleen Betsko and Rachel Koenig. Trans. Alberto Minero. New York: William Morrow, 1987. 184–99.
———. *La malasangre. Del sol naciente. Teatro 1.* Buenos Aires: Ediciones La Flor, 4th edition, 2008.
García Canclini, Néstor. *Culturas híbridas. Estrategias para entrar y salir de la modernidad.* México, D.F.: Grijalbo, 1989.
———. *La globalización imaginada.* Buenos Aires: Paidós. 4th ed. 2008.
Genovese, Alicia. *La doble voz. Poetas argentinas contemporáneas.* Buenos Aires: Editorial Biblos, 1998.
———. "Poesía y posición del yo: Juan L. Ortiz, Juan Gelman, Olga Orozco." *Hispamérica: Revista de literatura.* 30.89 (2001): 15–28.
Genovese, Alicia, and María del Carmen Colombo. "Del viaje sin límites a la profundidad del detalle (entrevista)." *Cyber Humanitatis,* 24 (7 Mar. 2007).
Giardinelli, Mempo. *Final de novela en Patagonia.* Barcelona: Biblioteca Grandes Viajeros, 2001.
Giles, Judy. *The Parlor and the Suburb. Domestic Identities, Class, Femininity and Modernity.* Oxford, New York: Berg, 2004.
Giella, Miguel Angel. *Teatro Abierto 1981. Teatro Argentino bajo vigilancia.* Vol. 1. Buenos Aires: Corregidor, 1991.
Girondo, Oliverio. *Obra.* Buenos Aires: Editorial Losada. 4th ed. 1992.
———. *Scarecrow & Other Anomalies.* Tr. Gilbert Alter-Gilbert. Riverside, CA: Xenos Books, 2002.

Gleber, Anke. "Female Flanerie and the Symphony of the City." *Women in the Metropolis. Gender and Modernity in Weimar Culture.* Ed. Katharina von Ankum. Berkeley, CA: California UP, 1997. 67–89.
Gottmann, Jean. *The Significance of Territory.* Charlottesville: UP of Virginia, 1973.
Grau, Cristina. *Borges y la arquitectura.* Madrid: Catedra. 4th ed. 1999.
Gray, Andrew. "Indigenous Peoples and Their Territories." *Decolonising Indigenous Rights.* ed. Adolfo de Oliveira. New York and London: Routledge, 2009. 17–44.
Graziano, Frank. *Alejandra Pizarnik: A Profile.* Frank Graziano, edition and introduction. María Rosa Fort, Frank Graziano, and Susan Jill-Levine, translations. Durango, CO: Logbridge-Rhodes, 1987.
Gregory, Derek. *Geographical Imaginations.* Cambridge, Oxford: Blackwell. 2nd ed. 1994.
Grewal, Inderpal, and Karen Caplan. *Scattered Hegemonies. Postmodernity and Transnational Feminist Practices.* Minneapolis, London: Minnesota UP, 1994.
Gropius, Walter. "Arquitectura functional." *Sur* 3 (1931): 155–62.
Grosz, Elizabeth. *Space, Time, and Perversion.* New York, London: Routledge, 1995.
Guy, Donna. *Sex and Danger in Buenos Aires. Prostitution, Family, and Nation in Argentina.* Lincoln: U of Nebraska P, 1991.
Harvey, David. "The Social Construction of Space and Time. A relational theory." *Geographical Review of Japan.* 67.2 (2006). 126–35.
———. *Social Justice and the City.* Baltimore: Johns Hopkins UP, 1973.
Heath, Stephen. *Questions of Cinema.* Bloomington: Indiana UP, 1981.
Heynen, Hilde. "Modernity and Domesticity. Tensions and Contradictions." *Negotiating Domesticity. Spatial Productions of Gender in Modern Architecture.* eds. Hilde Heynen and Gülsüm Baydar. London, New York: Routledge, 2005. 1–29.
hooks, bell. "Choosing the margin as a space of radical openness." *Yearning: Race, Gender and Cultural Politics.* Boston: South End, 1990. 145–53.
Hortiguera, Hugo. "Fabulando el presente: La normalización de los discursos de desvío y el thriller folletinesco en los medios argentinos de comunicación." *Ciberletras,* 18 (2007). Online.
Hortiguera, Hugo, and Carolina Rocha. Introduction. *Argentinean Cultural Production during the Neoliberal Years (1989–2001).* Lewiston, Australia: Edwin Mellen, 2007. 1–25.
Huyssen, Andreas. *After the Great Divide: Modernism, Mass Culture, Postmodernism.* Bloomington, IN: Indiana UP, 1986.
———. *Twilight Memories: Making Time in a Culture of Amnesia.* New York: Routledge, 1995.
Iglesia, Cristina. *Islas de la memoria. Sobre la autobiografía de Victoria Ocampo.* Buenos Aires: Ediciones Cuenca del Plata, 1996.
Iparraguirre, Sylvia. Personal Interview. June 26, 2008.
———. *La tierra del fuego.* Buenos Aires: Alfaguara, 2001.
———. *Tierra del fuego. An Historical Novel.* Trans. Hardie St. Martin. Canada: Curbstone Press, 2000.
———. *Narrativa breve.* Buenos Aires: Alfaguara, 2005.

———. "Quise contar la ciudad del Menemismo, sin nombrarlo." *Página 12, Cultura y Espectáculos*. November 15, 2007. Online edition March 9, 2008.

Iparraguirre, Sylvia, and Florian Von Der Fecht. *Tierra del Fuego. Una biografía del fin del mundo*. Buenos Aires: El Ateneo, 2000.

Jáuregui, Carlos. "Writing Communities on the Internet." *Latin American Literature and Mass Media*. 288–97.

Jelin, Elizabeth. "Los movimientos sociales en la Argentina contemporánea: Una introducción a su estudio." *Los nuevos movimientos sociales. Mujeres. Rock nacional. Derechos humanos. Obreros. Barrios*. ed. Elizabeth Jelin. Buenos Aires: Centro Editor de América Latina, 1989. 13–40.

Jelin, Elizabeth, and Victoria Langland. Introducción. "Las marcas territoriales como nexo entre pasado y presente." *Monumentos, memoriales y marcas territoriales*. eds. Elizabeth Jelin and Victoria Langland. Buenos Aires: Siglo XXI editors, 2003.

Kamenszain, Tamara. *El texto silencioso. Tradición y vanguardia en la poesía sudamericana*. México: Universidad Nacional Autónoma de México, 1983.

———. *La boca del testimonio. Lo que dice la poesía*. Buenos Aires: Grupo Editorial Norma, 2007.

Kaminsky, Amy. *Argentina. Stories for a Nation*. Minneapolis, London: Minnesota UP, 2008.

———. *After Exile. Writing the Latin American Diaspora*. Minneapolis, London: Minnesota UP, 1999.

———. "The Presence in Absence of Exile." *Reading the Body Politic. Feminist Criticism and Latin American Women Writers*. Minneapolis: Minnesota UP, 1993. 27–46.

Kaplan, Caren. "Introduction," "Becoming Nomad. Poststructuralist Deterritorializations," and "Postmodern Geographies. Feminist Politics of Location." *Questions of Travel. Postmodern Discourses of Displacement*. Durham, London: Duke UP, 1996. 1–26, 65–100, 143–87.

———. "Deterritorializations." *The Nature and Context of Minority Discourse*. Ed. Abdul R. JanMohamed and David Lloyd. New York, Oxford: Oxford UP, 1990. 357–68.

King, John. *Sur. Estudio de la revista literaria argentina y su papel en el desarrollo de una cultura, 1931–1970*. Trans. Juan José Utrilla. México: Fondo de Cultura Económica, 1989.

Koshar, Rudy. "Seeing, Travelling, and Consuming: An Introduction." *Histories of Leisure*. Oxford, New York: Berg, 2002. 1–24.

Kozameh, Alicia. *259 saltos, uno inmortal*. 2nd ed. Córdoba, Argentina: Narvaja. 2006.

Krauss, Rosalind. *The Originality of the Avant-Garde and Other Modernist Myths*. 10th ed. Cambridge, MA: MIT P., 1996.

Kristeva, Julia. *Powers of Horror. An Essay on Abjection*. Trans. Leon S. Roudiez. New York: Columbia UP, 1982.

Kuhnheim, Jill. *Gender, Politics and Poetry in 20th Century Argentina*. Gainesville: UP of Florida, 1996.

———. *Textual Disruptions. Spanish American Poetry at the End of the Twentieth Century*. Austin: U of Texas P, 2004.
Landow, George P. "Hypertext and Critical Theory." *Hypertext 3.0. Critical Theory and New Media in an Era of Globalization*. Baltimore: Johns Hopkins UP, 2006. 53–68.
Lange, Norah. *Cuadernos de infancia*. Buenos Aires: Losada, 1937.
———. *45 días y 30 marineros*. Buenos Aires: Editorial Tor, 1933.
———. *Estimados congéneres*. Buenos Aires: Editorial Losada, 1968
———. *Los dos retratos*. Buenos Aires: Domingo Viau, 1956.
———. *Personas en la sala*. Buenos Aires: Editorial Sudamericana, 1950.
Larkosh, Christopher. "Translating Woman: Victoria Ocampo and the Empires of Foreign Fascination." *Translation and Power*. eds. Maria Tymoczko and Edwin Gentzler. Amherst and Boston: U of Massachussetts P, 2002. 99–121.
Larson, Catherine. *Games and Play in the Theater of Spanish American Women*. Lewisburgh, PA: Bucknell UP, 2004.
Lavrin, Asunción. *Women, Feminism, and Social Change in Argentina, Chile, and Uruguay, 1890–1940*. Lincoln: U of Nebraska P, 1995.
Lefebvre, Henri. *The Production of Space*. Trans. Donald Nicholson-Smith. Malden, MA: Blackwell, 2005.
Legaz, María Elena. *Escritoras en la sala. (Norah Lange. Imagen y memoria)*. Córdoba, Argentina: Alción Editora, 1999.
Le Guin, Ursula K. and Diana Bellessi. *The Twins, The Dream*. Houston: Arte Público P, 1996.
Levisman, Martha. *Bustillo. Un proyecto de "arquitectura nacional"*. Buenos Aires: Archivos de Arquitectura Contemporánea Argentina, 2007.
Livon-Grosman, Ernesto. "La literatura de viaje: género, naturaleza y nación." *Geografías imaginarias. El relato de viaje y la construcción del espacio patagónico*. Rosario, Argentina: Beatriz Viterbo editora, 2003.
Lois, Carla Mariana. "La invención del desierto chaqueño. Una aproximación a las formas de apropiación simbólica de los territorios del Chaco en los tiempos de formación y consolidación del estado nación argentino." *Scripta Nova. Revista Electrónica de Geografía y Ciencias Sociales*. 38 (1999). August 29, 2009.
Loss, Jacqueline. "Cosmopolitanisms between the Americas." *Cosmopolitanisms and Latin America. Against the Destiny of Place*. New York: Palgrave Macmillan, 2005. 1–42.
Ludmer, Josefina. *Las culturas de fin de siglo en América Latina*. Rosario, Argentina: Beatriz Viterbo editora, 1994.
Magnarelli, Sharon. *Home Is Where the (He)art Is: The Family Romance in Late Twentieth-century Mexican and Argentine Theater*. Lewisburg, PA: Bucknell UP, 2008.
Majstorovic, Gorica. "Cosmopolitanism and the Nation: Reading Asymmetries of Power in Victoria Ocampo's 'Babel'." *A Contracorriente. Una revista de historia social y literatura de América Latina* 3.3 (2006): 47–64.
Malharro, Martín and Diana López Gijsberts. *La tipografía de plomo. Los grandes medios gráficos en la Argentina y su política editorial durante 1976–1983*. La Plata: Ediciones de Periodismo y Comunicación, 2003.

Martín-Barbero, Jesús. *De los medios a las mediaciones. Comunicación, cultura y hegemonía*. México: Ediciones G. Gill, 1987.

Martínez, Martha. "Tres nuevas dramaturgas argentinas: Roma Mahieu, Hebe Uhart y Diana Raznovich. *Latin American Theatre Review*. 13.2 (1980): 39–45.

Mansilla, Lucio V. *Una excursión a los indios ranqueles*. Buenos Aires: Peuser, 1964.

Marchant, Elizabeth. "From Consumption to Production: Victoria Ocampo as Cultural Critic." *Critical Acts. Latin American Women and Cultural Criticism*. Gainesville: Florida UP, 1999. 46–79.

Masiello, Francine. *The Art of Transition. Latin American Culture and Neoliberal Cities*. Durham, London: Duke UP, 2001.

———. *Between Civilization and Barbarism. Women, Nation, and Literary Culture in Modern Argentina*. Lincoln, London: U of Nebraska P, 1992.

———. "Este pobre fin de siglo: Argentina's Ten Years of Democracy." *Latin American Postmodernisms*. ed. Richard A. Young. Amsterdam, Atlanta: Rodopi, 1997. 239–55.

———. "Estado, género y sexualidad en la cultura de fin de siglo." *Las culturas de fin de siglo en América Latina*. Rosario: Beatriz Viterbo, 1994. 139–49.

———. "In Search of the Nomad's Shadow." *Luisa Futoransky y su palabra itinerante*. Comp. Esther Gimbernat González. Uruguay: Ediciones de Hermes Criollo, 2005. 41–55.

———. "La naturaleza de la poesía." *Revista de Crítica Literaria Latinoamericana* 29.58 (2003): 57–77.

———. "Scribbling on the Wreck." *Telling Ruins in Latin America*. eds. Michael J. Lazzara and Vicky Unruh. New York: Palgrave Macmillan, 2009. 27–37.

McLoughlin, Kate. "Introduction." *Memory, Mourning, Landscape*. Amsterdam, New York: Rodopi, 2010. ix–xiv.

Massey, Doreen. *Space, Place and Gender*. Minneapolis: U of Minnesota P. 4th ed. 2005.

Mercado, Tununa. *En estado de memoria*. España: Seix Barral, 2008.

Mills, Sara. *Discourses of Difference. An Analysis of Women's Travel Writing and Colonialism*. London, New York: Routledge, 1991.

———. "Gender and Colonial Space." *Feminist Postcolonial Theory. A Reader*. New York: Routledge, 2003. 692–719.

Mignolo, Walter. "The Many Faces of Cosmo-polis: Border Thinking and Critical Cosmopolitanism." eds. Sheldon Pollock, et al. *Cosmopolitanism*. Durham, London: Duke UP, 2002. 157–87.

———. "Linguistic Maps, Literary Geographies, and Cultural Landscapes." *The Places of History. Regionalism Revisited in Latin America*. ed. Doris Sommers. Durham: Duke UP, 1996. 49–65.

Mitchell, W. J. T. "Imperial Landscape." *Landscape and Power*. Chicago, London: U of Chicago P, 1994. 2–34.

Molloy, Sylvia. *Acto de presencia. La escritura autobiográfica en Hispanoamérica*. Trans. José Esteban Calderón. México: Fondo de Cultura Económica, 1996.

Mohanty, Chandra Talpade. *Feminism without Borders. Decolonizing Theory, Practicing Solidarity*. Durham: Duke UP, 2003.

Monteleone, Jorge. "La zona áurea. Los cuentos de Sylvia Iparraguirre." Sylvia Iparraguirre, *Narrativa breve*. Buenos Aires: Alfaguara, 2005. 13–28.
Moore, Henrietta L. "Of Texts and Other Matters." *Space, Text and Gender. An Anthropological Study of the Marakwet of Kenya*. London: Cambridge UP, 1986. 73–90.
Morello-Frosh, Marta. "La ficción se historifica: Cortázar y Rozenmacher." *Revista de Crítica Literaria Latinoamericana*. 3.5 (1977): 75–86.
Mulvey, Laura. "Visual Pleasure and Narrative Cinema." *Feminisms. An Anthology of Literary Theory and Criticism*. eds. Robyn R. Warhol and Diane Price Herndl. 2nd ed. New Brunswick, NJ: Rutgers UP, 1993. 432–42.
Muschietti, Delfina. "Las mujeres que escriben: aquel reino anhelado, el reino del amor." *Nuevo Texto Crítico* 4 (1989): 79–102.
Nari, Marcela. *Políticas de maternidad y maternalismo político*. Buenos Aires: Editorial Biblos, 2004.
Navarro Floria, Pedro. "Un país sin indios. La imagen de la Pampa y la Patagonia en la geografía naciente del estado Argentino." *Scripta Nova. Revista Electrónica de Geografía y Ciencias Sociales*. 51.1 (1999). August 29, 2009.
Negroni, María. *El sueño de Úrsula*. Buenos Aires: Seix Barral, 1998.
———. *El testigo lúcido. La obra de sombra de Alejandra Pizarnik*. Rosario: Beatriz Viterbo editora, 2003.
———. *El viaje de la noche*. Madrid: Editorial Lumen, 1994.
———. "Ir volver / de un adónde a un adónde." *Poéticas de la distancia. Adentro y afuera de la literatura argentina*. eds. Sylvia Molloy and Mariano Siskind. Buenos Aires: Grupo Editorial Norma, 2006. 23–33.
———. *Islandia. A Poem by Maria Negroni*. Trans. Anne Twitty. New York: Station Hill, Barrytown, Ltd., 2001.
———. *La anunciación*. Buenos Aires: Seix Barral, 2007.
———. *Museo negro*. Buenos Aires: Grupo Editorial Norma, 1999.
———. *Night Journey*. Trans. Anne Twitty. Princeton, New Jersey: Princeton UP, 2002.
———. Personal interview March 5, 2008.
Newman, Kathleen. *La violencia del discurso. El estado autoritario y la novela política argentina*. Buenos Aires: Catálogos Editora, 1991.
Neyret, Juan Pablo. "De alguien a nadie. Metáforas de la escritura de la historia en *La tierra del fuego*, de Sylvia Iparraguirre." *Espéculo. Revista de Estudios Literarios*, 29. http://www.ucm.es/info/especulo/numero29/sylviaip.html. 9 Mar. 2009.
Niedermaier, Alejandra. *La mujer y la fotografía. Una imagen espejada de autoconstrucción y construcción de la historia*. Buenos Aries: Leviatán, 2008.
Nigro, Kirsten F. "Textualidad, historia y subjetividad: Género y género." *Latin American Theatre Review* 26.2 (1993): 17–24.
Nora, Pierre. "Between Memory and History: Les Lieux de Mémoire." *History and Memory in African-American Culture*. Trans. Marc Roudebush. New York, Oxford: Oxford UP, 1994. 284–300.
Nouzeilles, Gabriela. "Desert Dreams: Nomadic Tourists and Cultural Discontent." Trans. Jens Andermann. *Images of Power. Iconography, Culture and State in Latin America*. New York, Oxford: Berghahn Books, 2005. 255–70.

———. "Patagonia as Borderland: Nature, Culture, and the Idea of the State." *Journal of Latin American Cultural Studies*. 8.1 (1999): 35–48.
Ocampo, Victoria. "Anna de Noailles y su poesía." *Testimonios. Series primera a quinta*. ed. Eduardo Paz Leston. Buenos Aires: Editorial Sudamericana, 1999. 13–28.
———. *Autobiografía I. El archipiélago. El imperio insular*. Buenos Aires: Fundación Victoria Ocampo, 2005.
———. *Autobiografía II. La rama de Salzburgo. Viraje*. Buenos Aires: Fundación Victoria Ocampo, 2005.
———. *Autobiografía III. Figuras simbólicas. Medida de Francia. Sur y Cía*. Buenos Aires: Fundación Victoria Ocampo, 2005.
———. "Costumbres." *Testimonios. Décima serie (1975–1977)*. 1977. Buenos Aires: Sur, 1978. 47–53.
———. *De Francesca a Beatrice. A través de La Divina Comedia*. Madrid: Biblioteca de la Revista de Occidente, 1928.
———. "Dejad en paz a las palomas." *Sur* 34 (1937): 84–86.
———. *Habla el algarrobo*. Buenos Aires: Sur, 1959.
———. "La aventura del mueble." *Sur* 1 (1931): 166–79.
———. "La historia viva." *Domingos en High Park*. Buenos Aires: Sur, 1936. 7–25.
———. "La mujer y su expresión." Buenos Aires: Sur, 1936.
———. "Mujeres en la academia." *Testimonios. Décima serie (1975–1977)*. 13–23.
———. "Sobre un mal de esta ciudad." *Sur* 14 (1935): 99–104.
Olea, Raquel. "Feminism: Modern or Postmodern?" *The Postmodernism Debate in Latin America*. Durham, London: Duke UP, 1995. 192–200.
Olivera-Williams, María Rosa. "Introducción" and "Vírgenes en fuga: pasión y escritura en tiempos de globalización." *El salto de Minerva: Intelectuales, género y estado en América Latina*. eds. Mabel Moraña and Maria Rosa Olivera-Williams. Frankfurt: Iberoamericana Vervuert, 2005. 11–28, 285–98.
Orta, Jorge, and Lucy Orta. "Antarctic Village: A Serious Shedworking Atmosphere." http://www.shedworking.co.uk/2007/10/antarctic-village-serious-shedworking.html. March 10, 2009.
Ortega, Eliana. "Sur Sur: Materia poética de Diana Bellessi". *Cyber Humanitatis*, 24 (2002). Online. Google 7 Mar. 2007.
Ortiz, Renato. "Globalización/mundialización." *Términos críticos de la sociología de la cultura*. Dir. Carlos Altamirano. Buenos Aires: Paidós, 2002.
Palmowski, Jan. "Travels with Baedeker. The Guidebook and the Middle Classes in Victorian and Edwardian Britain." *Histories of Travel*. 105–30.
Pellettieri, Osvaldo. "Diálogo de apertura." *El teatro y su crítica*. Buenos Aires: Galerna, Facultad de Filosofía y Letras de la Universidad de Buenos Aires, 1998.
———. *Historia del Teatro Argentino en Buenos Aires. El Teatro Actual* (1976–1998). vol. 5. Buenos Aires: Galerna, Facultad de Filosofía y Letras de la Universidad de Buenos Aires, 2001.
———. "Teatro argentino: Historia y crisis." *Teatro argentino y crisis (2001–2003)*. ed. Osvaldo Pellettieri. Buenos Aires: EUDEBA, 2004. 9–23.

Perloff, Marjorie. "Avant-garde or Endgame?" *Radical Artifice. Writing Poetry in the Age of Media.* Chicago, London: U of Chicago P, 1991. 1–28.

———. "The Invention of Collage." *Collage.* ed. Jeannine Parisier Plottel. New York: New York Literary Forum, 1983. 5–47.

Perlongher, Néstor. "Los devenires minoritarios. "Debates críticos en América Latina. *36 Números de la Revista de Crítica Cultural 1990–2008.* Santiago, Chile: Editorial ARCIS, ed. Cuarto Propio, Revista de Crítica Cultural, 2008. 165–75.

Perkowska, Madgalena. "Rememoración y reescritura desde los márgenes de la historia y la nación en *La tierra del fuego* de Sylvia Iparraguirre. *Historias híbridas. La nueva novela histórica latinoamericana (1985–2000) ante las teorías posmodernas de la historia.* Madrid: Iberoamericana Vervuert, 2008. 183–221.

Piglia, Ricardo. "Sarmiento the Writer." *Sarmiento. Author of a Nation.* 127–44.

———. "Sobre *Sur*." *Crítica y ficción.* Buenos Aires: Seix Barral-Planeta, 2000. 77–80.

Pile, Steven. *The Body and the City. Psychoanalysis, Space and Subjectivity.* New York: Routledge, 1996.

Pizarnik, Alejandra. "En esta noche, en este mundo." *Obras completas. Poesía y prosa.* Ed. Cristina Piña. Buenos Aires: Corregidor, 1999.

Pollock, Griselda. "Modernity and the Spaces of Femininity." *Vision and Difference. Femininity, Feminism, and the Histories of Art.* London, New York: Routledge, 1988. 50–90.

Pollock, Sheldon, et al. "Cosmopolitanisms." *Cosmopolitanism.* eds. Sheldon Pollock, et al. Durham, London: Duke UP, 2002. 1–14.

Popen, Shari. "Aesthetic Spaces/Imaginative Geographies." *A Boal Companion. Dialogues on Theatre and Cultural Politics.* eds. Jan Cohen-Cruz and Mady Schutzman. New York: Routledge, 2006. 125–32.

Potvin, Claudine. "De-Scribing Postmodern Feminism." *Latin American Postmodernisms.* 221–37.

Pratt, Mary Louise. *Imperial Eyes. Travel Writing and Transculturation.* 1992. London, New York: Routledge, 2003.

———. "¿Por qué la virgen de Zapopan fue a Los Ángeles? Reflexiones sobre la movilidad y la globalidad." *Sujetos en tránsito: (in)migración, exilio y diáspora en la cultura latinoamericana.* eds. Á. Fernández Bravo, F. Garramuño y S. Sosnowski. Madrid, Buenos Aires: Alianza Editorial, 2003. 29–57.

Prieto, Adolfo. *La literatura autobiográfica argentina.* Buenos Aires: Argentina, 2003.

———. *Los viajeros ingleses y la emergencia de la literatura Argentina, 1820–1850.* Buenos Aires: Fondo de Cultura Económica. 2nd ed. 2003.

Prebisch, Alberto. "Una ciudad de América." *Sur* 1 (1931): 216–20.

———. "Precisiones de Le Corbusier." *Sur* 1 (1931): 179–82.

Probyn, Elspeth. "Travels in the Postmodern: Making Sense of the Local." *Feminism/Postmodernism.* New York, London: Routledge, 1990. 176–89.

Puga, Ana Elena. *Memory, Allegory, and Testimony in South American Theater. Upstaging Dictatorship.* New York, London: Routledge, 2008.

Puga, Lidia. "Malvinas: La guerra de la información." *La tipografía de plomo.* eds. Malharro and López Gijsberts, 2003. 187–218.

Quevedo, Luis Alberto. "Política, medios y cultura en la Argentina de fin de siglo." *Los noventa. Política, sociedad y cultura en América Latina y Argentina de fin de siglo.* Buenos Aires: EUDEBA, 2da. Edición 1999.

Rama, Angel. "La ciudad letrada." *La ciudad letrada.* Hanover, NH: Ediciones del Norte, 2002. 23–39.

Raznovich, Diana. Casa Matriz. *Teatro americano actual.* Madrid: Casa de América. 81–118.

———. *De la cintura para abajo. Dramaturgas. En la escena del mundo.* Buenos Aires: Editorial Nueva Generación, 2004. 78–124.

———. *From the Waist Down.* Trans. Shanna Lorenz. *Holy Terrors. Latin American Women Perform.* 42–72.

———. *Inner Gardens. Defiant Acts. Four Plays by Diana Raznovich.* eds. Diana Taylor and Victoria Martínez. Drawings Diana Raznovich. Trans. Nora Glickman, Victoria Martínez, and Lidia Ramirez. Lewisburg: Bucknell UP, 2002. 53–95.

———. Jardín de otoño. Teatro americano actual. 11–77.

———. *Manifiesto 2000 del humor femenino.* Marlène Ramírez-Cancio and Shanna Lorenz, trans. *Holy Terror. Latin American Women Perform.* eds. Diana Taylor and Roselyn Constantino. Durham and London: Duke UP, 2003. 27–42.

———. *MaTRIX, Inc. Defiant Acts. Four Plays by Diana Raznovich.* Trans. Victoria Martínez and Lidia Ramírez. 99–127.

Richard, Nelly. *The Insubordination of Signs. Political Change, Cultural Transformation, and Poetics of the Crisis.* Trans. Alice A. Nelson and Silvia R. Tandeciarz. Durham and London: Duke UP, 2004.

Rocha, Carolina. "Literary Petites Histories: Santo oficio de la memoria and La madriguera." *Argentinean Cultural Production during the Neoliberal Years.* 37–57.

Rock, David. *Argentina 1516–1987. From Spanish Colonization to Alfonsín.* 2nd ed. Berkeley: U of California P, 1987.

Roffé, Reina. *La rompiente.* Córdoba: Alción Editora, 2005.

———. "Versos de ultramar." *Seqüana* barrosa. 9–10.

Rose, Gillian. *Feminism and Geography. The Limits of Geographical Knowledge.* Minneapolis: U of Minnesota P, 1993.

———. "Performing Space." Human Geography Today. Ed. Doreen Massey, John Allen, and Philip Sarre. Malden, MA: Polity Press, 1999. 247–59.

Rotker, Susana. *Captive Women. Oblivion and Memory in Argentina.* Trans. Jennifer French. Minneapolis: U of Minnesota P, 2002.

Rosman, Silvia N. "Of Travelers, Foreigners and Nomads: The Nation in Translation." *Latin American Literary Review* 25.51 (1998): 17–29.

Santos, Lydia. *Kitsch Tropical. Los medios en la literatura y el arte en América Latina.* Vervuert: Iberoamericana, 2004.

Sarlo, Beatriz. *Buenos Aires, una modernidad periférica.* Buenos Aires: Nueva Visión, 1988.

———. *Jorge Luis Borges, un escritor de las orillas.* Buenos Aires: Seix Barral, 2003.

———. *Jorge Luis Borges: A Writer on the Edge.* John King, ed. London: Verso, 1993.

———. *La máquina cultural: maestros, traductores y vanguardias*. Buenos Aires: Ariel, 1998.
Sassen, Saskia. *Los espectros de la globalización*. Trans. Irene Merzari. Buenos Aires: Fondo de Cultura Económica, 2003.
———. *A Sociology of Globalization*. New York: W.W. Norton and Company, 2007.
———. *Territory, Authority, Rights. From Medieval to Global Assemblages*. Princeton, Oxford: Princeton UP, 2006.
Scarry, Elaine. *The Body in Pain. The Making and the Unmaking of the World*. New York, Oxford: Oxford UP, 1985.
Schild, Verónica. "New Subjects of Rights? Women's Movement and the Construction of Citizenship in the 'New Democracies'." *Cultures of Politics. Politics of Cultures. Re-visioning Latin American Social Movements*. Eds. Sonia E. Alvarez, Evelina Dagnino, and Arturo Escobar. Boulder, CO: Westview, 1998. 93–117.
Schwartz, Jorge. *Vanguardia y cosmopolitismo en la década del veinte. Oliverio Girondo y Oswald de Andrade*. Rosario, Argentina: Beatriz Viterbo Editora, 1993.
Schwartz, Marcy. *Invenciones urbanas. Ficción y ciudad latinoamericanas*. Buenos Aires: Corregidor, 2010.
———. "Paris under Her Skin." *Writing Paris. Urban Topographies of Desire in Contemporary Latin American Fiction*. Albany: State U of New York P, 1999. 115–43.
Schwartz, Marcy, and Mary Beth Tierney-Tello. *Photography and Writing in Latin America. Double Exposures*. Alburquerque, NM: New Mexico UP, 2006.
Scolnicov, Hannah. *Women's Theatrical Space*. Cambridge, MA: Cambridge UP, 1994.
Sherman, William. "Stirrings and Searchings (1500–1720)." *The Cambridge Companion to Travel Writing*. eds. Peter Hulme and Tim Youngs. Cambridge, UK: Cambridge UP. 2005. 17–36.
Silverman, Kaja. *The Acoustic Mirror. The Female Voice in Psychoanalysis and Cinema*. Boomington: Indiana UP, 1988.
Siegel, Kristi. "Women's Travel and the Rhetoric of Peril. It Is Suicide to Be Abroad." *Gender, Genre, and Identity in Women's Travel Writing*. New York: Peter Lang, 2004. 55–72.
Sierra, Marta. "Oblique Views: Artistic Doubling, Ironic Mirroring, and Photomontage in the Works of Norah Lange and Norah Borges." *Revista Canadiense de Estudios Hispánicos* 29.3 (2005): 563–84.
Smith, Sidonie. *A Poetics of Women's Autobiography. Marginality and the Fictions of Self-Representation*. Bloomington: Indiana UP, 1987.
Smith, Sidonie and Julia Watson, eds. "Introduction. Mapping Women's Self-representation at Visual/Textual Interfaces." *Interfaces. Women. Autobiography. Image. Performance*. Ann Arbor: Michigan UP, 2002. 1–46.
Sommer, Doris. UP, 1991. *Foundational Fictions: The National Romances of Latin America*. Berkeley: California UP, 1991.
Sontag, Susan. "The Image-World." Int. Elizabeth Hardwick. *A Susan Sontag Reader*. New York: Farrar, 1982. 349–67.
———. *Regarding the Pain of Others*. New York: Farrar, Straus and Giroux, 2003.

Soja, Edward. *Postmodern Geographies. The Reassertion of Space in Critical Social Theory*. 8th ed. London, New York: Verso, 2003.

———. "Thirdspace: Expanding the Scope of the Geographical Imagination." *Human Geography Today*. Ed. Doreen Massey, John Allen and Philip Sarre. Cambridge, UK: Polity. 260–78.

Spain, Daphne. *Gendered Spaces*. Chapel Hill: U of North Carolina P, 1992.

Stone-Mediatore, Shari. "Storytelling and Global Politics." *Reading across Borders. Storytelling and Knowledges of Resistance*. New York: Palgrave Macmillan, 2003. 125–59.

Storni, Alfonsina. *Nosotras…y la piel. Selección de ensayos de Alfonsina Storni*. Compilación y prólogo de Mariela Méndez, Graciela Queirolo y Alicia Salomone. Buenos Aires: Alfaguara, 1998.

Suleiman, Susan Rubin. *Subversive Intent. Gender, Politics and the Avant-Garde*. Cambridge, MA: Harvard UP, 1990.

Szurmuk, Mónica. *Women in Argentina. Early Travel Narratives*. Gainesville: Florida UP, 2000.

Taylor, Diana. *Disappearing Acts. Spectacles of Gender and Nationalism in Argentina's "Dirty War."* Durham and London: Duke UP, 1997.

———. "Fighting Fire with Frivolity: Diana Raznovich's Defiant Acts." *Defiant Acts. Four Plays by Diana Raznovich*. eds. Diana Taylor and Victoria Martínez. Lewisburg: Bucknell UP. London: Associated University Press, 2002. 23–37.

———. "Performing Ruins." *Telling Ruins in Latin America*. 13–26.

———. *Theatre of Crisis. Drama and Politics in Latin America*. Kentucky: Kentucky UP, 1991.

———. "The Theatre of Diana Raznovich and Percepticide in *El desconcierto*." *Latin American Women Dramatists. Theatre, Texts, and Theories*. eds. Catherine Larson and Margarita Vargas. Bloomington and Indianapolis: Indiana UP, 1998. 113–25.

Taylor, Diana, and Roselyn Costantio, eds. "What Is Diana Raznovich Laughing at?" *Holy Terrors: Latin American Women Perform*. Durham: Duke UP, 2003. 73–92.

Thurschwell, Pamela. Introduction. *Literature, Technology and Magical Thinking, 1880–1920*. Cambridge: Cambridge UP, 2001.

Tierney-Tello, Mary Beth. *Allegories of Transgress and Transformation. Experimental Fiction by Women Writing Under Dictatorship*. New York: State U of New York P, 1996.

Tinajero, Araceli. "Orientalismo en el modernismo. Algunas consideraciones críticas." *Orientalismo en el modernismo hispanoamericano*. West Lafayette, IN: Purdue UP, 2004. 6–33.

Tompkins, Cynthia Margarita. *Latin American Postmodernisms. Women Writers and Experimentation*. Gainesville, FL: Florida UP, 2006.

Turner, James. *The Politics of Landscape. Rural Scenery and Society in English Poetry (1630–1660)*. Cambridge: Harvard UP, 1979.

Unruh, Vicky. *Performing Women and Modern Literary Culture in Latin America*. Austin: U of Texas, 2006.
Upstone, Sara. Introduction. "The Politics of Post-Space." *Spatial Politics in the Postcolonial Novel*. Farnham, England: Ashgate, 2009. 1–24.
Viñas, David. *Indios, ejércitos y frontera*. Buenos Aires: Santiago Arcos, 1983.
Warf, Barney, and Santa Arias. Introduction. *The Spatial Turn. Interdisciplinary Perspectives*. London, New York: Routledge, 2009. 1–10.
Wilson, Elizabeth. *The Contradictions of Culture. Cities, Culture, Women*. London: Sage, 2001.
Zandstra, Dianne Marie. *Embodying Resistance. Griselda Gambaro and the Grotesque*. Lewisburg, PA: Bucknell UP, 2007.
Zusman, Perla, and Sandra Minvielle. "Sociedades geográficas y delimitación del territorio en la construcción del Estado-Nación argentino." http://educ.ar/educar/site/educar/lm/.../sociedades_geograficas.pdf December 29, 2010.

Index

Adán Buenosayres (Marechal), 29
Adorno, Theodor, 108
Aguilar, Gonzalo, 38, 41–2
Alberdi, Juan Bautista, 116, 126
Alexander, Jacqui, 7
Alfonsín, Raúl, 80
Alsina, Valentín, 118, 208n2
Altamirano, Carlos, 127–8
Anaya, Jorge Isaac, 205n7
Andermann, Jens, 2, 11, 117–20, 208n4
Andrews, Joseph, 125
Ansermet, Ernst, 25, 43, 45
"Antarctic Village Project," 113–14
Arab Mind, The (Patai), 54
Arambel-Guiñazú, María Cristina, 43
Argentinean Color Television (ATC), 64
Artaud, Antonin, 77, 107, 110, 207n22
autobiography, 17, 22–6, 29–32, 35–7, 61, 127–8, 132, 200n5, 201n11, 202n25, 209–10n11
Avelar, Idelber, 189–91
Avellaneda, Nicolás, 118, 208n3

Barletta, Leónidas, 65
Barrancos, Dora, 15
Barros, Pía, 209n8
Bartra, Roger, 146
Baudelaire, Charles, 144
Baydar, Gülsüm, 31, 33
Belgrano Rawson, Eduardo, 152
Bellessi, Diana, 14, 19, 115, 138, 152, 181, 197–8, 211n19, 211n3, 211–12n5

Crucero Ecuatorial, 158, 161–2
El JardínI, 158, 162–3, 174–5
La rebelión del instante, 164
Mate Cocido, 158, 164, 173–5
Sur, 9–10
Tributo del mudo, 158, 161–2
Benítez-Rojo, Antonio, 5
Benjamin, Walter, 33, 77–9, 89, 99, 108, 144, 190, 207n23
Bhabha, Homi, 6, 130, 210n14
Bianco, José Pepe, 46
Bignozzi, Juana, 164
Blunt, Alison, 4, 22–3, 42, 103
Boal, Augusto, 65
Bond Head, Francis, 125–6
Borges, Jorge Luis, 9–10, 31–2, 34, 43, 177, 185, 187, 192, 201n12, 204n4, 214n20
Borges, Norah, 32
Bourdon, Albert, 48
Boyle, Catherine, 87
Braidotti, Rossi, 152, 186–7
Bridges, Roy, 213n13
Bussi, Antonio Domingo, 112
Bustillo, Alejandro, 41, 44
Butler, Judith, 55
Button, Jeremy, 123, 126–7, 129–31, 136–8, 208n5, 209n10, 210n13

Caamaña, Raquel, 12
Cahun, Claude, 36
Caplan, Karen, 145

Cárcamo-Huechante, Luis, 159–60
Carroll, Lewis, 140
Carter, Margaret, 205n9
Césaire, Aimé, 179
Chapman, Anne, 148–9, 211n4
Chatwin, Bruce, 119
Chercow Repetto, Fenia, 12
"chupado," 204n3
Churapuña, Rosemarie, 16
Clifford, James, 203n30
Colombi, Beatriz, 11, 56
Colombo, María del Carmen, 162
Coni, Gabriela, 12
Cornejo Polar, Antonio, 5
Cortázar, Julio, 80, 153, 176, 185, 204n4, 213n11
Cucurto, Washington, 115

Darwin, Charles, 119–20, 126, 128–30, 209n10
De Lauretis, Teresa, 83, 97, 99, 102–3, 111, 197
De Man, Paul, 32, 60–1
Deleuze, Giles, 16, 115, 133, 140
Derrida, Jacques, 85, 90
Dickerman, Leah, 207n23
Dirty War, 18, 66, 68, 81, 89, 93, 104, 108
Divine Comedy, 55–6, 202n24, 203n29
Dolan, Jill, 99
Domínguez, Nora, 29, 200n5
Dowling, Robyn, 22–3, 42
Drieu La Rochelle, Pierre, 25, 60, 202n24

Echeverría, Esteban, 1–3, 19, 78, 117–18, 126
Estrada, Ángel de, 56
Estrella Gutiérrez, Fermín, 26

Facio, Sara, 202n23
Falklands War, 80, 82, 204–5n5
Faulkner, Thomas, 128
Feitlowitz, Marguerite, 64, 70–1, 81, 89, 204n3

Felski, Rita, 26, 52, 200n7, 203n27
Fernández Bravo, Álvaro, 5, 11
First Biennial of the End of the World. *See* Primera Bienal del Fin del Mundo
Fitz Roy, Robert, 120, 126, 129, 132, 136, 208n5
Forcinito, Ana, 152–3, 175, 183, 186
Foucault, Michel, 4–5, 16, 18, 66–7, 72–4, 79, 94, 111, 163, 211n2
fourth wall, 65, 81
Franco, Jean, 12
Frank, Waldo, 25, 41–6
Frankfurt School, 102, 108
Freud, Sigmund, 18, 33, 66–7, 69, 72, 205n9
Friedman, Alice, 53
Friedman, Susan Stanford, 10
Futoransky, Luisa, 9, 19, 115, 139–40, 157, 197–8, 213n11, 212–13, 214n17
Babel, Babel, 158, 175–8
De Pe a Pa o de Pekín a París, 14, 176, 212n10
Inclinaciones, 168, 175, 184–5
Manifiesto 2000 del humor femenino, 106
Partir, Digo, 158, 179
Prender de Gajo, 14, 158, 175, 180–5
Seqüana barrosa, 158, 185
Son Cuentos Chinos, 14, 176

Gache, Belén, 14, 18, 115, 121–4, 139–55, 168, 210–11n18
Diario de una luna cannibal, 121, 123–4, 140, 144–55, 159
El libro del fin del mundo, 124, 141–4
Escrituras nómadas, 124, 139–41
Luna india, 124, 148
Lunas eléctricas para una noche sin luna, 124, 147–8
Seqüana Barrosa, 185–6
Galtieri, Leopoldo Fortunato, 82, 205n7

Gambaro, Griselda, 14, 18, 65–6, 93, 98, 100–1, 108, 111–12, 203–4n2, 205n8
  Antígona furiosa, 67, 72–3, 79–91
  Del sol naciente, 67, 72, 79–86, 204–5n5
  El campo, 67
  Ganarse la muerte, 68
  Información para extranjeros, 69–72
  La malasangre, 67, 72–3, 78–83, 88–9, 101
  Las paredes, 67, 69–72
García Canclini, Néstor, 114
Gelman, Juan, 164, 170, 175, 185
gendered modernity, 203n27
Gendered Spaces (Spain), 7
Genovese, Alicia, 162, 170, 198
geographical imagination, 3–4, 10, 139, 210n16
Giardinelli, Mempo, 115, 120
Giles, Judy, 52
Girondo, Oliverio, 13, 29, 35, 37–8, 43, 45, 201n15
Gleber, Anke, 90
globalization, 18, 94, 113–15, 121–2, 133–4, 140, 146–7, 153, 155, 160–1, 167, 180, 184–8, 211–12n5, 212n8
Gómez de la Serna, Ramón, 43, 45
González Lanuza, Eduardo, 34, 201n12
Gottman, Jean, 118–19
Grau, Cristina, 32
Gray, Andrew, 119
Gregory, Derek, 4
Grewal, Inderpal, 145
Gropius, Walter, 47
Grosz, Elizabeth, 35
Groussac, Paul, 56
Guattari, Félix, 16, 115, 133, 140
Guebel, Daniel, 115
Gusinde, Martin, 148, 211n3

Harvey, David, 4, 205n10, 212n7
Heath, Stephen, 96
Hernández, Felisberto, 185
Hernández, Ibis, 147

Hernández, José, 82
heterotopias, 4, 18, 66, 111, 163, 211n2
Heynen, Hilde, 40, 203n31
Hortiguera, Hugo, 101, 146, 206n17, 207–8n1
Housewives Union, 15
Hudson, W. H., 119
Humboldt, Alexander Von, 126, 213n13
Huyssen, Andreas, 98, 107–8, 206n16

Idle Days in Patagonia (Hudson), 119
imaginary geographies, 1, 3, 10–12, 80, 83, 115, 161, 177, 197
In Patagonia (Chatwin), 119
Iparraguirre, Sylvia, 14, 18, 115, 168, 208n5, 209n9 , 209n6–7, 210n13
  La tierra del fuego, 121–39, 152, 153, 155, 210n15, 211n19

Jáuregui, Carlos, 124, 153
Jeanneret, Charles-Édouard (Le Corbusier), 41, 46–7, 53
Jelin, Elizabeth, 15

Kamenzsain, Tamara, 183
Kaminsky, Amy, 69, 121–2, 127, 200n6, 213n11
King, John, 51
Koshar, Rudy, 56
Kozameh, Alicia, 80, 86
Krauss, Rosalind, 33, 37
Kristeva, Julia, 77, 106
Kuhnheim, Jill, 181, 184–6, 214n18
Kushigian, Julia, 213n12

Landow, George, 140
Lange, Norah, 17–18, 22–42, 52, 59, 61, 66, 200n5, 201n13, 201n15, 202n20
  45 días y 30 marineros, 22–3, 26–7, 35–8
  Antes que mueran, 23
  Cuadernos de infancia, 23, 26, 29–35
  Estimados congéneres, 23
  Los dos retratos, 23, 26, 32–5
  Personas en la sala, 23, 26, 32–3

238 • Index

Lanteri, Julieta, 13
Larkosh, Christopher, 58
Lavrin, Asunción, 199–200n3
Le Corbusier. *see* Jeanneret, Charles-Édouard
Lefebvre, Henri, 3–4, 6, 13, 65, 215n23
Legaz, María Elena, 29–30
Lenin, Vladimir, 207n23
Livon-Grosman, Ernesto, 11, 120
Loss, Jacqueline, 203n30
Ludmer, Josefina, 106

Maetzu, María de, 57
Magnarelli, Sharon, 75
Majstorovic, Gorica, 49, 57
Mansilla, Lucio V., 116–18
Marchant, Elizabeth, 55, 200n5
Marechal, Leopoldo, 29
Martín Fierro, 25, 28, 31, 37–9, 82, 200n5
Martín-Barbero, Jesús, 102
Martínez, Julián, 55, 60
Masiello, Francine, 12–14, 16, 22, 24, 38, 60, 80, 102, 114, 125, 155, 159, 166, 175, 182, 185–7, 200n4–5, 206n18, 210n15
Massey, Doreen, 8–9, 161, 169, 175, 213n14
materialized spatiality, 2–3
Mazzotti, José Antonio, 159–60
McLoughlin, Kate, 181–2
Melville, Herman, 119, 126, 135, 209n7
Menem, Carlos, 100–1, 109, 122, 160, 167, 207–8n1, 209n6
Mercado, Tununa, 86, 115
Mignolo, Walter, 139–40, 154
Mills, Sara, 93
Minvielle, Sandra, 2, 117
Mistral, Gabriela, 57
Mitchell, W. J. T., 135
Moby-Dick (Melville), 119, 126–7, 135
Mohanty, Chandra, 7, 212n7

Molloy, Sylvia, 30, 55, 61, 200n5, 203n29, 209–10n11
Monroe, James, 199n1
Monteleone, Jorge, 123, 174
Moore, Henrietta, 43, 199n2
Moreira, Juan, 65
Morello-Frosh, Marta, 204n4
Moreno, César Fernández, 164
Moreno, Francisco, 120
Mulvey, Laura, 95, 99
Mussolini, Benito, 202n24
Muzzili, Carolina, 12

Nari, Marcela, 27, 52, 103, 200n9
naturalization of motherhood, 27, 52
Navarro Floria, Pedro, 119
Navy Mechanics School (ESMA), 64, 92–3, 206n15
Negroni, María, 9, 14, 19, 115, 157–60, 214–15n22
El viaje de la noche, 158, 188–9, 195–6
Islandia, 158, 187–98, 214n21
Museo negro, 194–5
Nelson, Theodor, 140
Newman, Kathleen, 91
Neyret, Juan Pablo, 123, 209n7
Nigro, Kirsten, 105
Noaille, Anna de, 202n24
Nora, Pierre, 82–3, 88, 181

object book, 124, 209n8
Ocampo, Victoria, 9–10, 17–18, 22–6, 66, 199n1, 200n5, 202n23–5
Autobiografía, 22–3, 42–3, 51–4, 56–61, 202n24–5, 203n29
De Francesca a Beatrice, 41, 55–6, 202n24, 203n29
Habla el algarrobo, 50–1
Sur, 9, 22, 41–59, 138–9, 158, 163–77, 211n19, 211–12n5
Testimonios, 23, 42, 53–4, 56–7
Olea, Raquel, 14–16, 40
Oliver, María Rosa, 22, 43, 45–6, 58

Operativo Independencia, 112, 207n24
Orozco, Olga, 170, 186
Orta, Jorge, 113
Orta, Lucy, 113
Ortega, Eliana, 139, 161, 165
Ortega y Gasset, José, 41–2, 55
Ortiz, Juan L., 166, 169–70
Ortiz, Renato, 121

Panunzi, Benito, 28
Partnoy, Alicia, 80
Patagonia, 11, 18–19, 113–55, 208n3–5, 209n9, 210n16
Patai, Raphael, 54
Pelletieri, Osvaldo, 109
Perkowska, Magdalena, 123, 126, 133, 209n7
Perloff, Marjorie, 212n9
Perlongher, Néstor, 16, 197
Perón, Eva, 51
Peronism, 51, 80, 82–3, 102, 191, 204n4
photography, 28–37, 99, 106–10, 125, 206n20, 206–7n21
Pigafetta, Antonio, 119, 128
Piglia, Ricardo, 50, 128
Pizarnik, Alejandra, 171, 184–6, 194, 197
Plotting Women (Franco), 14
Poe, Edgar Allan, 144
poetry, 157–98
Pollock, Griselda, 39, 201–2n19
Postmodern Geographies: The Reassertion of Space in Critical Social Theory (Soja), 4
postmodernism, use of the term, 13–14
power maps, 2, 117
Pratt, Mary Louis, 107, 109, 211–12n5, 213n13
Prebisch, Alberto, 41, 48
Prieto, Adolfo, 125–6, 202n25, 209n7
Primera Bienal del Fin del Mundo (First Biennial of the End of the World), 113, 124

Probyn, Elspeth, 10
Production of Space, The (Lefebvre), 4, 215n23
Puga, Ana Elena, 71–2, 74–5, 87

Rama, Angel, 197, 215n23
Ramírez, Ariel, 82
Raznovich, Diana, 14, 18, 65–8, 91–112
  Casa matriz, 68, 103–5
  De atrás para adelante, 68, 105–6, 109–10
  De la cintura para abajo, 68, 94, 106–11
  Jardín de otoño, 68, 94–103, 107–8, 111
  Manifiesto 2000 del humor femenino, 106
Richard, Nelly, 13, 89
Riedemann, Clemente, 152
Riveros, Juan Pablo, 152
Robbe-Grillet, Alain, 30
Roca, Julio A., 118, 125, 147, 210n16
Rock, David, 116
Roffé, Reina, 86, 185
Romanticism, 2
Roosevelt, Franklin, 46
Rosas, Juan Manuel de, 51, 67, 75, 78, 210n15
Rose, Gillian, 4, 10, 72, 79, 83–4, 94, 106, 150, 151, 160, 169, 188–9
Rotker, Susana, 19

Safranchik, Graciela, 115
Salgueiro, Bernardo, 16
Santos, Lydia, 49
Sarlo, Beatriz, 40, 54, 55–7, 127–8, 201n17, 201–2n19
Sarmiento, Domingo Fuastino, 2, 116–18, 126–8, 134–6, 209n7, 210n16
Sassen, Saskia, 121–2
Scarry, Elaine, 85
Schwartz, Jorge, 39
Schwartz, Marcy, 28–9, 91, 176, 178, 183, 213n11, 214n17

Scolnicov, Hannah, 18, 66, 80
Siegel, Kristi, 37
Siscar, Cristina, 120
Siskind, Mariano, 41–2
Smith, Sidonie, 25, 201n11
social construction of space, 2
Social Justice and the City (Harvey), 4, 205n10
Soja, Edward, 2–4, 6, 65, 205n10, 210–11n18, 212n7
Sommer, Doris, 43, 74–5
Sontag, Susan, 36–7, 107–9, 206n20, 206–7n21
Space, Place and Gender (Massey), 8
space as text, 199n2
Spain, 58, 68, 201n12, 209n8
Spain, Daphne, 7
spatialization, 4–6, 9, 12, 16–17, 84, 125, 166
Spatial Politics in the Postcolonial Novel (Upstone), 6
spatial turn, 4, 205n10
Stieglitz, Alfred, 46–7
Storni, Alfonsina, 12, 27, 97, 200n10
Strejilevich, Nora, 80
Suleiman, Susan Rubin, 28
Szurmuk, Mónica, 11, 35

Tagore, Rabindranath, 203n28
Taylor, Diana, 67, 71, 75, 84, 87–8, 90, 92, 95, 99–100, 106–7, 205n8
Teatro Abierto, 18, 65, 100
Temple, Edmond, 125
territorial consciousness, 2, 119
theater, 18, 49, 64–72, 77, 80–7, 94–112, 191–3, 207n22
Theater of the Oppressed, 70
Thénon, Susana, 197
third space, 6–7, 205n10
Tierney-Tello, Mary Beth, 28, 72
Tierra del Fuego, 113, 117, 121–40, 144–7, 151, 152, 163, 167, 173, 208n3, 209n9, 210n16

Tinajero, Araceli, 213n12
Tompkins, Cynthia, 14
transition, 114–15
travel writing, 11–12, 27, 35–9, 54–6, 61, 119–28, 151, 154, 166, 176–80, 209n7, 213n13
Turner, James, 165
Turner, Joseph Mallord William, 135

Ultraismo, 201n12
Unruh, Vicky, 23, 27–8, 35, 52–5, 57, 200n5, 201n16
Upstone, Sara, 6
urbanism, 41–2, 47–9, 57
Urondo, Francisco, 164
Usuhaia Prison, 146, 149

Valenzuela, Luisa, 115
Victorica, Benjamín, 118
Voyage of the Beagle, The (Darwin), 119, 126, 128, 130, 209n10

Wallerstein, Immanuel, 7
Walser, Robert, 144
War of the Triple Alliance, 116
Watson, Julia, 25
Whitman, Walt, 162
Wilson, Elisabeth, 201–2n19
Women in Argentina: Early Travel Narratives (Zsurmuk), 22
Woolf, Virginia, 23, 25, 57
World Cup, 63–4, 1978
World War II, 42, 47, 52
Wright, Frank Lloyd, 53

Yrigoyen, Hipólito, 41
Yupanki, Atahualpa, 82

Zandstra, Dianne Marie, 85
Zeballos, Estanislao, 120
Zsurmuk, Mónica, 22
Zusman, Perla, 2, 117

GPSR Compliance

The European Union's (EU) General Product Safety Regulation (GPSR) is a set of rules that requires consumer products to be safe and our obligations to ensure this.

If you have any concerns about our products, you can contact us on

ProductSafety@springernature.com

In case Publisher is established outside the EU, the EU authorized representative is:

Springer Nature Customer Service Center GmbH
Europaplatz 3
69115 Heidelberg, Germany

www.ingramcontent.com/pod-product-compliance
Lightning Source LLC
LaVergne TN
LVHW051913060526
838200LV00004B/126